The European Business Environment: France

Edited and translated by Robert Crawshaw

in collaboration with Jean-Yves Eglem

INTERNATIONAL THOMSON BUSINESS PRESS

I⊕P®An International Thomson Publishing Company

London ● Bonn ● Boston ● Johannesburg ● Madrid ● Melbourne ● Mexico City ● New York ● Paris
Singapore ● Tokyo ● Toronto ● Albany, NY ● Belmont, CA ● Cincinnati, OH ● Detroit, MI

The European Business Environment: France

Copyright © 1997 Robert Crawshaw

First published 1997 by International Thomson Business Press

I(T)P® A division of International Thomson Publishing Inc.
The ITP logo is a trademark under licence

British Library Cataloguing-in-Publication Data
A catalogue record for this book is available from the British Library

First Edition 1997

Typeset by LaserScript, Mitcham, Surrey
Printed in the UK by TJ International Ltd, Padstow, Cornwall

ISBN 0–415–10535–8

International Thomson Business Press

Berkshire House   20 Park Plaza
168–173 High Holborn   14th Floor
London WC1V 7AA   Boston MA 02116
UK   USA

Contents

List of tables, figures and *encadrés*

TABLES

FIGURES

ENCADRES

List of contributors

Sandra Bellier-Michel qualified in clinical psychology and political science, and is a consultant in human resource management. A former teacher at the *Ecole Supérieure de Commerce de Paris* and the University of Geneva, she currently holds a teaching post at the *Institut des Sciences Politiques*, Paris.

Joël Broustail is a graduate of the *Ecole Normale Supérieure* and the *Ecole des Hautes Etudes Commerciales* as well as an *agrégé* in history and in management science. He is an adviser to the French Ministry of Education, a member of the French national commission on human rights and teaches strategic management at the *Ecole Supérieure de Commerce de Paris*.

Loïc Cadin is a graduate of the *Ecole des Sciences Sociales, Economiques et Commerciales* and holder of a PhD in human resource management. He is head of the Department of HRM at the *Ecole Supérieure de Commerce de Paris* and having had a variety of managerial responsibilities in the Danone and Bull groups, his present research interests are in the field of competency management.

Robert Crawshaw is a lecturer in French at Lancaster University where he is director of studies for degrees in management and modern languages. He was formerly Director of European Relations for The Management School and academic adviser to the European Commission.

Jean-Yves Eglem is a *Docteur d'Etat* in economics and a qualified accountant. He teaches accounting and financial analysis at the *Ecole Supérieure de Paris* where he was formerly Director of Research.

Marie-Pierre Fénoll-Trousseau teaches labour law at the *Ecole Supérieure de Commerce de Paris* where she is director of studies for the Masters programme in publishing management.

Frédéric Fréry teaches strategic management at the *Ecole Supérieure de Commerce de Paris* and holds a doctorate in management from the University of Paris.

Bernard Galambaud is director of studies of the Masters programme in human and organisational management at the *Ecole Supérieure de Commerce de Paris*. He is also scientific director of the Paris research institute *Enterprise et Personnel*.

Patrick Gilbert teaches management development at the *Ecole Supérieure de Commerce de Paris* and is Associate Professor at the *Centre National des Arts et Métiers* and the University of Geneva. Formerly responsible for human resource development for the Matra Group, he is now a director of research at the *Institut Entreprise et Personnel*, Paris.

Guy Groux holds a *Doctorat d'Etat* in political science and is currently research director at the *Centre National de la Recherche Scientifique*. He is responsible for courses on management and politics at the *Ecole Supérieure de Commerce de Paris*.

Jyoti Gupta is a member of the faculty at the *Ecole Supérieure de Commerce de Paris*, Dean of the School of Management of the Asian Institute of Technology, Thailand, and Editor of *The Journal of Euro-Asian Management*.

Sylvie Hébert is *Docteur d'Etat* in law and a graduate of the University of Columbia and the *Institut d'Etudes Politiques*. She teaches business law at the *Ecole Supérieure de Commerce de Paris*, where she is also director of studies of the Masters programme in law and international management.

John Kennedy is a chartered accountant and *expert-comptable*. He is director of studies of the Masters in audit and consulting at the *Ecole Supérieure de Commerce de Paris* where he also teaches international financial analysis.

Renaud de Maricourt is a graduate of the *Institut d'Etudes Politiques* and holder of an MBA from Northwestern University, Illinois. He is responsible for MBA course in strategic marketing and Japanese management as well as for the foundation programme in marketing at the *Ecole Supérieure de Commerce de Paris*.

Annie Médina is a Paris barrister and a specialist in contract and labour law She teaches business law at the *Ecole Supérieure de Commerce de Paris*.

Carla Mendoza is a graduate of the *Ecole des Hautes Etudes Commerciales*. Holder of a doctorate and a *Diplôme d'Etudes Approfondies* in strategic management, she is presently director of studies in accounting and financial management at the *Ecole Supérieure de Commerce de Paris*.

Philippe Spieser is a graduate of the *Ecole des Hautes Etudes Commerciales* and the *Institut d'Etudes Politiques* with a doctorate and a *Diplôme d'Etudes Approfondies* in economics. He coordinates finance courses for the Masters programmes at the *Ecole Supérieure de Commerce de Paris* where he is head of the Department of Finance and Accounting. He is author of numerous articles published by the French finance association (*AFFI*) and of a book *La Structure des Taux d'Intérêt* (1992).

Benoit Heilbrunn is a graduate of the *Ecole des Hautres Etudes Commerciales* and a holder of DEAs in marketing, semiology and philosophy. He was formerly associate professor at the *Ecole Supérieure de Commerce de Paris* and lecturer in marketing at University College Dublin. He is currently *chargé de conférences* at the *Ecole Supérieure de Commerce de Lyon*.

Series editors' introduction

European Business Environments

Robert Crawshaw and Stephen Fox

This book, part of a series which includes separate publications on the business environments of France, Germany and the UK, appears at a moment when the future of European union is being widely called into question. The belief that closer trans-European integration in education and training is required in order to respond to an increasingly international business environment is being undermined by pressures to reduce public spending. On a larger scale, the debate on European Monetary Union has raised questions as to whether the sacrifice of national economic control by individual member states will be outweighed by the advantages of a single currency area, doubts which public discussion on the subject has done little to dispel and less to inform. The relationship between economic cooperation within Europe and that between states on an international scale is increasingly under review. It is argued by some that the 'global marketplace' has overtaken the concept of a European Community in terms of economic importance. Countries are better able to respond to the challenge of world competition on an individual basis than if they carry the collective burden of regional disparities within a wider Europe.

Yet the concept of European unity will not go away. The importance of maintaining political and economic equilibrium in the face of new national configurations on the Eastern borders of the continent is all the more pressing as a consequence of the high level of unemployment which is dogging the Western nations. The interdependency of European economies means that companies must continue to increase their capacity to operate across national boundaries. At the level of multinational groups, this implies regarding West Europe as a unitary field of operations. For small and medium-sized enterprises, it means facilitating expansion and export to other member states in the Union as well as more widely afield. In short, the importance of the single European market has not been diminished by the shrinking boundaries of global trade. On the contrary, the improvement of communications and the growing efficiency of distribution have enhanced Europe's identity as a discrete region of the world.

It is incontrovertible, however, that the struggle between the different models of global capitalism is vividly illustrated by the different approaches to national economic management current in France, Germany and the United Kingdom.

These differences are explored most cogently by Michel Albert in his now classic book *Capitalisme contre Capitalisme* and are reflected in the study for the Royal Institute of International Affairs, *Britain, Germany and 1992: the Limits of Deregulation* by Woolcock, Hodges and Schreiber. Both analyses date from the year 1991. Following the Rhodes summit of 1988, that year appears in retrospect to signal a heightened sense that a fundamental choice had to be made if the Europe of the post-1992 era was to be based on a common social and economic foundation. In both studies, the option of convergence between the three main West European economies was opposed to that of accepting their differences in economic principles and management practices.

From a primarily economic standpoint, one view was that Europe could be cast in the mould of a free trade area characterised by a lack of government involvement in corporate affairs and most public services – an unlikely scenario, given the traditional belief of the French in the civic responsibility of the state and the commitment on the part of the Germans to the *Ordnungspolitik* which formed the strength of their economy. On the other hand, from a more *dirigiste* perspective, a socially regulated community might emerge in which the German model of controlled intervention would dominate – by regional government in the management of local affairs and by banks and trade unions in corporate decision-making. To a greater or lesser extent, other states would be satisfied to compromise with German hegemony whilst preserving their cultural and political identities within a reconstituted political structure.

As Woolcock *et al.* saw it, a compromise between these two political and economic philosophies was the likely outcome, not out of respect for consensus, but as the result of a common reluctance to accept federal regulation of work practices at the European level. Within this context, the principles of the strongest European economy – that of Germany – would dominate. In Albert's eyes, this would be a positive development. France was faced with a choice between the law of the corporate jungle marked by low public investment and short-termism which characterised what he termed the 'Anglo-Saxon' model and the stability, social purpose and cost-effectiveness which he saw as the prerogative of the *rhénan* system. He hoped that France would opt to maintain her long-standing tradition of forward planning and state regulation which he saw as complementary to *Ordnungspolitik*. He could not have reckoned on the extent to which his native country's balance of payments deficit and the *franc fort* policy of alignment with the Deutschmark would threaten her own institutions by inducing a more monetarist and hence *laissez-faire* approach to economic management.

Even in a climate of compromise, both Albert and Woolcock not surprisingly portray Britain as lying at the liberal end of the political–economic continuum against the background of a Franco-German alliance. Britain has sought both further deregulation and increased competition within Europe, having unilaterally made its own markets more open than those of other member states. For the sake of free market principles, the country has apparently been unconcerned about sacrificing corporate sovereignty to foreign investors even to the extent of allowing its public utilities to be taken over by its European partners. However, in those countries where competition is still regulated through state intervention, it is not clear that UK firms have found corporate success so easy.

Whatever the outcome of the debate between deregulation and *dirigisme*, national differences continue to run deep and permeate every aspect of corporate and national life. It remains to be seen exactly what this means in terms of the social and economic structures which will shape the business environments of the different European countries in the new millenium. If European unity means anything in terms of business administration, it must be to promote the ability on the part of citizens generally and of managers in particular to cope with diversity and difference, and to turn these factors to commercial advantage. Whatever the economic pressures for convergence and compromise and however uneven the pace of progression towards closer European union, the essential importance of understanding the fabric of national business environments remains undiminished. The objective of the *European Business Environments* series is to make this field of knowledge more accessible to students of management and practising businessmen.

Much has been written about the most appropriate form of education and training required to develop qualities of cultural adaptability alongside the fundamental technical and professional knowledge demanded of international managers. There is a growing literature on European management culture, much of which takes a comparative perspective and includes an analysis of behaviour in organisations in a number of different European countries. Equally, there have been a number of publications which attempt to provide an overview of business practice on a country-by-country basis, either as an everyday practical guide for the businessman or woman or in order to provide more 'in-depth' analyses of the countries concerned. Others too approach the topic of Europeanisation from the perspective of a single management 'discipline'. This is particularly true of the more 'technical' or professional fields such as accounting and marketing.

The *European Business Environments* series seeks to combine these approaches. Acknowledging the profound cultural differences already referred to between France, Germany and the UK, the series devotes a single volume to each of the three countries concerned. All three volumes, however, follow a common template based on the academic disciplines which together constitute the field of management studies. The aim of the series is not simply to provide a business person's guide to each individual country, but to offer an accessible introduction to the business environments of the countries concerned from a series of academic perspectives.

An original feature of the series is the fact that, although it is published in English with the editors of each volume being British nationals, each book is written by a team of academics who are natives of the country concerned, the academics being specialists in the disciplines which they represent. Thus, the perspective on, for example, business law in Germany will be that of a German academic and will reflect the style and analytical approach which is characteristic of that academic culture. In this respect, the series is not designed to replace or directly to compete with existing publications which seek to describe and compare European management practices. It aims to complement these texts and to fulfil a need which is not so far being met for the benefit of students following courses in European management at undergraduate, postgraduate or post-experience levels.

Insofar as each volume covers five more or less discrete areas of academic specialisation, the series is intended as much as a source of reference as a collection of individual studies to be read in their entirety. For example, the non-specialist student of management in France may have a particular interest in French business law but may not need to have a complete overview of the French accounting system. It is hoped that the series will be used eclectically in response to the different needs of individual programmes. Explanatory tables are provided in the text and each chapter includes recommendations for further reading within the specialist field concerned as well as useful sources of documentation. In addition to an index, each volume also contains a glossary of technical and specialist terms designed to enable non-native students to familiarise themselves with essential vocabulary as well as abbreviations and acronyms in current usage.

The series as a whole has been a joint enterprise between the publishers, Thomson International Business Press, the series and volume editors and the teams of academics in the three countries so far covered. It has involved extensive translation and editorial work over a three-year period and has enhanced the working relationships between the partner institutions engaged on the project. It is our hope that the series makes a worthwhile contribution to the available educational literature in the field and that, within its own limited sphere, it furthers the cause of European cooperation in the area of European management education.

Lancaster
July 1996

Volume editor's introduction

The French Business Environment

Robert Crawshaw

This book went to press at a time when France was undergoing what many saw as a crisis of confidence in the state. Unemployment stood at between 13 per cent and 14 per cent and was as high as 60 per cent in certain parts of the country for those leaving school with no qualifications. The social security system was heavily in debt and could no longer survive without massive government support. The budget deficit represented more than 6 per cent of national income. Serious economies in public spending linked to high interest rates were necessary for France to maintain a stable political relationship with Germany in the period leading up to the proposed adoption of a single European currency. There was disillusionment with the intellectual élite who governed the country, the product of a hierarchical educational system which the state had created over the years to act as the guardian of republican values and the guarantee of rational planning. It seemed that the very foundations of the French state and its capacity to restore the country to what the population would consider to be a satisfactory level of economic prosperity and social stability were being called into question.

Yet France is one of the most prosperous countries in the world. During the early 1990s, its companies were consistently successful in terms of export performance and foreign acquisitions. In terms of the number of firms in the top 200 worldwide, and as a function of GNP, France is in fourth position behind the USA, Japan and Germany. It is acknowledged to have one of the most highly developed and effective transport infrastructures of any country in Europe, if not the world. Its reputation for investment and innovation in research and design is outstanding. Its physical geography, remarkable for its diversity and natural beauty, together with its exceptional cultural and architectural heritage make it, per capita, one of the most popular tourist destinations in the world. To the visitor, the economic difficulties which the country is having to confront seem almost like a mirage until he/she is confronted by the bitter reality of the metropolitan suburbs.

The truth is that, unlike the United States, France can no longer mortgage its domestic overdraft against its overseas assets. The cost of financing the country's national deficit will steadily increase and will become progressively harder to bear as its population ages and its active human resource diminishes. The medium-term future for France, like that for West Europe as a whole, is challenging and arduous. It is not hard to understand why France's leaders should look to maintaining a stable economic and political alliance with her great neighbour so that together they can benefit from the growth potential on their Eastern borders and buttress themselves against domination by Japan, North America and the competition from the emerging economies of Malaysia and China.

The problem is that economic stability comes at a high price in terms of social well-being and forcibly overrides the traditionally humanitarian principles of the French State. High interest rates limit companies' capacity to invest whilst insecurity about jobs acts as a brake on consumer spending. The salaries and social protection which companies can afford for their employees are correspondingly constrained. It is tempting for France, as for Germany, to ignore the eligibility criteria laid down by the Maastricht Treaty for the adoption of a single European currency and to maintain, if not increase, current levels of public spending. Yet the perspective of enhanced confrontation between national economies, with the combined threats of increased inflation and competitive devaluations ever-present on the horizon, hardly appears to provide a credible future for West Europe as a secure political and economic environment.

Increasingly, therefore, the French state has had to turn to the corporate sector for medium-term economic and social solutions to deep-seated national and international problems. In 1983, in the wake of two successive devaluations and a large-scale programme of nationalisation, the government relied on individual enterprise and rapid growth linked to tight control of the money supply to resolve the difficulties induced by economic instability and overregulation of business by the state. Today, once again, but in a much harsher global climate, it is mainly business which is being called on to provide training and short-term employment for school leavers whilst bearing the brunt of social security, local taxes and health provision. At the same time, companies are expected to increase productivity levels and raise exports still further in order to generate national income. Large-scale publicly supported industries such as computing (Bull), parts of the railways (SNCF) and motor manufacturing (Renault) are being privatised or merged with multinational corporations in order to remove them from the state's balance sheet. Domestic consumption is being promoted by providing tax incentives to encourage ever-thrifty citizens to realise their savings and buy French products.

For businesses themselves, the pressure is unremitting, the only way out of the morass being a judicious combination of cost-cutting and growth. Cost-cutting means in practice downsizing – redundancies and rationalisation linked to the outsourcing, or franchising of essential services such as research, supply of technical equipment, distribution and manufacture of components. In this way, it is the outlying company which bears the risk, in competition with others, and relieves the core firm of the social responsibility and cost of a larger and less flexible organisation. Clearly this tendency is not confined to France but is a general feature of European business which is changing the nature of work and is linked to the development of internationalisation. One consequence of the decentralisation which has accompanied downsizing is that the functional definition of tasks is giving way to management by project in which the essential competence required by middle management is that of coordinating a range of unstable variables within and outside the organisation. Basic issues such as design specifications, quality control, levels of demand and timing must be flexibly combined by integrating the operations of a number of different agencies, increasingly on an international scale and in a context of great uncertainty (see Crozier 1989; Dany and Lemetais 1993; Duchéneaut 1995)

At the growth end, the choices for large groups are limited but clear – concentrate on particular sectors and expand the market share in those spheres which correspond to the strengths of the company and which have the highest potential (Péchiney's drive on food packaging), improve relationships with the key global purchasers in the company's field of operations (Valéo's partnership with Honda), exploit major untapped world markets (Lafarge-Coppée in Central Europe and Airbus in China) and expand internationally through merger and takeover (Danone in Central and South America). There are signs that the period of major cost-cutting is drawing to a close and that the strategy of larger French firms is to regroup and to look towards expansion as the major source of long-term survival. After a period of renewal following the low point of 1993, forecasts for 1996 were relatively optimistic for a number of sectors: the automobile industry – including parts and accessories, building and construction, communication, electronics, computing, clothes and fashion, mechanical goods and services. Less positive were the prognoses for food and agriculture, chemicals, insurance, iron and steel, transport, tourism, and, above all, textiles, which are heavily affected by competition from East Asia. Nevertheless, in October 1995, the average growth level in all sectors was estimated at around 3 per cent (*Le Nouvel Economiste* no. 1021, novembre 1995).

The problem for French companies which have ambitious plans to expand abroad is a long-standing one: the lack of capitalisation. Despite a tradition of high state investment in industrial development in which France was third in the world in 1990 behind the United States and Japan, the current shortfall is linked to the fact that, despite major growth in the 1980s, Paris is still a relatively small financial marketplace. The capacity for investment by the general public remains limited. One of the most significant features of the French business environment is the inbred relationship between the public and private sectors which rely on each other's financial support to prop themselves up (*endogamie*). Large state-run companies invest in private firms, including banks, which in turn tie up large amounts of capital in relatively high risk expansionist schemes proposed by large French-owned groups. It only requires one major project of this kind to fail to place a bank such as the Crédit Lyonnais in serious financial difficulties and thus to destabilise the position of the state-owned corporation. The only alternative to this dangerously circular interdependency is to raise money abroad, through acquisition or flotation on foreign stock markets, a line taken by an increasing number of French firms.

The strong links between the state and private sectors nevertheless still predominate in France and reinforce a sense of national identity in the way in which French business operates. A solid infrastructure linked to chambers of commerce and business associations ensures that support facilities such as research, product testing, information on overseas markets and education and training are available to companies of all sizes, both regionally and nationally. At the same time, the growing need for large groups to consolidate their positions in the manner just mentioned has led to a greater dependency on the activities of small and medium-sized enterprises as providers of technological know-how or essential components. In terms of employment capacity, the proportion represented by SMEs/SMIs within French industry as a whole increased from 42 per cent to 50.5 per cent during the 1980s with an increasing tendency for smaller companies to be acting as subsidiaries of groups (*L'Entreprise* 1992).

During the 1990s the status of SMEs/SMIs has shifted as groups have shed subsidiaries in order to reduce costs, a tendency which has had the dual consequence of strengthening the potential importance of small companies for the national economy while making them much more vulnerable to competition and to pressure from their clients. Inevitably, the downsizing of groups in the early 1990s led to a marked increase in the level of small business failure, at first among the smallest firms but then in 1992–3 extending to companies with more than 100 employees. There was little room for forward planning in what directors saw as a depressingly hostile environment. Of the 100 directors of SMIs in the Rhône-Alpes region interviewed by the *Institut de Recherche en Entreprise* of the Groupe ESCLyon, 70 per cent were incapable of saying for sure whether their firm would survive the following twelve months (Silvestre *et al.* 1995).

Once again, the options for smaller units are limited. For those in more traditional sectors such as textiles, furniture and mechanical equipment, one strategy has been to attempt to establish and sustain a privileged relationship in a specialist 'niche', particularly one involving technological expertise, so that a state of mutual dependency can exist between the company and the principal 'client'. A related approach is to use the client's international expansion as a means of ensuring the SME's own penetration of foreign markets. The competitiveness of the environment has caused the groups which are the main clients of SMEs/SMIs to force down prices and make survival even harder. There has therefore been a tendency for smaller companies to attempt to form regional alliances so as to resist the top-down pressure of market forces.

As far as internationalisation is concerned, a clear distinction appears to exist between companies which view expansion outside France as an absolute necessity for survival and those for which it is simply not a feasible option. Certainly, successful internationalisation is difficult for companies with limited human resources at the managerial level. There may be a growing awareness that diversification and foreign expansion offer the only avenues to growth. However, despite the support at regional level for commercial agreements with developing economies, notably China and South America, the lack of expertise within SMEs/SMIs and the inability to plan on the time-scale necessary to establish successful overseas partnerships frequently make it hard for smaller enterprises to carry such strategies through.

The most dynamic areas and the ones which carry the greatest potential for growth for SMEs/SMIs are not surprisingly those involving technological expertise. Where such forms of expertise have specialist applications, they can provide a firm basis for a long-standing relationship based on trust and experience. It is clear that the future business environment for smaller companies will depend not only on the stable performance of the larger firms, but also on the ability of the managers and entrepreneurs at the head of smaller units to innovate and be flexible in their response to market demand. Once again, issues of technology management will need to be at the forefront of training programmes as will learning how to cope with unexpected variables in a context of rapid change.

As Crozier (1989) puts it, '*une logique nouvelle*' is needed in order to meet the challenges of post-industrial society and, as he sees it, whatever her structural problems, France is as well equipped as any developed country to do so successfully. It is hardly the object of this book to hazard a description of what that 'logic' should consist of, though certain of the central ideas proposed by Crozier and others are summarised in the concluding chapter. Rather, *The French Business Environment* aims to provide the reader with an essentially practical insight into the way in which business in France operates. In so doing, the book begins with an overview of the economic conditions of the recent past and considers the relationship between French traditions and institutions and the country's present economic performance. Next, it considers the particular characteristics of the French marketplace and the role and culture of marketing as an activity in France. Brief summaries of the accounting system and the operations of the financial sector lead to a chapter on the interaction between law and business practice. Finally, the volume examines developments in the field of organisational culture and human resource management including an insight into industrial relations.

In offering this overview, *The French Business Environment* aims essentially to provide a 'technical' introduction to the context of commercial activities in France. It may plot basic tendencies but, given its broad scope, it cannot provide detailed analyses of the different fields of expertise which it examines. As such, it is designed to be consulted alongside other publications with analagous, if somewhat different, objectives. These are referred to in the bibliography and at various points in the text. The central issue of how macro-economic changes at the national level impinge on organisational structures and practices within enterprises remains an underlying theme which has already been touched on and runs through the text as a whole. However, except in the first chapter, it is rarely made explicit and is only confronted in the conclusion's tentative statements about the future pressures to which the French business environment, like those of other European countries, will have to respond.

A book of this kind cannot claim to offer more than a limited perspective on an ever-changing cultural and economic kaleidoscope. With this in mind, the introduction and conclusion were written as a *mise en contexte* for the volume as a whole. It is hoped that the reader will consider them jointly as a summary which places the *French Business Environment* in a broader, if more subjective frame.

Lancaster
July 1996

Acknowledgements

There are many people without whom this project would never have been realised and to whom thanks are due: Rosemary Nixon, who first gave encouragement and support to the concept of a series on the European business environment using colleagues from different European countries, the then *Délégué à la Recherche* of the *Ecole Supérieure de Commerce de Paris,* Jean-Yves Eglem, who embraced the idea and formed a team from amongst the staff of the school, Loïc Cadin, also of the *ESCP,* who took responsibility for assembling the contributors for the human resource management section of the book and of course the contributors themselves who were always courteous and friendly, despite the embarrassing gulf which existed between their level of expertise and mine. It was a particular pleasure to work with Philippe Spieser on the first chapter of the book and to find that ideas which seemed at first like fantasies or anecdotes lent themselves to apparently rational economic explanation for which sound statistical evidence could always be found.

It was also reassuring to be able to count on the generosity of colleagues such as Stephen Ackroyd, Alexandrine Cerfontaine, John O'Hanlon, and Nick Snowden for their readiness to comment on early drafts of the manuscript and supply bibliographical information as well as on the insights of fellow editors Stephen Fox, Nigel Reeves and Helen Kelly-Holmes. My thanks are also due to Antoine de Bucy for his time and his shrewd analysis, to Rosemary Anderson, Claire Backhouse and Andrea Fish for their patience and word-processing skills.

Finally, I am grateful to our editors, Dominic Recaldin and Julian Thomas of Thomson International for their drive, unfailing support and sound experience. While accepting full responsibility for inaccuracies, misperceptions and omissions, I can only hope that the final version of the text is worthy of the effort and commitment of the original contributors who are its true authors.

Robert Crawshaw
Lancaster
July 1996

Translator's note

As recent research has indicated, the boundaries between translation and adaptation are, to say the least, indeterminate. Instead, the word 'rewriting' is often used to capture the process which is involved in recreating a source text in the context of a target culture. This is certainly the case for *The European Business Environment: France*. The original French versions of the contributions have been substantially edited, reduced, modified and in some cases combined in order to make the text more accessible to a non-specialist English speaking readership. Overlap in content has as far as possible been avoided, except where it was felt that it served to consolidate the reader's knowledge and insight into the subject matter. At the same time, a certain uniformity of style has been imposed on the disparities of the source texts as an inevitable consequence of the final version's being the responsibility of a single author.

Nevertheless, as was agreed with the authors/editors/translators of the companion volume on Germany, every effort has been made to respect the distinctive character of the series, namely that the style, structure and orientation of the original contributions were those of national experts in the disciplines concerned: economics, research and technology, marketing, finance and accounting, law, human resource management and the sociology of organisations. In the case of *The European Business Environment: France*, two colleagues from the *Ecole Supérieure de Commerce de Paris*, Jean-Yves Eglem and Loïc Cadin, were responsible for assembling a team from amongst staff at the school. They worked with the editor in maintaining contact with the individual contributors and in reviewing the original manuscripts. These were intermittently recast in their present form over a two and a half year period. Because of the constraints of space, the volume of the coverage had to be substantially reduced. Inevitably, the completeness of the overview has to some extent been compromised. In the chapter on law, for example, it was agreed to give priority to the main legal factors involved in setting up a firm in France and to the impact of the legal environment on employment and conditions in the workplace. Here, more than in any other of the fields, the chapter does little more than provide an introduction to the subject matter, leaving the reader free to follow up areas which need to examined in greater depth. The tone of the chapters varies, not simply because each was originally written by a different author, but because the content and focus were in each case different in kind. In all cases, the aim has been to respect the intention of the contributors, yet to convey their ideas in a clear and readable style.

Robert Crawshaw
Lancaster
July 1996

1   The cultural and economic context

Robert Crawshaw and Philippe Spieser

FRANCE AND THE FRENCH

It is difficult, if not impossible, to gain a satisfactory understanding of the French economy without taking account of certain traits which are inherent in the French character, culture and way of life. Many features of the country's economic structure and development can only be explained with reference to France's historical past and to the French nation's image of itself. Despite the obvious dangers of invoking ethnic stereotypes, a multiplicity of sociological studies and political analyses have attempted to capture in recent years the relationship between shifts in the economic climate, the structure of corporate organisation and the changing 'mentality' of French society (see in particular Albert 1991, Zeldin 1983 and, in more popular vein, *Francoscopie*, the biennial studies of trends and attitudes in French society compiled by Georges Mermet). Many of these studies have as their reference points fundamental historical principles which have governed the idiosyncratic relationship between the individual and the state in France for the last four hundred years, principles which still permeate many aspects of French life. The French are individualists, yet, as organisational theorists such as Crozier and d'Iribarne have pointed out, they have traditionally respected formal social structures based on clearly articulated, hierarchical precepts inherited from a feudal and monarchic past. Despite their self-preoccupation, they believe implicitly in the state as guardian of the collective good. The machinery of the Republic acts as protector of the personal rights and freedoms of the citizen and as provider of education, capital and managerial expertise for the country's most prestigious commercial organisations. Of all the nations in Europe, the French are perhaps the best adapted, temperamentally and culturally, to the obligations and relationships of a mixed economy. Clearly however, these long-lasting traits are subject to continuous change and one of the most compelling aspects of the French business environment is the way in which the traditional features of French organisations are responding to the social pressures of the global economy.

In general the developments of the last twenty years have shown an increasing tension between, on the one hand, the combined influences of mass media, modernism and technological advance and, on the other, the diversity of cultural traditions which still predominate in different parts of the country. As elsewhere in the world, modern communications have imposed a superficial uniformity on certain aspects of the French way of life, a uniformity symbolised by such features of global culture as fast food, international television channels and hotel chains, the American penetration of the film industry and Minitel, the on-line, interactive data service. Yet strong regional differences in France still lurk beneath a veneer of pseudo-Americanised materialism, coupled to a sense of national identity which goes back to the revolution of 1789 and beyond.

Despite Paris's being the cradle of modernism and the avant-garde, an architectural showpiece and one of the world's focal points for intellectual renewal, French society as a whole is still, in many ways, deeply conservative and resistant to the impact of political change. As de Tocqueville (1856/1904) was one of the first to point out, one of the great paradoxes of the 1789 revolution was that, far from abolishing the administrative structures of the *ancien régime*, its long-term outcome was to reinforce them. The organisation of local communities, for example, medieval in origin, was strengthened to such an extent by the First Republic that it has survived all more recent attempts at reform. Despite the law of July 1971 recommending a reduction in the number of *communes* (currently 36,700 – the highest number of local government units of any industrial country), only a dozen of them accepted to merge. Similarly, important state institutions such as the *Conseil d'Etat*, the *Cour des Comptes* or the *Grandes Écoles* have outlived the many different regimes which have been in power since their foundation.

More recently, successive changes of government during the 1980s and early 1990s have been accompanied by apparently radical alterations of course in economic policy and political ideology. Yet despite the apparently momentous movements between state and private ownership during the 1980s, accompanied by two devaluations of the French franc and shifts in the level of interest rates, the main infrastructure of social and economic institutions in France has remained intact. There have been few major educational reforms since the Second World War. The syllabus is still determined centrally by the state and enforced through a rigid system of inspection; teachers are nominated to schools by central government. The training and recruitment of officers to the *Corps d'Etat*, the senior administrative echelons of the French civil service, is essentially unchanged while the prestige of state employment as a whole (*la fonction publique*) has survived the fascination with private ownership and enterprise which swept over the country during the mid-1980s – doubtless aided by the high and durable levels of unemployment.

Inheritance in France is still strictly protected and inheritance tax is low. A citizen making a will is not free to choose the beneficiaries of his estate, a majority of which must pass to his close family. A substantial number of French households still do not pay income tax. The high ratio of savings relative to domestic earnings is a reflection of French people's tendency to invest in

Encadré 1: *Les Corps d'Etat*

The *Corps d'Etat* are the senior administrative bodies which advise and regulate the government of the French State. The military connotations of the word *corps* derive from the Napoleonic era (1799–1815) and the term relates to the council's main function which is to oversee the major arms of the legislature and the civil service – foreign affairs, the "interior" and, most prestigious of all, finance. Access to senior posts in the *Grands Corps* is gained almost exclusively via the *Ecole Nationale d'Administration* (ENA), the civil service *grande école* which is often used to complete specialist education undertaken at another school, typically an *Ecole des Sciences Politiques* (*Sciences-Po*). The *grandes écoles* are advanced, specialised institutions of higher education which are peculiar to France and are often seen as symbolising the principle of élitism within French government and society – including management. Ever since the establishment in the seventeenth century, the *Ecole des Ponts et Chausées*, there has been a strong emphasis on engineering, a focus reflected in institutions such as the *Ecole des Mines* and, most prestigious of all, the *Ecole Polytechnique*, founded by Napoleon to provide technical training for senior officers of the *Grande Armée*.

Policy proposals presented by the *Corps d'Etat* are regulated through the joint agencies of the *Conseil d'Etat* and the *Cour des Comptes*. The *Conseil d'Etat* (founded in 1799) is the Republican successor to the King's Council (*Conseil du Roi*) of the *ancien régime*. It is responsible for advising the government on administrative and legal matters. The texts of all laws proposed by the government are subject to the prior scrutiny of *Conseil d'Etat*. The *Conseil d'Etat* is also the senior court of appeal in France. It passes final judgement on cases referred to it by the *Tribunal Administratif*, typically those brought by citizens or private organisations against the state administration.

The *Cour des Comptes* (founded in 1807) is the inheritor of the institution established by Philippe le Bel in 1314. It has two roles:

- to audit state accounting procedures;
- to act as an appeal court for beneficiaries of the social security system and for public and private associations which are in receipt of public subsidies.

The *Conseil d'Etat* and the *Cour des Comptes* are hugely prestigious institutions of the French State and recruit their members largely from the *Ecole Nationale d'Administration*.

tangible goods (real estate, land or gold) rather than to purchase securities on the financial market. Despite a marked decline in the 1980s, the national domestic saving fund ('SICAV') is still the most active in the world relative to the size of the population. At the end of 1993, savings accounted for nearly 3,000 billion francs against a GNP of about 7,000 billion.

Even though many of the major French corporations are ostensibly in the private sector, there are close ties between senior management and officials of government as well as a movement of personnel in both directions. It is for this reason that the successive shifts from private ownership to nationalisation (1982–3) and back again (1986 and 1993) had only a limited effect on the internal structure and administration of the companies themselves.

Demographic factors

Traditionally, the growth in the French population has been slow. This was partly through self-regulation encouraged by the government in line with the Malthusian principle that a population's rate of increase should not exceed the growth rate of its productivity (Ariès 1973; Leroi-Ladurie 1975). According to this principle it is possible to assert that, in the period following the Second World War, France had the highest potential for economic growth of any European country. It also meant that the post-war baby boom caused less demographic imbalance in France than in other countries such as the UK. In a highly publicised advertising campaign, the French government continued to promote increased natality through special family benefit schemes until at least the end of the 1970s. The initiative was only partly successful. The density of the native French population relative to the physical size of the country is still relatively low and has made the French economy dependent on the contribution

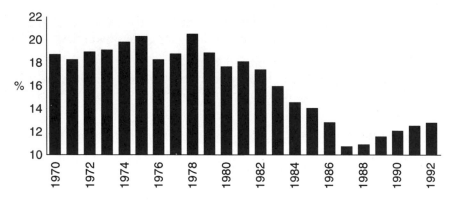

Figure 1.1 Savings in France as a percentage of disposable income (1970–92)

Source: INSEE

of immigrants and foreign visitors to manufacturing output. According to 1993 figures, there were 4.8 million foreigners resident in France. Nearly half of these lived in the Paris area representing 18.5 per cent of the population of the capital. Moreover, France's traditionally low birth rate has not prevented the country suffering from the same problem of demographic imbalance as other European nations, the consequence of the post-war boom and increased life expectancy. This will lead to the inevitable collapse of the French national pension scheme if no measures are taken. It is likely that in the near future, France will be forced to move from the traditional system of state-funded retirement benefit (*répartition*) to one which more closely resembles the private investment schemes prevalent in the US and Japan (*capitalisation*).

As in other European countries, the demographic imbalances in France have made the problem of unemployment among young people all the more significant for the country's medium-term future. In May 1994, unemployment in France reached nearly 3.4 million, representing 12.7 per cent of the active population, a rise of more than 1 per cent since May 1993.

After decades during which the major economic priority was inflation, unemployment has become the key criterion of electoral success and was the main cause of the crushing defeat suffered by the centre-left alliance in March 1993. In practice, however, there is little difference in the economic strategy adopted by recent governments other than that between defenders of an exchange rate policy which involves shadowing the Deutschmark, with the deflationary consequences which that entails, and supporters of a more flexible economic policy implying greater national independence from the rest of Europe. This distinction is a seam which runs through French society as a whole and cuts across the former political divide between right and left.

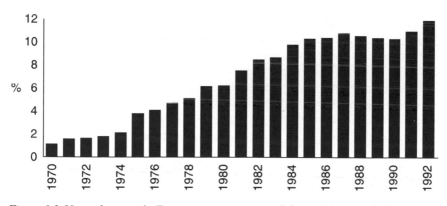

Figure 1.2 Unemployment in France as a percentage of the working population (1970–1992)

Source: *INSEE*

Table 1.1 Unemployment in OECD countries as a percentage of the working population (1983–92)

	1983	1984	1985	1986	1987	1988	1989	1990	1991	1992
Germany	7.7	7.1	7.1	6.4	6.2	6.2	5.6	4.9	4.4	4.8
Belgium	12.1	12.1	11.3	11.2	11.0	9.7	8.0	7.2	7.1	7.8
Spain	17.0	19.7	21.1	20.8	20.1	19.1	16.9	15.9	16.0	18.1
France	8.3	9.7	10.2	10.4	10.5	10.0	9.4	8.9	9.4	10.2
Ireland	14.0	15.5	17.0	17.1	16.7	16.2	14.7	13.4	14.9	16.1
Italy	8.8	9.4	9.6	10.5	10.9	11.0	10.9	10.3	9.9	9.9
Netherlands	12.0	11.8	10.6	9.9	9.6	9.2	8.3	7.5	7.0	6.7
Portugal	7.9	8.4	8.5	8.5	7.0	5.7	5.0	4.6	4.1	4.1
UK	12.4	11.7	11.2	11.2	10.3	8.6	7.2	6.8	8.7	10.0
Canada	11.8	11.2	10.4	9.5	8.8	7.7	7.5	8.1	10.2	11.2
USA	9.5	7.4	7.1	6.9	6.1	5.4	5.2	5.4	6.6	7.3
Japan	2.6	2.7	2.6	2.8	2.8	2.5	2.3	2.1	2.1	2.2
EU	10.3	10.7	10.9	10.8	10.6	9.9	9.0	8.4	8.7	9.4
OECD	8.5	8.0	7.8	7.7	7.3	6.7	6.2	6.1	6.8	7.4

Source: OECD

Physical imbalances

In many ways, respect for tradition in France is inseparable from an acceptance of the country's regional diversity. Any movement towards cultural homogeneity in France has taken place against the odds as a result of the imposition of power from the centre. France is a large and profuse country by European standards, both from a physical and a demographic point of view. Continental France, the biggest country in Western Europe, covers 551,695 km². This is significantly more than the area of Spain (520,000 km²), or even of the united Germany (390,000 km²). Despite the self-evident heterogeneity of other European countries such as Germany, Italy, Spain and the United Kingdom, the physical diversity of France, reflected in its landscapes, architecture and regional culture, is still one of its most significant national characteristics and is matched by the contrasts in population density between urban and rural communities.

These contrasts are overshadowed by the traditional domination of the Paris region which, with its 11 million inhabitants (against Lyon's 2.3 million), still accounts for 60 per cent of GNP. It has been commonplace to take account of the broad division of the country into the wealthier and more industrial eastern half and the comparatively more agricultural regions of the west and south. At one level this image of France is being modified through the development of ancient regional centres such as Toulouse, Bordeaux, Nantes or Rennes. Nevertheless, the physical contrast between town and rural *commune* remains. In about 80 per cent of the country, the level of population is still less than 100 inhabitants per square kilometre. What has changed is the national economy's traditional dependence on agriculture. Although France's rural populations still cling to

No. of inhabitants	Growth 1962–8 (%)	Growth 1982–90 (%)

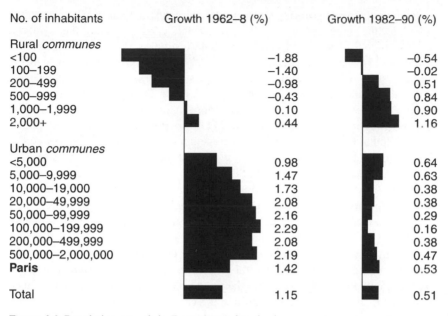

	Growth 1962–8 (%)	Growth 1982–90 (%)
Rural *communes*		
<100	–1.88	–0.54
100–199	–1.40	–0.02
200–499	–0.98	0.51
500–999	–0.43	0.84
1,000–1,999	0.10	0.90
2,000+	0.44	1.16
Urban *communes*		
<5,000	0.98	0.64
5,000–9,999	1.47	0.63
10,000–19,000	1.73	0.38
20,000–49,999	2.08	0.38
50,000–99,999	2.16	0.29
100,000–199,999	2.29	0.16
200,000–499,999	2.08	0.38
500,000–2,000,000	2.19	0.47
Paris	1.42	0.53
Total	1.15	0.51

Figure 1.3 Population growth in France's rural and urban *communes*
Source: *INSEE*

identities which are rooted in the farming traditions of individual provinces, in 1993 agricultural products represented only 6.3 per cent of GNP.

Outside Paris, the physical dispersal of economic forces within France has meant that an efficient road and rail transport network is essential. Ironically, it is this which continues to give the French farmers and railway employees a disruptive power which is out of all proportion to their real contribution to the national economy. It has also conferred a duality on many French people's attitudes to the countryside. The efficiency of the transport network has meant that it has become progressively more common to live in the country and to retain a sense of rural locality while travelling long distances to an urban place of work. In this respect, modernisation has enhanced many French citizens' consciousness of traditional values while improvements in infrastructure have focused attention on town and country planning issues (*l'aménagement du territoire*). The need has arisen to lessen the mobility of rural populations – particularly that of young people – and to limit the risk of social disturbance arising out of excessive concentrations of unemployed citizens in towns and cities. Government initiatives are promoting mixed uses of the countryside by encouraging the growth of 'greenfield' industry, commercial activity and tourism.

At the same time, sophisticated communications have brought about a convergence in the population's lifestyle and have, if anything, enhanced the role of Paris as the administrative and commercial heart of France. The centralised power of the state remains embodied by the capital despite the symbolic decentralisation of a limited number of state institutions such as the school for senior civil servants, the *Ecole Nationale d'Administration* (*ENA*), which has controversially moved to Strasbourg. France is still marked by major imbalances in the distribution of state investment. Under the Socialist administrations of 1981–6 and 1988–93, the main urban transport projects were concentrated on Paris, as were the state initiatives in medical provision and cultural development. The public funds allocated to the Bastille opera house accounted for 90 per cent of the total budget for French opera as a whole. At the same time, local taxes have undergone a substantial increase. Since 1993, the cost of 'lower secondary' education (ages 11–16) supplied by the *collèges* has been met by the *commune*, while that of the *lycées* (ages 16–18) has remained at the level of the *département*. This led to a huge rise in local taxation in 1992–3 while state taxes remained constant. The physical reallocation of national resources, a recurrent theme in France's history, has once again become a major political element in planning the country's economic future. While the enduring status of the *commune* and the executive authority of the *maire* are the main bastions of local identity in France, their very multiplicity tends to reinforce the centralising power of the state.

Despite or perhaps to some extent because of these changes, it is fair to say that the innate conservatism of the French has survived the political and financial turbulence of the last decade. However, it would obviously be an exaggeration to claim that French culture and traditions have not been marked, perhaps indelibly, by the garish materialism of the 1980s. Attitudes to religion, marriage and family life, food and leisure, have not stopped evolving, despite the recession. In different ways, these contrasts, which are an integral feature of contemporary life in France, are reflected in the culture and organisation of companies which have been forced to respond to higher level changes in the economic environment.

Changing models of management

According to d'Iribarne (1989), the traditional respect for hierarchies based on merit, an inheritance of the social structure under the '*ancien régime*', represented what he called a '*logique de l'honneur*' shared by a management class whose idealised sense of superiority and solidarity had been instilled by a highly selective educational system.

In the field of management, the notion of a meritocratic and technological élite groomed to govern the state, plan its infrastructure and build its physical amenities has been grafted onto the patriarchal system which, until the 1960s, still conditioned the ownership and organisation of firms (Szarka 1988). In the 1980s, the view of management as a 'profession' sought to rival, in career terms, even the huge prestige of the *Corps d'Etat* and to eclipse the executive status of highly qualified engineers within French industry. This development, part of a state-

Encadré 2: The administrative strata

There are four main levels of administration in France: the *état*, or state, the *région*, the *département* and the *commune*. The law passed on 2 March 1982 significantly modified their different responsibilities. Article 5 in particular gave *communes* and *régions* the authority to adapt social and economic policy determined by central government, provided that they respected a number of basic principles.

The *communes* are in charge of local administration, particularly of public works and the organisation of public services. They are free to create public services which they regard as essential to community life provided that these do not duplicate those created by the *état* and the *régions*. Their budget is based on four local taxes but consists mainly of state subsidies. The main problem of the *communes* is that they are too numerous (36,700 in all, of which 28,000 consist of less than 500 inhabitants). The consequence is that funding is too widely dispersed and thus too limited in each case to carry out serious measures.

The law of 1982 transferred responsibility for a number of public services from central government to the *départements*. These included part of secondary education (the *lycées* are financed at departmental level) and roads (since 1982, *routes nationales* have in fact become *routes départementales*). Like the *communes*, the *départements* suffer from financial shortages, being subsidised principally by central government. Their policies are affected by the high representation of the 'green' party on departmental councils, one reflection of the influence of rural inhabitants on the management of the local economy.

However, it is perhaps at the level of the *région* that the effects of the 1982 law were most significant. Under its new status of *'collectivité territoriale'*, the *région* was granted full competence to manage what are referred to as *dépenses de fonctionnement*. These include measures to promote employment through the disbursement of state subsidies to companies and responsibility for transport, training, housing and construction.

The effect of the law of 1982 has been to involve citizens more closely in the process of government and it has underlined the important role played by local politics in the economic and social development of the country as a whole. However, the relative complexity of the system encourages conflict between the different levels of government, while the degree of autonomy delegated to the *régions* increases the likelihood of mismanagement and the recurrence of the financial scandals (*affaires*) which are a regular feature of French political life.

Encadré 3: Hierarchy and honour's logic

'We should honour those in high rank (*Les Grands*) because they are high ranking while we are lowly and because there are others who are more lowly than ourselves who honour us' (La Bruyère 1665). In translating this tradition of caste under the *ancien régime* into a modern, industrial context, d'Iribarne was at pains to point out in his now classic book, *La Logique de l'Honneur* (1989), that the predominant culture of a typical French organisation is not simply hierarchical. According to d'Iribarne, it is based rather on respect for the individual's dignity and freedom of action within boundaries which are defined by role. Within French culture, abstract powers of reasoning are seen as more 'noble' than the responsibility of applying ideas in practice. Hence the deference which attaches to the status of *cadre* (see Barsoux and Lawrence 1990) and the level of education which such posts traditionally demand. However, for d'Iribarne, *noblesse* is distinct from *honneur* which may apply to any role whatever its status such that a spirit of mutual respect between different hierarchical strata supports both the principle of hierarchy and that of equality between individuals.

---

supported drive to promote entrepreneurship, was accompanied by the rapid expansion of management education, resulting from the successful development of *Instituts Universitaires de Technologie* (*IUT*) and the growth of regional business schools largely financed by chambers of commerce. There is now a measure of overlap between the major hierarchical categories just outlined. The sons and daughters of the heads of family firms are motivated to attend the senior schools of engineering and administration so as to add intellectual and professional prestige to the rights and duties of inheritance. Alternatively, a careerist aspiring to a senior management position is likely to seek a qualification from a *Grande Ecole de Commerce*, though the growth of management education in the 1980s has greatly increased the flexibility of the system.

The outcome of these tendencies has been to reduce the aura of exclusivity surrounding the *grandes écoles*, while, at the same time, the perception of the management process has itself undergone a substantial change. There has been a reaction, particularly by the owners of hard-pressed small and medium-sized enterprises (SMEs), against the patronising style of management cultivated by an 'élite' cadre trained in the *grandes écoles*. The level of technical expertise developed in the best of these schools has given way to more pluralistic management concepts based on personal competencies and performance goals (see Chapter 10). There is scepticism towards the universal value of the élitist principle. As in other areas of government, the traditional assumption that high-quality management education will itself resolve national balance of payments and productivity problems has to some extent been undermined. The recent dominance

---

Encadré 4: The Grandes Ecoles de Commerce

From the early nineteenth century, the traditional sectors of the *grandes écoles* – humanities and pure mathematics (*Ecole Normale Supérieure*), art and design (*Ecole des Arts et Métiers*), engineering and agriculture (*Institut National d'Agronomie*) and electronics (*Ecole Centrale*) – have been extended to include business and management. The *Grandes Ecoles de Commerce* of which the first was the *Ecole Supérieure de Commerce de Paris* (founded 1819) followed by its more prestigious sister school, the *Ecole des Hautes Etudes Commerciales* (*HEC* – founded 1881) now number 42 and are funded principally by regional chambers of commerce. They must, however, respect certain administrative and academic conditions, determined originally by the national ministry and regulated by a council known as the *Chapitre des Grandes Ecoles* which sanctions curricular reforms, conditions of membership, etc.

The *grandes écoles* are considered to provide the most effective training for senior management posts in France. Entry is via a fiercely competitive examination (*concours d'entrée*) and follows two years intensive preparation post-*baccalauréat* at specially designated *lycées* (*classes préparatoires*). Indeed it is extremely hard to accede to a top management position in France without a *Diplôme de Grande Ecole* the status of which as a management qualification exceeds a university degree even at postgraudate level.

---

of management and the traditional superiority of élite forms of training in administration and engineering have therefore both been called into question. As in the United Kingdom, it is acknowledged that the industrial training sector in France has been underdeveloped and that the qualifications of skilled workers and technicians need to be upgraded within the education system.

Nevertheless, the proportion of senior managers having a broad educational culture is higher in France than in any other European country. If the management profile is changing, it is because of the need for managers with wider social and interdisciplinary experience who are free of national and intellectual prejudices. Executives are increasingly more international, either because they have been educated outside France or because they are themselves foreigners. The advent of a new generation of managers, the increasing importance of SMEs as a source of recruitment and the rise in the number of mergers and takeovers between national and international companies have demanded not only knowledge related to specialist issues, but also more diverse skills – communicative, intercultural and technological. The recession in Europe has been a key factor in hastening the change in the skills requirements of middle and senior management in France – as in other European countries. The depth of the economic crisis of the early 1990s and the sharp rise in unemployment have meant that many graduates of the best schools have not been offered the opportunities which, in former times, they would have taken for granted as a natural right. In France alone, the number of job offers for managers fell from 98,000 in 1989 to 27,000 in 1993.

At the same time, a significant change of attitude has taken place during the last fifteen years towards the social responsibilities of senior management, a reflection of the more wide-ranging shifts in attitude towards the nature of entrepreneurship. Entrepreneurs are now held to be legally accountable to the public at large for the probity of their actions. Leading figures in business who attained the status of national heroes in the 1980s are currently involved in much publicised investigations into the ethics of their financial dealings. A new climate of 'equity' has permeated company dealings, an atmosphere which complements the harsh measures which middle management has had to implement during the difficult period which followed the 'boom years'.

'Downsizing' has led of necessity to much greater flexibility in the workplace with managers having to take on a range of functions for want of resources to satisfy specialist requirements on a tailor-made basis. This tendency, combined with that of 'outsourcing' by larger firms – closing down less profitable 'in-house' activities and purchasing equivalent expertise or base products from franchised suppliers – had by 1994 to some extent stemmed the flood of SME closures and was contributing to a resurgence of management opportunities in sales and computing. At the same time, evidence of graduate recruitment patterns in the first half of the 1990s suggested that the movement towards service industries which had been a major feature of the rise in the number of SMEs in the 1980s had, broadly speaking, been consolidated (Warwick University, 1993).

Management and the wider social context

These features of the French economic and social environment imply a society which, despite the pressures for change, has retained many of its centralising and élitist educational traditions. The institutions which still uphold these traditions have had to accommodate economic forces which have imposed more pluralistic patterns of employment. Changes in attitude towards training and management qualifications have taken place against a background of tentative recovery from recession. The upheavals of the 1980s have had a dual effect. On the one hand, the increased availability of globally marketed goods and advances in communication and technology have homogenised certain aspects of the French

Table 1.2 Corporate bankruptcies in France (in thousands) (1983–93)

1983	1984	1985	1986	1987	1988	1989	1990	1991	1992	1993
22.23	25.02	26.40	27.77	30.72	35.06	41.74	47.12	52.97	57.78	65.47

Source: INSEE

way of life. On the other, the 'unreality' of the enterprise culture, and its ultimate failure to sustain economic growth, have heightened the need to 'rediscover' regional differences and so regain a sense of 'permanence'. In economic terms, this has meant stimulating local development and diversifying land use, while respecting local traditions. On the demand side, there are signs that products in which utility and durability take precedence over 'design' are increasingly finding favour with French consumers (see Chapter 2).

At the same time, the widespread fall in levels of employment following the boom of the 1980s has undermined established management structures. The increase in flexibility and personal autonomy which has become essential to managers' professional survival has been accompanied by a sense of exclusion and marginalisation felt by those out of work. The political instability and growing disillusionment with government's inability to solve wider economic problems have led to a resurgence of nationalism, and, as in other European countries, have induced a feeling of scepticism towards international, and more specifically European, ideals. In a referendum held in 1992, the French population only approved the Maastricht Treaty on European Union by the narrowest of margins. They were openly hostile to elements in the worldwide General Agreement on Tariffs and Trade (GATT) agreement, most notably the clauses relating to certain agricultural products and those concerning the global deregulation of media products such as films and television programmes. Thus as the swing to the right in the 1994 European elections and the strikes and civil disorder of 1995 have demonstrated, the drive towards modernity has not eradicated a more deep-seated belief in the importance of economic and cultural independence, a trait which has always been part of French national identity.

However, the developments of the last fifteen years have radically affected the intellectual and entrepreneurial climate in France. By the end of the 1980s, France, unlike the UK, had created a new managerial class, a '*bourgeoisie nouvelle*', caricatured by the left and the conservative right as a European technocracy. Its archetype was the internationally minded professional entrepreneur, forward looking and optimistic about the future. In the 1990s, these 'new managers', having largely supplanted the traditional *patrons* of former generations, have lost the confidence and *élan* which they inherited from the previous decade. Deprived of job security and coping with the daily uncertainties of restructuring which have undermined established hierarchies, the French manager of the late 1990s is striving to maintain a sense of direction and rationality in a period of change.

THE FRENCH ECONOMY: A BRIEF OVERVIEW

France's recent economic history

In the broadest terms, it is possible to view the recent economic history of France as falling into two main periods: from the beginning of the twentieth century to the end of the Second World War and from 1945 to the present day. The main feature of the first period was the impact of low population levels, compounded by the effects of the First World War. This, combined with deflationary policies and political doctrines which favoured a closed economy, accounts for the relative weakness of the French economy during the first half of the twentieth century, but also for the preservation of a huge potential for growth which the country was then in a good position to exploit. The history of the second period

---

Encadré 5: 'Le Plan'

The French national economic plan, universally known as 'Le Plan', is a document drawn up by the state in which the major lines of future social and economic policy are laid down for the medium term. Although much less significant now than when it was first introduced in 1947, Le Plan still symbolises the interrelationship between the public and private sectors in France which brands the country as the archetype of a mixed economy. It bears the hallmark of French intellectual tradition in that it represents a holistic vision or framework which lends coherence or structure to individual measures undertaken by the state.

The original Plan, drawn up by Jean Monnet for the purposes of rebuilding the French economy after the war, was linked to the state takeover of the major sectors of industry – Renault cars, Air France, the coal mines, electricity and gas, insurance and banking. As such, it became inseparable from the France of the Fourth Republic (1947–58) and the early years of the Fifth Republic (1958–) under the Presidency of Charles de Gaulle. Since 1973, when Valéry Giscard d'Estaing acceded to the presidency, the influence of Le Plan has waned, though, as is shown by this and other chapters, the tradition of central state intervention in private enterprise and more generally in the development of economic infrastructure, including research, remains a dominant force in French culture and society.

Le Plan is drawn up by a council (Commissariat Général) established by the Conseil d'Etat in full collaboration with the major agencies of social and economic activity – the trade unions, the employers' federation (CNPF) and the banks and insurance companies. Since 1947, there have been ten plans of which only the first three and the fifth under de Gaulle have had a decisive influence on the direction taken by the French economy. Despite de Gaulle's pronouncement that the fifth plan should represent a serious moral commitment ('ardente obligation') for the country, subsequent plans have not been binding on companies but have laid down the conditions under which financial support may be made available in different spheres of activity.

is one of dramatic but fluctuating growth characterised by the themes of reconstruction, liberalisation and European cooperation in the wake of a significant post-war baby boom.

After the period of reorganisation in the immediate aftermath of the Second World War, France entered the 30-year phase of growth widely known as '*les trente glorieuses*', lasting from 1950 to the first oil crisis of 1973. However, although during this period France benefited from a high growth rate, the country's favourable economic development was accompanied at first by considerable political instability and a high rate of inflation which was linked to the pressures of reconstruction and European cooperation. This was due in some measure during the 1950s to the high degree of central state planning of the economy which was nevertheless essential in order to establish a sound basis for future development. The need for less regulation was underlined in reports by Sadrin-Wormser (1958) and Rueff (1959) whose recommendations were accepted by the incoming administration under the presidency of de Gaulle. Thus, from 1958, with the phase of reconstruction effectively completed, France entered a period of less constrained economic activity in which the government, by promoting growth, could be said to have given France a 'new deal'.

The post-1958 phase of France's post-war economic development also coincided with the opening up of the French economy following the signature of the Treaty of Rome in 1957. The movement towards free trade within Europe was not universally welcomed by the *Conseil National du Patronat Français* (*CNPF*), which feared that the French economy would not be able to resist the shock of external competition. The fact that it did so was due essentially, as we have seen, to a combination of favourable demographic trends and a sound economic base. The astonishing expansion of the French economy from 1960 to 1973 was accompanied by a high degree of investment and a low rate of

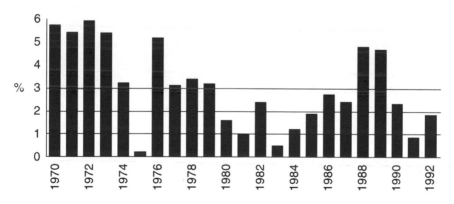

Figure 1.4 Annual growth of French GNP (1970–92)

Source: *INSEE, Comptes Nationaux*

unemployment, and by the progressive withdrawal of the '*Le Plan*' following the election of Georges Pompidou to the presidency in 1969.

The period from 1974–93 is more varied and can be divided into two main parts:

- The first (1974–80), coinciding with the presidency of Giscard d'Estaing, is the phase of absorption of the first oil crisis. During this period, France tried to rediscover its former rate of growth in the face of inflation and rising unemployment.
- The second (1981–93) – the 'Mitterrand years' – has led to a period of perhaps lasting unemployment, low growth and varied economic policy. A substantial increase in the money supply in 1981–2 was accompanied by a comprehensive investment programme leading to two devaluations of the franc. This was followed sharply by three years of harsh budgetary constraint followed by a phase of euphoria between 1986 and 1990. Since 1990, economic policy has been dominated by the need to reduce the budget deficit to 3 per cent of GNP in line with criteria laid down by the Maastricht Treaty and to minimise the risk of inflation.

The 1980s were therefore extremely lively and variegated years with boom leading to restriction followed by caution and a short period of sustained economic growth. The economic environment was briefly buoyed up by the end of the cold war and the effects of German reunification. This last event provided early prospects for French exports creating an unexpected external surplus in 1991 and 1992, but these were soon replaced by depressionist trends caused by the general rise of interest rates in Europe.

The period beginning in 1993 appears to have marked another break in the economic history of France. The high level of unemployment continues to rise and is unlikely to fall to pre-1973 levels in the foreseeable future. This has inevitable long-term consequences for the budgetary deficit in the sense that the public sector borrowing requirement (PSBR) includes not only the public funds raised by the state itself and the financial requirements of local authorities but also the cost of benefits which is increased by high levels of unemployment. The problem of reducing unemployment is not eased by the apparent mismatch of the educational system to the economic needs of the country. Although the quality of traditional education in France and of that provided for the managerial élite has been a significant residual factor in accounting for the country's growth rate, it has failed in recent years to provide a dominant advantage in technologically based areas faced with competition from the Far East and Pacific Rim countries. It now seems clear that the adaptability of the French economy through the flexibility of its workforce is the single most important challenge of the years to come.

The contribution of residual factors to France's economic growth

One of the main features of Solow's (1956) model for analysing rates of growth was to give greater prominence to the influence of education and training on economic growth. He represented this 'invisible' element of growth as a 'residual factor'. Not surprisingly, traditional factors of production cannot in themselves account for the fluctuations of the French economy since the beginning of the century. Apart from changes in the external economic climate, it is necessary to recognise the development of knowledge and know-how within a population as well as certain underlying structural features of a society such as technological progress. It is only recently that the importance of residual factors has been fully appreciated, a fact which has led to serious political debate, in France and elsewhere in the Western world, about the cost-effectiveness of the educational system relative to State investment, particularly in the wake of the irresistible rise in unemployment. Education has accounted for an ever-increasing proportion of the state budget, yet in 1994, 23 per cent of the population under the age of twenty-five was unemployed against only 10 per cent in Germany, an increase of almost 4 per cent in less than two years. It has become increasingly clear that the relationship between levels of education and national economic performance is not a direct one and the issue is the subject of deep controversy worldwide in view of the strain placed on levels of public spending throughout the Western world.

It seems that despite France's impressive achievements in specialised fields of education which have led to the constitution of a highly qualified élite, educational investment has been less effective in developing a combination of technical and managerial skills at middle and lower levels. This has traditionally been an area in which Germany has excelled. However, Europe as a whole suffers from a lack of competitiveness in the field of technical education and training where it has been overtaken in levels of knowledge and efficiency by newly industrialised countries elsewhere in the world. In France, as in other major European countries, there is a quantitative and qualitative lack of intermediary industrial skill which is seriously threatening what has historically represented a 'residual' advantage.

Underlying structural factors

The superficial conclusion of any structural analysis of the French economy in recent times is that it has developed in the post-war period from an economy based on small industry and agriculture to one dominated by services and multinational groups.

However, although in the first instance the modernisation process created jobs, it has proved not to provide a secure basis for long-term employment and has made the underlying problems in the economy if anything more acute.

Table 1.3 Services in France as a percentage of GNP

1980	1985	1992
59.0	66.8	71.1

Source: *INSEE*

The composition and quality of the workforce

Statistical evidence of recent changes in the composition of the workforce allows the following broad conclusions to be drawn:

- Although, clearly, the level of education has not ceased to progress since the beginning of the century and has evidently made a substantial contribution to growth, the government initiatives of the early 1970s and 1980s appear not to have been as successful as they should have been given the level of investment.
- Generally speaking, despite obvious exceptions, a worker is more productive in mid-career than at a younger or more advanced age. In this sense, the age structure of the French workforce improved in the period after 1973 as a generation of executives born in the post-war baby boom came to power.
- The active contribution of women to the workforce has increased progressively and is still doing so, a fact which implies that women's skill levels are also rising. Although, in the last thirty years, this has also been a feature of other European economies, it is more marked in France than in the UK, Germany or the Netherlands, reaching 45.8 per cent of the working population in January 1990. The average level of education for women is now superior to that of men. Moreover, the tertiary sector is more open to the type of highly skilled manual jobs which employ a high proportion of women. However, while 75 per cent of 'office workers' are female, women only account for 29.5 per cent of senior executives and members of the 'intellectual' professions.

It should be noted that 54 per cent of jobs are accounted for by the services and trading sectors and that the only categories to undergo an increase are white collar workers, commercial executives and the so-called 'intellectual' professions. As we have seen, another important feature of the workforce is the proportion of foreigners. At 6.3 per cent of the active population, it remains the highest in Europe, even though the overall number of officially registered foreign workers decreased from 1.08 million in 1979 to 690,000 in 1992. Unemployment among foreign workers has risen considerably faster than among French citizens, a fact which explains in part and is a function of the increase in racial prejudice. Immigrants' countries of origin have remained largely unchanged for twenty years and derive in large measure from France's colonial past, particularly in North Africa, with Algerians representing 19 per cent, and Moroccans 13 per cent of the non-French workforce; 46 per cent are EU citizens.

Foreign workers in France are concentrated in the construction sector, represent 18 per cent of the workforce and generally have a low level of qualification with 57 per cent being 'unskilled' workers. The problems of immigration in France, as in other northern member states of the European Union, have been exacerbated by the freedom of mobility enshrined in the European Single Market Act introduced in 1993 (the Schengen Agreement). Although the immigrant populations are different in France, Germany and the UK, and the tensions which they arouse are specific to each culture, immigration in all three countries represents one of the single most important issues which each society has had to face as it has grappled with the problem of rising unemployment.

Whatever the composition of the workforce, the fact remains that, to an even greater extent than in other European countries, unemployment has been the most enduring problem faced by successive French governments since 1973. As in the UK, more and more of the unemployed are young and unskilled or, on the other hand, experienced people in late middle age who cannot easily find another job. The problem has proved particularly intractable in the 1990s since the option of artificially boosting the growth rate, as happened in France under the Socialists in the early 1980s, and, disastrously, in the UK in 1988, has not been open to recent French governments, whatever their political persuasion, because of the recession elsewhere in the world. Paradoxically, the problem has been exacerbated in the mid-1990s by the interdependence of the different European economies. The effect of being tied too closely to the development of other member states of the Union has meant that France, like Spain and Italy, and, until recently, the UK, has had to respond to fluctuations in the German

Table 1.4 Origins of foreign workers* in France and Germany in 1989

Country of origin	France	Germany
Greece	–	116.4
Italy	103.8	206.6
Portugal	413.3	42.5
Spain	101.5	67.3
Other EC	88.7	
Total EC	707.3	–
Austria	–	–
Finland		–
Turkey	65.0	651.6
Yugoslavia	30.7	329.3
Algeria	258.5	–
Morocco	187.0	–
Tunisia	76.2	–
Others	269.1	526.9
Total	**1593.8**	**1940.6**

Source: INSEE

Note: *Figures in thousands

economy. On the other hand, too great a divergence between the national partners of the European Union would lead to even greater external disequilibrium, making it impossible to plan for steady growth (see Bensahel *et al.* 1992.

The changing structure of the business sector

Underlying the structural features which have affected the composition and productivity of the workforce and equally significant to them have been the changing contributions to the national economy made by different sectors. France is now to a large extent a service economy. In terms of value added, the four sectors which contribute the most to tertiary output are:

● public administration;
● distribution and commerce;
● market support services to industry;
● real estate and buildings.

Together, in 1992, they accounted for 49 per cent of GNP, against 23.9 per cent for industry and only 3.4 per cent for agriculture. Across sixteen other sectors, the level of contribution has altered profoundly over the last ten to fifteen years and clearly reflects the changing structure of the French economy. If we compare the annual growth rates of various sectors between 1983 and 1992, remarkable differences appear. Financial services, for example, increased by 82 per cent while, during the same period, household durables fell by 13 per cent. Shifts such as these have clearly had lasting effects on the growth rate and the crisis of the 1990s can in part be explained by the fall in demand for 'traditional' goods. Industry in the strict sense only accounts for 20 per cent of paid employment, 24 per cent if food, agriculture and energy are taken into consideration. Moreover, France's progress towards a post-industrial economy seems to be accelerating and will continue in the future to have a negative effect on the level of employment.

Nevertheless, certain French industrial groups now rank among the biggest in the world. In terms of sales, French companies represented nine out of the top 100 in 1993, and thirty-three out of the top 500 – the same number as Germany. The European Union as a whole had 139 in the top 500, USA 153 and Japan 120. Renault, the top French group, was ranked thirtieth in the world, Peugeot, Elf, EDF and CGE (electricity and engineering) between fortieth and forty-fifth.

Three remarks in particular can be made about these groups:

● Only two are genuinely private companies (Peugeot and CGE) while two are state owned (Renault and EDF), though the legal status of Renault is subject to frequent review. The two main petroleum groups (Elf and CFP-Total) are under mixed ownership though the state holds approximately 50 per cent of the shares. Here again, the state's holding has diminished through the public's right to buy shares in Elf, a process of privatisation completed in 1994.

- These groups are related to only one sector – the automotive (car) industry, a fact which demonstrates how vital car production is for the French economy. Table 1.5 shows the distribution of the top seven French companies between the different sectors.

  Among the seventeen groups whose turnover is more than 50 billion francs, there are three public utilities, La Compagnie Générale des Eaux, France-Télécom and the Post Office. However, the size of the services sector, normally a net creator of jobs, has not led to a significant reduction in the scale of unemployment since, with certain notable exceptions such Air France and the Régie Autonome des Transports Parisiens (RATP), the drive for greater efficiency has led to downsizing in most sectors.

- The position held by French firms in the international hierarchy is due to a drive by the French government to promote external growth and to a multinationalisation process which is extremely recent. In line with the removal of all barriers to the free movement of capital from 1 January 1993, the French Treasury has lifted the requirement that all inward and outward flows of capital be subject to government authorisation, a measure which has assisted French groups such as Rhône-Poulenc or Péchiney to become truly multinational. In addition, it is worth noting that there is a close link between the size of French groups and their export performance. The biggest firms are the biggest exporters which means of course that they make the biggest contribution to the balance of payments surplus.

Table 1.6 shows that over the eleven-year period between 1982 and 1993, the top exporting firms have remained unchanged. It is also interesting to note that 90 per cent of French exports is accounted for by only 50 of the 125,000 French firms which export.

External imbalances and the exchange rate

France is one of the most commercially active countries in the world, being the fourth largest exporter behind the USA, Japan and Germany. However, France's

Table 1.5 The top ten French firms by turnover (in 1000m) in 1993

1.	ELF Aquitaine	209.7
2.	EDF	183.6
3.	Renault	169.8
4.	Alcatel-Alsthom	156.3
5.	Générale des Eaux	147.6
6.	PSA Peugeot Citroën	145.4
7.	Total	135.5
8.	France Télécom	127.0
9.	Carrefour	123.2
10.	Lyonnaise des Eaux	93.6

Source: *INSEE*

Table 1.6 The top ten French exporters in 1982 and 1993

	1982	1993
1.	Renault	Renault
2.	Peugeot	Peugeot
3.	Airbus	Airbus
4.	Citroën	Citroën
5.	IBM France	IBM France
6.	Michelin	EDF
7.	Union Sidérurgique	AVSA
8.	Valluorec	Sollac
9.	Alsthom	Snecma
10.	Thomson	ELF

Source: *Le Nouvel Economiste*

external balance of trade has always been problematical, despite dramatic growth levels between 1960 and 1990. Between 1983 and 1993, France's average rate of growth was 1.4 per cent against 1.9 per cent for the UK and the Netherlands, 2.6 per cent for Spain and 4.2 per cent for Ireland. Between 1970 and 1990, imports grew by 800 per cent against 650 per cent for imports. Currently, imports represent about 25 per cent of GDP and exports only a little less, whereas at the beginning of the 1960s they stood at 1 per cent. Some 60 per cent of France's trade is with EC countries; 55 per cent is with only five countries in the world (Germany, Italy, the UK, Belgium and the USA), whereas until the 1950s France's external trade was concentrated mainly on its colonies.

Generally speaking, France runs a deficit on its balance of trade in goods while invisibles remain in surplus. However in 1992, for the first time since 1986, France registered a surplus in its balance of payments due, in the main, to a fall in French investment abroad and an improvement in the balance of services. Thus the country's current account has traditionally been in balance

Table 1.7 Annual rates of growth (%) for OECD countries (1970–90)

	1970	1980	1985	1986	1987	1988	1989	1990
Belgium	6.4	4.1	0.8	1.6	2.3	4.5	4.0	3.4
France	5.7	1.6	1.9	2.5	2.3	4.2	3.9	2.8
Germany	5.0	1.4	1.9	2.3	1.5	3.7	3.8	4.1
Italy	5.3	4.2	2.6	2.5	3.0	4.1	3.1	2.6
Spain	4.1	1.2	2.3	3.2	5.5	5.1	5.0	3.5
Netherlands	5.7	1.5	3.4	2.6	0.4	2.7	4.1	2.9
UK	2.3	−2.3	3.7	3.8	4.6	4.6	2.1	1.5
EC/EU (12)	4.6	1.4	2.4	2.7	2.6	3.9	3.4	2.9
Canada	2.6	1.1	4.7	3.2	4.0	4.3	2.9	1.0
Japan	9.5	4.2	4.9	2.4	4.6	5.7	4.8	6.1
USA	−0.3	−0.1	3.3	2.7	3.4	4.4	2.5	2.7
OECD	**3.1**	**1.5**	**3.4**	**2.6**	**3.4**	**4.4**	**3.3**	**2.7**

Source: *INSEE*

with deficits being recorded on the capital side, the overall balance of payments of a country being derived from that of 'visible goods' (i.e. commercial exchanges), exchange of services, and inflows and outflows of capital resulting from payments for goods and services and long-term financial settlements. If the exchange of services exceeds that of commercial trade, then an economy can be described as a 'service economy'. The last figure in particular (the balance on financial exchanges) acts as a measure of the attractiveness of an economy for foreign investors (i.e. if the figure is negative, it implies that a country is exporting more capital than it is importing). Since the 1980s, France has increased its attractiveness for investors. It was in 1988 that trade in services rose to a level equal to 50 per cent of trade in goods.

The way that France registers its balance of payments implies that the commercial balance is in equilibrium when exports represent more than 95 per cent of imports. Exports are accounted 'free on board' (FOB), that is shipping and delivery costs are excluded, while in accounting for imports, transport and insurance costs are included. France's balance of trade went seriously into the red in 1974 following the first oil crisis. It progressively worsened in subsequent years reaching 62 billion francs in 1982. In the second half of the 1980s it became positive, fell again after 1990, and then recovered as a consequence of German reunification which led to a massive rise in demand from France's main European partner. The extent of these movements and the rapidity of their succession underline the fact that France's economy, like that of any other European country, can no longer be out of phase with that of its main partners without running the risk of increasing its trade deficit. In practical terms, this means that the level of France's exports must be more responsive to demand from its trading partners than is the demand for imports in response to internal growth. In other words, France, like any other country wishing to show a positive balance of payments must be less dependent on other economies than other economies depend on it.

Apart from fluctuations in the balance of trade, there are significant weaknesses in the composition of the goods and services exchanged. Exports have tended to remain reasonably consistent, concentrating on specific industrial sectors such as cars and chemicals, agro-industrial and agricultural products. The composition of imports on the other hand has changed radically since 1949. Over the last forty years, the French market has progressively opened up to the importation of foreign products. Between 1949 and 1990, the proportion of total imports represented by industrial goods rose from 45.4 per cent to 80 per cent. Inevitably, the size of other sectors simultaneously decreased, from 16.7 per cent to 5 per cent for agricultural products, 16.6 per cent to 7.5 per cent for the agro-industrial sector, and 21.3 per cent to 10.6 per cent for energy. The progression of these trends was interrupted by the increases in the world price of oil which revealed the extent of France's dependence on external sources of energy. The relative decline in energy imports can be explained by France's substantial investment in nuclear power and, to a large extent, could be said to justify it in strictly economic terms.

France is no exception to the general rule that the main consequence of a fragile trade situation is that there is less margin for manoeuvre in economic policy. Any increase in public consumption risks promoting a degree of disequilibrium which becomes progressively harder to correct. Such a situation leads to the type of 'stop-go' policies which marked the transition in the UK from the 1970s to the 1980s and affected France to a lesser extent in the early 1980s. Internal growth must therefore be kept in line with export levels. Alternatively, the temptation of imposing import controls is always present, but carries with it the more serious threat of reprisals from a country's main trading partners.

Thus, in general terms, at least five main features characterise France's position as a trading nation:

- **France's dependence on imported energy**   This acts as a constraint on the economy despite substantial reductions in cost, the price being dependent on the exchange rate of the dollar.
- **The underdevelopment of agricultural industry**   This means that there is inadequate transformation of farming produce. Although, as a traditionally agricultural nation France has a high level of primary produce, its industry for converting this into foodstuffs or other products is relatively small.
- **A steady fifteen-year deterioration in the country's industrial trade surplus**   This trend appears to have been arrested since 1991 due in part to the consequences of German reunification which, as we have seen above, has temporarily provided France with a new market opportunity. At the same time, the fragile situation of the industrial sector is in marked contrast with the buoyant state of trade and transport services. Although these sectors promote the production of industrial goods like trucks and lorries, these products are extremely sensitive to short-term fluctuations in the economy and to fierce foreign competition. For instance, the biggest French producer of lorries and commercial vehicles (Renault Véhicules Industriels) was forced to find an overseas partner, Volvo, only to have its proposed merger with the Swedish car manufacturer fall through at the last moment.
- **A relative improvement in competitiveness due to a progressive reduction in labour costs**   The recent decline in the rate of increase in labour costs has led to a better balance of trade and a larger share of the international market, and has generally safeguarded the position of the French franc within the European Monetary System, despite moments of crisis such as that of August 1993. Once learned, this lesson is hard for governments to forget, despite its negative consequences for domestic demand and the risk of industrial unrest which can all too easily follow – as the events of 1995 clearly demonstrated. Nevertheless, despite having been reduced, the traditional weakness in the French balance of trade still exists since France exports relatively less to developing countries than it did fifteen years ago.
- **An effort to stabilise the balance of trade by controlling the exchange rate**   This has followed the successive shocks of two devaluations in 1981

Table 1.8 Percentage annual change in the rate of increase of unit labour costs in France (1980–92)

1980	1981	1982	1983	1984	1985	1986	1987	1988	1989	1990	1991	1992
15.3	14.3	14.1	10.0	8.2	6.6	4.3	3.5	4.0	4.9	5.4	4.0	3.2

Source: INSEE

and 1983. A policy of shadowing the Deutschmark has replaced the experimental strategy of the 1981 Socialist government in which devaluation was presented as a deliberate means of gaining competitive advantage. Although, to a limited extent, this may have been a confidence boosting preparation for the period of austerity and subsequent growth which followed, in the immediate term it led to more inflation, an increased deficit in the balance of trade and a serious upset in the French tradition of close macro-economic regulation. However, the more recent policy of stable exchange rates has been put under extreme pressure by the combined forces of recession, high German interest rates and the vagaries of international currency speculation. These are of course maladies which have afflicted all European countries since 1991 and it has only been through extensive depletion in France's foreign reserves that the country's exchange rate policy was able to weather the storm of 1993. In this, France has shown a consistency lacking in the UK, Spain and Italy. Whether this consistency will eventually pay off remains to be seen. It is one significant indicator of the tension between France's desire for independence in agreements on world trade and the need to safeguard the stability of its relationship with its European partners, in particular Germany. The regulation of exchange rates has, however, made it easier for France to control another long-standing problem, that of inflation.

Controlling inflation

France's success in controlling inflation, like that of the UK, has corresponded to the slowing down of the rate of increase in labour costs referred to above and, despite failures in other areas, has been one of the most impressive successes of the country's recent economic performance. Yet over the twentieth century as a whole, the level of prices in France has risen dramatically. During the First World War, prices rose by 250 per cent. They doubled between 1919 and 1939 despite a progressive fall during the Great Depression of the 1930s. In the period between 1945 and 1960, prices again multiplied by eight, thus effectively increasing 160-fold between 1913 and 1960. In that year, a *nouveau franc,* equal to 100 old francs, was finally introduced. Since that time, inflation has slowed down significantly.

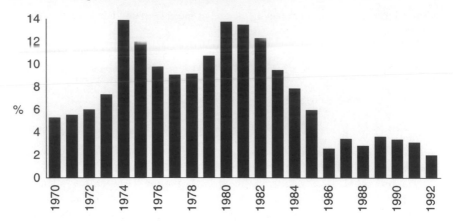

Figure 1.5 Mastering inflation: the inflation rate in France (1970–92)

Source: INSEE

Table 1.9 Annual percentage change in retail prices in OECD countries (1960–90)

	1960	1965	1970	1975	1980	1985	1987	1988	1989	1990
Germany	1.4	3.4	3.4	5.9	5.4	2.1	0.2	1.2	2.7	2.6
Spain	1.5	13.2	5.7	17.0	15.6	8.8	5.2	4.8	6.7	6.7
France	3.5	2.5	5.3	11.8	13.5	5.8	3.1	2.7	3.6	3.4
Italy	2.3	4.6	5.0	17.0	20.9	9.1	4.7	5.0	6.2	6.4
UK	1.0	4.8	6.4	24.0	18.0	6.0	4.1	4.9	7.7	9.4
EC/EU (12)	–	3.9	5.0	14.5	13.8	6.1	3.3	3.6	5.3	5.6
USA	1.6	1.7	5.9	9.1	13.4	3.5	3.6	4.0	4.8	5.3
Japan	3.6	6.6	7.7	11.7	8.0	2.0	0.1	0.6	2.2	3.1
OECD	**1.8**	**2.9**	**5.6**	**11.8**	**14.1**	**5.1**	**3.2**	**3.5**	**4.6**	**5.2**

Source: INSEE

Since 1991, for the first time in forty years, inflation levels in France have been lower than those in Germany. As a side-effect of the 'new relationship' between the two countries, France has gained a share in the very competitive German market. French people have begun to feel that they can compete with their neighbours and long-standing rivals on equal terms. The so-called 'virtuous circle' which had been a feature of Germany's rising prosperity – containment of costs leading to an external surplus leading in turn to a revaluation of the currency – has also become a feature of the French economy. Having once achieved this, it makes it very difficult to identify a new economic policy which would enable the country to recover more quickly from the recession of the early 1990s than that of further reducing labour costs and thereby slowing down internal growth.

Even though it would be dangerous to conclude that inflation has been radically and definitively eradicated in France, it is certain that, in the mid-1990s, the extreme mechanisms which caused it to rise in the past have been abandoned. The regulation of the exchange rate since 1983, and, more recently, the holding down of wages, have been directly linked to stricter monetary controls. It is a basic tenet of economics that control of the money supply, the exchange rate of a currency and inflation are closely linked. Limiting the amount of money provided for the economy maintains its value in real terms and, if linked to solid future prospects, should increase the confidence of foreign investors. In support of this argument, economists also cite the relationship between the 'twin deficits' – the budget deficit and the external deficit. These combine to boost inflation, first because excess demand places pressure on prices and second because excess imports undermine the real value of the currency. The tighter budgetary policy linked to high levels of output which successive French governments have maintained since the mid-1980s made it easier to control the money supply until the sharp fall in world trade in 1992–3. This was perceived as a crisis in France and caused receipts to fall well below estimated levels.

The monetary policy of the newly elected President Jacques Chirac came under further pressure in 1995. The attempt by the Prime Minister, Alain Juppé, to reduce the budgetary deficit from a level approaching 5 per cent led to widespread public unrest which emphasised the acute difficulty within a highly developed economy of simultaneously reducing state expenditure, engineering growth and maintaining social stability.

The rise in the Public Sector Borrowing Requirement (PSBR) since 1992, a problem France shares with other European countries, has been shocking given the already high level of state revenue. After a period between 1970 and 1973 during which direct taxation (*prélèvement obligatoire*) stabilised at around 35 per cent, it rose dramatically from 35.7 per cent to 44.6 per cent between 1973 and 1984. It then settled at around 44 per cent of GNP between 1984 and 1992. Since 1985, it has become an objective of government policy to reduce income tax, which would necessarily imply a reduction in public spending. However, given the present levels of unemployment and the traditional dependence of the French population on the health and social security systems, there is clearly a limit to the amount that social contributions can be cut back.

Table 1.10 France's public sector borrowing requirement as a percentage of GNP (1981–93)

1981	1982	1983	1984	1985	1986	1987	1988	1989	1990	1991	1992	1993
2.03	2.53	3.44	3.61	3.39	2.91	2.60	1.76	1.68	2.30	2.89	3.04	3.90

Source: INSEE

CONCLUSION: EMERGING FROM CRISIS IN A NEW EUROPE

As is well known, the crisis in world trade which hit Europe in the years following 1992 was the biggest since the Second World War. Although the symptoms have been the same throughout the continent, each country has been affected differently in terms of unemployment rates, levels of inflation, external balances and public deficits. While in 1993 Germany registered a fall in GNP of 1.9 per cent, France, in the words of Alain Peyrefitte's best selling book *Le Mal Français* (1974), could be said to be suffering from a 'French disease' which is different in kind from that of its British neighbours, though its economic impact is broadly similar. This 'disease' can be analysed from a relative and an absolute point of view.

In many ways, when compared to its European partners, France is facing problems as serious as those of any other country in the Union. While Germany has had difficulties coping with the immediate consequences of reunification, it is likely that the country's residual strengths will once again make it the dominant economy in Europe at the end of the century, notwithstanding the internal social issues caused by imbalances in standard of living, unemployment and frustration on the part of the population living in the western part of the country at having to accept a relatively lower level of prosperity. Competition with France's great neighbour will quickly become tougher as the investment in the former East Germany begins to reap rewards. Already by the end of 1993, the Volkswagen factory at Zwickau in Saxony was the most profitable in the group and was achieving standards of quality on a par with the Japanese. Having effectively opted out of the European Exchange Rate Mechanism, the United Kingdom has overcome the predominant recessionist tendencies before its European partners and has succeeded, albeit superficially, in reducing the level of unemployment. It remains to be seen how firmly founded Britain's recovery really is. Italy, despite its deep political crisis, is showing a positive balance of trade. Among the larger European countries, only Spain is showing signs of profound economic difficulties with uncontrollably high unemployment, excessive levels of borrowing and an unfavourable balance of trade. In the long run, France will not find it any easier than its partners to conform to the conditions of the Maastricht Treaty, a challenge which will be further complicated by the entry of other European countries to the Union.

On the other hand, certain of the long-standing weaknesses of the French economy have been overcome, most notably the vulnerability to inflation and the over-readiness to have recourse to protectionism. Even in the aftermath of the events of November 1995, the economic policy of both the Socialists and the right-wing alliance, which can be summed up as *la politique du franc fort*, is only likely to be questioned if there is no improvement in the unemployment situation. However, although it is extremely improbable that the French government will adopt any policy which puts at risk the country's relationship with Germany, the extent to which the population as a whole will continue to

---

Encadré 6: EMU – the Maastricht criteria

The conditions for entry to a European Union based on a single currency laid down by the 1991 Maastricht Treaty are:

1 Each member state must attain a sufficient degree of price stability. This is represented by an annual rate of inflation which should be not more than 1.5 per cent above that of the average of the three countries with the lowest rate.
2 The public deficit must be below 3 per cent of GNP unless it is showing a progressive decrease.
3 The currency must respect a narrow margin of fluctuation according to the terms of the European Monetary System and should not have been devalued for at least two years prior to joining the Union.
4 Public debt must be less than 60 per cent of GNP.
5 The long-term interest rates should not be more than 2 per cent higher than the average of the rates of the three countries showing the greatest price stability.

---

favour closer *rapprochement* with Europe remains an open question. One of the most important problems which French governments must tackle now and in the future is the cost of the education system and its 'return' in terms of the French economy's ability to create lasting jobs. Put simply, the question is: how can an educational system which is so expensive leave so many people out of the labour market? One answer would be to overhaul the social and fiscal system so as to reduce the high level of social contributions. This narrowing of the gap between gross and net wages would diminish firms' employment costs but would make it essential to reduce the burden on the social security budget by partially removing healthcare and pensions from the public sector, a complete reversal of the policy followed by the centre-left governments of the 1980s. Finally, it will be necessary for a higher proportion of people than at present to pay direct taxes. At present only 50 per cent of total households do so, a proportion which represents the middle class on whose support all governments depend. The future of the French business environment will be directly determined by the political courage of governments in facing up to these challenges which imply redefining the traditional relationship between the French population and the state.

SELECTED TEXTS

Albert, M. (1991)
Attali, J. (1994)
Barsoux, J.-L. and Lawrence, P. (1990)
Birnbaum, P. (1993)

Bremond, J. and Bremond, G. (1990)
Cayrol, R. (1994)
Gordon, C. (1995)
Guigou, E. (1994)
Mermet, G. (1995)
Szarka, J. (1992)
Weil, P. (1991)
Zeldin, T. (1983)

See Bibliography

2 Consumers, products, markets and the marketing process

Renaud de Maricourt and Benoit Heilbrunn

Like most other advanced countries, France is entering the post-industrial era. The effects of this process, which has been steadily accelerating since the beginning of the 1980s, have sometimes been painful, as much for the economic and industrial infrastructure as for society itself. As far as companies are concerned, it has meant much greater flexibility in production methods, a substantial cutback in manpower in the secondary sector and a loosening of organisational structures in response to changes in the external environment. These consequences have been combined with the growing significance of information as a source of power (Badot and Cova 1992). Like other West European countries, France has recently experienced difficulty in safeguarding employment levels, training young people, maintaining its balance of payments and modernising its structures. In seeking answers to two overriding questions – Is it possible to control unemployment? Where does the country stand in relation to the European Union? – the country has taken at least three major steps: to control inflation, to give higher priority to investment and to cut back on public spending.

FRENCH SOCIETY AND THE MARKETPLACE

In his book *Mythologies* which appeared in 1957, Roland Barthes outlined a number of myths which he claimed were the symbolic cornerstones of French society after the Second World War – the Catholic priest, '*L'abbé Pierre*', the potency of '*le bifteck et les frites*', '*le Tour de France*', the then avant-garde 'Citroën DS' and the new multi-purpose material '*le plastique*'. After almost forty years, with only slight modifications (*le football* has replaced *le Tour de France* and the *Twingo* the Citroën DS), these myths still remain intact in the French imagination. Nevertheless, in other important respects, the images of French society differ considerably, not simply from those sketched by Barthes, but also from the picture presented eight years later by Georges Pérec (1965). These more recent shifts in French behaviour are recorded in the biennial sociological portrait of France drawn up by Gérard Mermet (1995).

National character and social values

As early as 50BC, in his *Gallic Wars*, Julius Caesar noted the Gauls' penchant for internecine squabbles and their taste for good food. Some 1,700 years later, in attempting to define the particular character of each of the European nations, Diderot described the French as '*léger*'. They were, he said, incapable of taking even the most important subjects seriously, least of all themselves and other people. Today, the traits most commonly associated with the French are refinement (the enjoyment of luxury), sophistication, gallantry, gastronomy and, more negatively, ethnocentrism and arrogance. A lexical survey carried out by *CREDOC* analysed the expressions given in reply to the question: What does the expression 'to be happy' mean to you? The most frequently recurring terms were: 'have', 'family', 'be', 'health', 'life', 'money', 'work', 'child'. The main concerns of the French are, in order of priority, health, family, money and work (see Table 2.1).

Are the French more or less happy than their European compatriots? A 1991 study attempted to determine an overall indicator of national happiness by asking: In general, are you very, generally, scarcely or not all satisfied with the life that you are leading? The results of the survey are shown in Table 2.2.

Table 2.1 The French view of happiness: some defining criteria

Good health	78%	An interesting job	19%
A successful domestic life	38%	A home which I like	5%
To have children	25%	None of the above	2%
Not to lack money	23%		

Source: *France Soir/CREDOC* October 1991

Table 2.2 Degrees of satisfaction with life in different European countries

	1973	*1980*	*1991*
Denmark	95	95	97
Netherlands	93	95	93
Germany	82	85	85
Belgium	73	88	88
UK	85	86	85
Luxembourg	79	92	94
Spain	–	70	78
Ireland	92	86	86
France	77	70	74
Italy	65	64	79
Portugal	–	50	73
Greece	–	58	53

Source: Eurobaromètre

Note: Figures represent the percentage of survey respondents describing themselves as 'very' or 'fairly' satisfied

In general, with the exception of France, there seems to be a positive correlation between the level of satisfaction and the level of economic development of the country concerned. Even though, according to the *INSEE* classification, 75 per cent of the French population live in 'reasonable' comfort, it seems that the pleasure of being French is more widely appreciated by foreigners than by the French themselves who are prey to a number of frustrations. The most prominent reasons for this dissatisfaction include the questioning of institutions (political parties, the unions, the church), the growing dehumanisation of the urban environment (more than 48 per cent of Parisians live alone), and, perhaps, nostalgia for the time when France played a leading role on the international stage.

CREDOC also questioned the French about the constraints under which they live: 41 per cent declared that they felt restricted by their spending capacity on holidays and leisure, 38 per cent on their budget for clothes, 31 per cent on that for household equipment and 20 per cent on the level of funds available for food. If they could have an increase in their purchasing power, the vast majority of those interviewed would give priority to holidays and leisure, a fact which reveals a clear development in the aspirations and desires of French society (see Table 2.3).

Over the last ten years, the French economy has suffered a number of structural shocks; most notable among these have been France's rapid internationalisation, the significant cutbacks in the profitability of industrial manufacturing (this represented 21.7 per cent of GNP in 1990) and the growing heterogeneity of the country's industrial infrastructure. During the 1980s, France lost one million industrial jobs. Conversely, the service sector grew fast. The main structural problem which confronted France in 1990 was therefore that the country's growth in productivity was approximately twenty times higher than that of its level of employment, an imbalance which would have stifling consequences for the economy in the years which followed. (At a purely anecdotal level, it is revealing to record a selection of positive and negative economic indicators for the year 1992 – see Table 2.4).

At the same time, France has entered a 'global economy' in which nationally based concepts of companies, jobs and investments no longer have any real meaning. In 1992, France became the leading centre of investment in the world. Although it only contributed 7 per cent to world trade, it attracted 12 per cent of global capital invested outside a country of origin. In that year, almost 85,000

Table 2.3 Where the French would spend their money in the event of a salary increase

Holidays and leisure	85.4%	Food	37.3%
Clothes	64.8%	Medical care	24.5%
Housing	57.3%	Drink, tobacco	8.3%

Source: *CREDOC*

Table 2.4 Some fields where France was number one in Europe in 1992

Contribution by nuclear power to total electricity	70%
Expenditure on health as a proportion of GNP	8.9%
Number of cinemas	4,441
Number of casinos	138
Annual consumption of alcohol per person	19 litres
Proportion of households owning a second residence	13%

Source: Mermet 1996

Note: Data relates to 1993

million francs were invested in French production by foreign firms. France itself was the second investor in the world with a total of 99,600 million francs being spent abroad. On the other hand, foreign capital was responsible for one-third of French export sales and accounted for one-quarter of salaries in the industrial sector. Furthermore, nearly two-thirds of the turnover of the top thirty French groups were due to international activity, primarily that of subsidiaries (36 per cent). In other words, in 1992, the jobs of more than one out of every two French employees were dependent on decisions made at the supra-national level.

Most of France's external trade is with the EU. In 1991, it accounted for 61.4 per cent of exports and 57.9 per cent of imports to metropolitan France. The strength of the European link varies according to the product. As regards imports, most energy-related products originate in distant countries; industrial purchases, however, are generally made from materials supplied by France's European neighbours. For exports, the opposite is true – the market for agricultural and food products is mainly restricted to the countries of the EU, while industrial products tend to be sold further afield.

Movement in the level of market share (imports over internal demand at standard prices) shows a fall in domestic supply in numerous sectors such as leather, textiles and automobiles and the maintenance of a dominant position in

Table 2.5 French imports as a percentage of national sales

	1974–8	*1980*	*1983*
Agriculture	14.5	14.3	15.2
Meat and dairy products	9.1	9.5	9.8
Chemical and pharmaceutical products	12.3	13.1	14.3
Household goods and equipment	40.0	44.2	53.0
Motor vehicles	23.4	26.9	32.4
Shoes and leather products	23.8	31.1	37.0
Textiles and clothing	21.5	26.9	32.4

Source: INSEE

other sectors such as agriculture and pharmaceuticals where there is only slight foreign penetration. Yet the French are so sensitive to the native origin of products that, according to a survey by the newspaper *Libération* in 1993, they are ready to pay 10 per cent more for a product if it is French. Given that the fact of publicising the 'Frenchness' of a product can lead directly to a purchase, it is possible in France to refer to the 'citizen consumer'.

Demographic factors

At the end of the Second World War, France had a population of 40.5 million inhabitants. This grew to 50 million in 1968 and by 1 January 1993 stood at 57.5 million for the metropolitan mainland. For several decades, France has had the fastest level of population growth of any country in Europe; yet it remains underpopulated relative to its surface area. According to *INSEE* forecasts, the French population will number between 65 million and 75 million inhabitants by the middle of the next century which represents a density of between 118 and 124 inhabitants per km^2.

Since the beginning of the 1980s, the national birth-rate has stabilised at about 760,000 births per year, that is at about 10 per cent less than what it was at the beginning of the 1970s. Moreover, the average age of women at the birth of their children is increasing. In 1990, it was 28.3 against 26.8 ten years earlier. The progress in pre-natal diagnosis having reduced the dangers of giving birth up to and beyond the age of 40, the number of births now being deferred amounts to nearly 100,000 per year. While 10 per cent of women remain childless, the average number of children per mother has stabilised for the last ten years at around 1.8. In 1991, life expectancy at birth was 81.1 for women (French women live on average longer than other women in 12 out of the 15 countries of the EU, hence France's higher level of widowhood) and 73 for men. The shorter life expectancy for men can partly be explained by medical causes and partly by factors relating to lifestyles (tobacco, alcohol, driving accidents) which affect men to a greater extent than women. Individual variables are still significant, however. A primary school teacher lives on average nine years longer than a manual worker.

As in all advanced countries, the population in France is gradually growing older. According to current projections, the proportion of men and women over

Table 2.6 French population by different age groups

	Less than 20	*20–64 years old*	*65 and over*
1946	29.5	59.4	11.1
1960	32.3	56.1	11.6
1980	33.2	54.0	12.8
1992	27.1	58.6	14.3

Source: INSEE

sixty will represent 34 per cent of the population in the year 2000, whereas it was only 16 per cent in 1950. During the 1980s, purchasing power shifted towards those in retirement who tend to consume less. A retired household receives a level of income per person which is 98.5 per cent of that of an individual in full employment while its per capita level of consumption is only 93.5 per cent. This ageing of the population presents society with a threefold problem, that of dependence (which presently affects 1.5 million elderly people), healthcare (8.3 per cent of GNP in 1991 against 3 per cent in 1950) and pensions.

At the strictly demographic level there are several other phenomena which are worthy of note. The first is the diminishing number of large families (with more than three children). This phenomenon can be explained by the fall in the birth-rate following the baby boom years (1945–70). Clearly this has affected all European countries but, as we have seen, it seems to have had less of an impact in France than elsewhere in Europe, probably as a result of a vigorous and well-coordinated policy promoting childbirth undertaken by successive post-war French governments. This comprised more generous family allowances, tax relief for large families and a special effort to provide childcare facilities for the benefit of working mothers (see also Chapter 1).

Between 1968 and 1990 the number of households increased by more than 37 per cent. Smaller in size than in the past, they now number in total 21.5 million. Some 5.8 million people live alone, including 1 million single mothers, a phenomenon due to the breakdown in the traditional family structure which is accompanied by the increase in single parent families, in the number of births outside marriage and in the rate of extra-marital cohabitation. In 1990, 27 per cent of households consisted of single individuals while single parent families represented 7.2 per cent of families overall.

Table 2.7 French population by age group: predictions to the year 2020

	0–19 (%)	20–59 (%)	60+ (%)	Total population (in millions)
1995	26.1	53.7	20.1	57.221
2000	25.5	53.7	20.8	58.226
2005	24.5	54.3	21.3	59.054
2020	22.0	50.1	28.0	60.541

Source: INSEE

Table 2.8 The average size of households in France

1962	3.10 people
1975	2.88 people
1990	2.57 people

Source: *Recensements de la population*, INSEE

The concept of the family has therefore been radically transformed and no longer corresponds to what it once was. Even though it may remain the dominant model, marriage has to some extent lost its status in France as the cornerstone of family life; 12 per cent of couples live together outside wedlock and this number rises to 30 per cent if only couples aged less than thirty are taken into consideration. It follows that there is a continuing increase in the number of babies born to non-married couples. These represented 30.1 per cent of births in 1990 against 11.4 per cent in 1984 – a telling comparison! Another interesting statistic is the rise in the number of children born to couples of which at least one of the parents is foreign, 15.3 per cent of the 533,000 legitimate children born in 1990. Studies on this topic demonstrate that immigrant parents tend to have more children than native French, but less than in their country of origin, pointing to the relative speed with which they adapt to the way of life of their new compatriots.

Finally, there has been an increase in the number of 'dual spending' households which consume more durable goods. In France today, families which spend the bulk of their income on life outside the home, that is on goods and services linked to personal welfare rather than to household goods, represent only 25 per cent of households nationally.

The changing state of employment

Not surprisingly, the structure of the working population has changed dramatically since 1950. The number of workers in the primary sector (agriculture) has declined considerably. After the war it represented almost 30 per cent of the population. By the dawn of the twenty-first century, it is estimated that it will have fallen to less than 4 per cent. The manufacturing sector absorbed this fluctuation in the workforce at first and expanded in the 1950s and 1960s. Subsequently, it has continued to decline in favour of the tertiary sector (services). Although the problem of unemployment became more acute in the early 1990s as a consequence of deindustrialisation and the decline in world trade, the size of its increase was due primarily to the fact that the tertiary sector could not absorb the labour surplus released by the other areas of the economy.

Another striking feature of the recent past has been the rise and subsequent fall in the number of managers which has accompanied the fall in the number of industrial and agricultural workers (see also Chapter 1). As has just been suggested, the latter group in particular declined dramatically from 31.5 per cent of the population just after the war to a mere 5 per cent in 1991.

Table 2.9 The French working population by sector of activity

Primary sector	5.5
Secondary sector	28.9
Tertiary sector	65.6

Source: *INSEE*

Table 2.10 The French working population by category

	1968		1991	
	Total	*Women*	*Total*	*Women*
Agricultural workers and farmers	11.5	12.8	5.0	4.4
Craftsmen, traders and owners of small companies	10.7	11.5	8.0	6.2
Managers and senior intellectual professions	5.1	2.5	11.6	8.4
Middle professions	10.4	11.4	20.1	20.3
Office workers	21.2	38.8	26.1	47.3
Manual workers	39.3	22.5	28.1	13.3
Others	1.8	0.5	1.0	0.1

Source: *INSEE*

Table 2.11 Women's employment as a percentage of the working population

1970	54.8%
1980	69.5%
1990	78.6%

Source: *INSEE*

As in other European countries, the increase in unemployment has had a significant impact on the stagnation of household consumption. Overall, a French family with one member out of work spends 25 per cent less than a family which is unaffected by unemployment. Other general trends in patterns of employment include:

- **The increase in irregular working hours**   In 1993, one out of every two people in employment regularly worked on Saturday, while Sunday working affected one employed person out of five. Night-time work was undertaken by 12 per cent of the working population.
- **The rise in the insecurity of work**   Some 8 per cent of people in work occupied short-term posts in 1993, twice the number registered in 1985.
- **The development of performance-related pay**   In 1990, reward based pay increases affected 2 million people in employment, against 600,000 in 1986 and accounted for more than 10 per cent of total salaries in small and medium-sized enterprises (SMEs).
- **The increasing gap in the job market between supply and demand**   To an ever-greater extent, new industries and services require a highly qualified and versatile workforce. However, this demand is not matched by the supply of human resource which is still characterised to an excessive extent by young people who have not entered the right educational stream or by an ageing and

underqualified workforce, well adapted to the high opportunity period of the 1960s and 1970s but less in tune with current needs.

- **The continuing decline in the length of the working week** Since July 1984, the length of the working week has hovered around an average of 39 hours while in 1969 it was 45.2 (see Chapter 5 on the legal environment). Part-time work is a significant factor in this development. It affects 11.8 per cent of working people, particularly women (23.4 per cent).

The French as consumers

The increase in disposable income has brought about a rise in consumption since the beginning of the 1970s, a rise which has been accentuated by the fall in the rate of saving; between 1959 and 1989 expenditure on food almost doubled, while spending on health multiplied by seven and that on leisure by four. However, the increase in consumption tended to slow down as a consequence of the stagnation in purchasing power which only increased by 1.7 per cent in 1992 and by 0.3 per cent in 1993.

In 1991, each household spent a total of 190,000 francs on consumer goods, that is an average of 72,000 francs per person. The main areas of expenditure were:

- **Food** There has been a decline in the extent of expenditure on food which, in 1993, represented on average less than 20 per cent of family income. This arises partly from the fact that people are tending to lead a less physically active way of life but is also partly due to the explosion of the agricultural and food sectors accompanied by more intense competition and the development of supermarkets.
- **Health** The social security system in France reduces by three-quarters the direct cost of health to the consumer. There has been an increase in the volume of goods and services purchased, a fact which has been masked by the reduction in the relative prices of pharmaceutical products, thanks to a squeeze on profit margins by laboratories and pharmacists.
- **Leisure** There has been a consistent progression in expenditure linked to the increase in leisure time and to spending on household goods. French

Table 2.12 Savings in France as a percentage of gross disposable income

1981	18.0
1983	15.9
1985	14.0
1987	10.6
1989	11.7
1991	12.6

Source: INSEE

people devote a quarter of their budget to expenditure of this kind, having a strong propensity to acquire property, particularly individual houses. The average size of property has shown an increase and there has been a growing concern for comfort.

The above developments are linked to relative price levels. Technology-based goods cost less thanks to growth in international competition and a rise in productivity due to technical progress, economies of scale and the benefits of experience. Thus, prices have fallen for products such as watches, tape recorders, computers and CD players but have risen for postage stamps, newspapers, cinema seats and hairdressing.

At the same time, in the last few years, there has been a change in purchasing behaviour characterised by the more systematic search for the lowest price or the 'best deal' and by the growing disloyalty towards national brands. French consumers react favourably to the development of distribution systems (sales depots, warehouses, bargain-price collections and the wide range of goods available in supermarkets). Some distributors, such as Leclerc or Monoprix,

Table 2.13 Patterns of household expenditure in France as a percentage of spending

	1959	1970	1980	1991	2000*
Food	36.0	26.0	21.4	19.2	16.5
Clothes	9.3	9.6	7.3	6.3	5.1
Residence	9.3	15.3	17.5	20.3	19.0
Furnishing and upkeep	11.2	10.2	9.5	7.7	8.7
Health	6.6	7.1	7.7	9.8	16.4
Transport and communication	9.3	13.4	16.6	16.1	15.7
Leisure, education, culture	5.4	6.9	7.3	7.6	8.6
Other	12.7	11.5	12.7	13.0	10.0

Source: INSEE

Note: *Figures for the year 2000 are projected

Table 2.14 Patterns of household expenditure in the USA, France, Japan, Germany and the UK as a percentage of spending

	USA	France	Japan	Germany	UK
Food products	13.1	19.4	20.4	16.5	21.1
Clothes	6.6	6.5	6.4	7.7	6.2
Housing	19.3	18.8	19.2	18.4	19.5
Furnishings and upkeep	5.6	8.1	6.1	8.8	6.9
Health	15.3	9.2	10.8	14.3	1.3
Transport and communications	14.5	16.8	10.2	15.1	17.7
Leisure, education, culture	10.0	7.3	10.2	9.0	9.5
Others	15.6	13.9	16.7	10.2	17.8

Source: INSEE

retail the products of reputed couturiers under their own brand name. Thus, loyalty to the image of the manufacturer is diminishing as is brand loyalty. In short, the French consumer has become an economist who makes decisions in order to maximise the use of personal resources.

Overall, there are signs of convergence between countries, despite certain exceptions: the Irish still devote 40 per cent of their budget to food against less than 20 per cent in countries such as Germany, France or the United States.

THE STRUCTURE AND ORGANISATION OF COMMERCIAL ACTIVITY

French attitudes towards marketing

As a country with a long tradition of self-sufficiency and a culture which still clings to a peasant way of life – although today farmers represent less than 6 per cent of the working population – French people have an ambiguous attitude towards commercial activities. Traditionally, peasants dislike and distrust businessmen whom they accuse of trying to rob them. In Greek and Latin mythology, Mercury, the god of trade and commerce, was also the god of thieves. The Christian church too was prejudiced in its attitude towards money and those who trade in it. Vestiges of this outlook still remain; marketing only established itself recently in France and has long been considered a less than serious activity which was secondary to more 'noble' disciplines such as engineering, research, production and, more recently, finance. French companies still suffer from shortcomings in marketing knowledge and techniques. They tend to be too rigid and insufficiently aggressive in foreign markets, and to show reluctance to invest in market research, after-sales services and even in advertising. Socially, a job in 'sales' is not highly rated; a 'sales person' is normally referred to as a 'commercial engineer'. What is sometimes referred to as '*l'esprit marketing*' – a combination of skills, an instinctive feel for the basic mechanisms of communication and exchange, the ability to put oneself in the position of another person and to adapt his/her point of view – is often missing in France, while it tends to be present to a much greater extent among populations with a commercial tradition. Such defects can be detected in the circumstances of daily interchange; clients or the users of public services are not spontaneously well received. They are considered with suspicion if their demand does not immediately correspond to the offer which the provider is ready to make.

Things are changing, however. The pressure of necessity is forcing companies to become aware of the importance of marketing in a modern economy. Firms are investing more heavily in marketing both in terms of money and human resources. The lessons of the North American experience are beginning to be assimilated. Close attention to technological detail, product testing, strategic planning and market forecasts have become tools which are in current use. In so far as functions create instruments, a marketing orientation, externally focused, which underpins all these methods and ensures their appropriate application, is gradually replacing the focus on production which has for so long predominated among the directors of French firms.

Market research

A study carried out in 1991 has shown that market research has shifted from being a support function to a position where it plays an integral role in the strategic activities of the company – a sign of the positive development in attitudes towards marketing in many firms in France. As a cerebral activity which demands little long-term investment, business-related research is extremely fragmented. There are well over 100 specialist institutes operating in this area, excluding the research departments of numerous companies, advertising agencies and firms of consultants which, apart from acting as subcontractors, occasionally carry out studies themselves. Table 2.15 gives the names of the main research institutes in 1992.

In the crisis-ridden atmosphere of 1992–3 which was marked by a slump in media advertising, investment in market research continued to increase, if only

Table 2.15 Principal market research agencies in France in 1992

Ranking	Name	Turnover (in million francs)	% change on previous year	Number of personnel
1	A C Nielsen	473.00	−4.8	850
2	SOFRES	298.00	+6.4	351
3	SECODIP (SOFRES group)	290.00	+4.7	620
4	Ipsos (CRCS Auxerre)	119.00	+4.7	150
5	Médiamétrie	115.00	=	75
6	BVA	109.74	+11.2	171
7	IMS France (medical sector only)	102.00	–	107
8	Research International	88.00	+8.6	100
9	GFK France	82.00	+64.0	150
10	MV2 Conseil (Publicis group)	75.00	=	63
11	ISL	73.00	=	100
12	TMO Consultants (INRA network)	72.00	+2.9	60
13	IFOP (Borçarse and the Parisot group)	64.00	+12.3	180
14	Insight (Ipsos group)	58.00	−14.7	57
15	Institut Français de Démoscopie (Cofremca)	52.00	=	70
16	Burke Marketing	51.20	+0.6	50
17	George Chetochine Conseil	47.00	+4.4	35
18	Novaction	37.00	+5.7	40
19	WSA (+ in Viro – SRC group)	33.85	+13.6	20
20	Louis Harris France	33.00	+32.0	24

Source: Syntec, *Editions de marché, Rapport annuel*, May 1993

by 1 per cent. The total market in 1992 was approximately 4,000 million francs. Although in 1991, too, the market only rose by 1 per cent, the average annual growth in this sector over the previous ten year period was around 14–15 per cent (9 per cent in real terms after inflation), representing a rate of growth four times higher than that of the economy as a whole. The present tendency is towards a relative decline in research into consumer products. This is balanced by the growth in the number of studies in the fields of telecommunications and new technologies in general, as well as in the sectors of medicine, public health, distribution and services, both private (banks and insurance) and public.

Another recent trend in the market research sector is that of concentration. Among the major agencies, Insight merged with Ipsos in January 1993 while the organisers of consumer panels, SECODIP, was taken over by SOFRES in 1992. There has also been a tendency for middle-sized institutes to specialise, a development which has come about both for reasons of quality and as a consequence of market pressures. Institutes which are more 'focused' on a particular sector or on a specific type of study enjoy a higher level of credibility with clients. There has been much talk of internationalisation. However, in practice, according to a report by Syntec, income from abroad only represented 10 per cent of turnover in France in 1992. It may well be the high cost of research which makes it difficult for the French to export.

The cost of research

It is certainly true that market research in France is expensive. According to a comparative study carried out by ESOMAR (1991), prices in France were 40 per cent above the European average for all types of study. The difference was particularly marked for group discussions (+68 per cent) and for in-depth analysis (+52 per cent). An interesting audit of BSN's research department based on 350 studies carried out in 1990–1 for twelve companies in the BSN group, showed that the average prices for qualitative studies were 3,700 francs per individual interview and 4,700 francs for focus groups. For quantitative research, the average cost per interview was about 305 francs for tables alone, and 395 francs if the findings were incorporated into a full report.

The crisis of the early 1990s has heightened competition, and somewhat stabilised prices. In 1993, for example, Ipsos was charging between 100 and 250 francs for quantitative research interviews (Lallemand and Jardin 1993). It is true that, contrary to other agencies, Ipsos conducts most of its interviews by telephone (68 per cent), and that the majority of these, being computer based, are less expensive than the traditional pen and paper method. The breakdown of costs for quantitative studies by Ipsos:

- the study itself – 40%;
- data collection – 50%;
- data analysis – 10%;

The complete process involves the analysis of the client's needs, the recommendation of an appropriate methodology, the formulation of questionnaires, data collection and the analysis of the results.

Methods and product types: current trends

A number of tendencies are dominating the types of study which are presently undertaken. These include:

- The shift from purely descriptive research to research which is predictive or explanatory – market simulations, forecasts for the performance of new models, positioning of new brands and advertising research.
- The replacement of *ad hoc*, highly focused studies by 'series-based' research including regular follow up studies based on set procedures which are progressively more international. These include, for example, studies into advertising impact and efficiency, company or brand image, and customer satisfaction.
- Improvements in the instruments of control in such areas as the length of time required to complete a study, the communication of information, reliability and the response to enquiries. New means of measurement have been developed based on information derived from the national census, while technical aids such as electronic scanners have replaced the analysis of questionnaires based on the traditional interview.
- The development of studies into customer satisfaction which, until 1990–1, were still relatively infrequent in France. These studies involve large industrial companies such as car manufacturers as well as services (banks, insurance) or public services (post, telecommunications). In order to cater for this new demand, Ipsos, for example, has created a company: Ipsos Unicab, which is specialised in this area of research (Lallemand and Jardin 1993).

There has also been a growth in the number of studies into social problems, notably those involving young people, the environment, aspects of social behaviour and tendencies in public attitudes. Similarly, studies measuring 'total quality' have followed the vogue of total quality control prevalent in many large firms. These studies have been as much external as internal and have frequently mixed qualitative and quantitative techniques. In general, there has been a merging of qualitative and quantitative studies, most notably in customer satisfaction surveys, advertising pre-tests and image studies.

As regards methods, France is ahead of other European countries in the field of qualitative research which, in 1991, represented approximately 30 per cent of turnover against 10 per cent in the UK, 22 per cent in Germany and 20 per cent for Europe as a whole. Telephone interviews, on the other hand, were lower than the European average representing about 15 per cent of turnover in 1990 against 17 per cent for the countries of Europe as a whole in that year and 19 per cent in 1991. However, the telephone is making ground as a means of carrying out research, thanks to its reduced cost and the fact that 88 per cent of households are now equipped. It has now become possible to obtain data direct from Minitel. At Ipsos, it is thought that door-to-door interviewing will soon be finished as a research method due to its cost, its relative danger, especially in Paris, and also to the increase in the number of working women which means that housewives are no longer a clearly identifiable marketing target group (Lallemand and Jardin 1993).

Other tools have also appeared:

- The computer-assisted telephone interview (CATI), in which the computer proposes a telephone number and dials it, after which a sequence of questions appears on the screen. The respondent reads the questions and enters the answers directly.
- The computer-assisted personal interview (CAPI) where researchers carry microcomputers on which questionnaires are pre-recorded and which directly enter the replies of the people interviewed. In 1993, Ipsos was equipped with 250 of these machines and carried out all its public research in this way.
- The interview without researchers, where the computer automatically dials the numbers of interviewees, reads out the questionnaire in a synthetic voice and records coded answers entered manually by the respondent according to instructions given by the computer. According to another system, which is still at the experimental stage, the questionnaire is recorded on cassette; the computer asks the questions and records the answers.

Scanners are being developed for panels of distributors and computers for panels of consumers. These advances free subjects from the constraints of pencil and paper and speed up the transmission of data. A system known as 'unified data analysis' should also shortly be launched (Géradon de Véra 1993). The system combines information on buying practice with data on television exposure. Since 1993, SECODIP has provided advertisers with a new instrument, 'Scannel', which allows shop sales, consumer purchases and the effectiveness of a TV spot to be analysed simultaneously.

These developments are not, of course, restricted to the French context. There is a tendency amongst different countries worldwide towards standardising methods which are in ever-greater demand by multinational firms seeking to compare data and results in the different markets in which they operate. This need is particularly acute in Europe where markets are progressively converging despite recent political and monetary setbacks. Companies are more and more conscious of the fact that it is no longer feasible for them to have commercial strategies, tariffs and positions in the marketplace which differ from one country to another. They need data on a group of countries and are anxious to realise economies of scale. This opportunity has been available to them for some time through the distributors' panel, Nielsen and its counterpart for consumers, Europanel. Standardisation is obviously harder for *ad hoc* studies, however, as a consequence of the cultural, linguistic and structural differences which persist between European countries, differences which extend to variations in approach and to ways of interpreting data. For quantitative studies, for example, it is extremely difficult to create questionnaires which can be accurately translated from one European language to another, while it is even harder to homogenise qualitative methods of analysis when cultural differences dominate group behaviour.

Distribution networks in France

Overall in 1992, the distribution sector in France employed 12.2 per cent of the active population and represented 11 per cent of GNP. The distribution boom which began in the 1960s continued throughout the 1980s, despite the implementation of the *Loi Royer* (December 1972) which sought to curb the growth in the size and number of supermarkets.

Increased concentration in retailing is a dominant trend which continues to progress at the expense of the small independent trader. However, within the wholesale group there are contrasting styles of development.

Hypermarkets and supermarkets

Not surprisingly, these are the types of unit which are growing most rapidly with hypermarkets being most active in food. In 1992, the ten first brand names in distribution all belong to this category which no longer includes a single town centre departmental store (*grand magasin*).

The most striking development in the last few years has been the rapid rise of the 'hard discounters'. The formula was introduced in France in 1979–80 by a subsidiary of Carrefour, ED, and only succeeded in breaking even in 1989 (Dupuis 1991). According to a recent survey, the progression of hard discounters between 1990 and 1993 was:

- 47 in 1990;
- 106 in 1991 (+126%);
- 282 in 1992 (+166%);
- 553 in 1993 (+96%).

Seven names dominate the sector:

- the three Germans – Aldi, Lidl and Norma;
- the Baud-Franprix group – ED, Leader Price;
- the Intermarché group – le Mutant and CDM.

The main features of these traders are:

- their relatively limited floorspace (674 m^2 average as compared with 953 m^2 for a classic supermarket);
- a limited range of basic products with a high turnover (600–900 references against an average of 2,500–3,000) and sold mainly under their own brand name;

Table 2.16 Sales outlets in France

Type of sales outlet	Overall			Food			Non-food		
	1980	1990	% change	1980	1990	% change	1980	1990	% change
Hypermarkets (+2,500 m²)	9.4	16.7	+77.7	14.5	25.9	+78.6	6.6	11.6	+75.8
Supermarkets (400–2,500 m²)	7.0	11.6	+65.7	17.0	26.5	+55.9	1.8	3.4	+88.9
Popular chains	2.2	1.4	−36.4	3.6	2.3	−36.1	1.4	0.9	−35.7
Small supermarket chains	3.8	1.7	−55.5	8.6	3.8	−55.8	1.2	0.6	−50.0
Large town centre stores	2.2	1.6	−27.3	0.8	0.6	−25.0	3.0	2.1	−30.0
Mail order	1.0	1.0	=	–	–	–	1.5	1.6	+6.7
All types wholesale	26.3	34.6	+31.6	44.6	59.2	+32.7	16.5	21.1	+28.5
Small independent retailers	4.6	3.2	−30.4	12.5	8.4	−32.8	–	–	–
Butchers	6.1	3.7	−39.3	17.8	10.4	−41.6	0.5	0.4	−20.0
Specialist retailers	3.5	3.0	−14.3	9.9	8.4	−15.2	–	–	–
Chemists	4.1	5.6	+36.6	0.0	0.2	–	6.1	8.5	+39.3
Other non-food specialists	31.7	30.8	−2.8	0.4	0.3	−25.0	48.4	47.6	−1.7
All types small retail	50.0	46.3	−7.4	40.6	27.7	−31.8	55.0	56.5	+2.7
Bakers	3.0	2.6	−13.3	8.6	7.2	−16.3	–	–	–
Cars	11.6	8.4	−27.6	–	–	–	17.7	13.0	−26.6
General	9.1	9.4	+3.3	6.2	5.9	−4.8	11.8	9.4	−20.3
Total retail sales	**955.5**	**1,986.6**	**+107.9**	**330.7**	**707.4**	**+113.9**	**624.8**	**1,279.5**	**+104.8**

Source: INSEE, 1991

Table 2.17 Leading French retailers and distributors

Ranking 1992		Sector	Turnover 1992 (in million francs)	% Turnover 1992/91
1	Carrefour	HM	117.14	+16.7
2	Leclerc	HM/SM	113.80	+34.0
3	Intermarché	SM	113.60	+5.7
4	Auchan	HM	85.13	+6.6
5	Promodès (Continent)	HM/SM	84.20	+10.3
6	Pinault-Printemps	GM/MP/VPC	70.23	+93.5
7	Casino	HM/SM	61.59	+45.3
8	Système U	SM	40.00	+6.7
9	Docks de France	HM/SM	32.06	+9.1
10	Galeries Lafayette	GM/MP	31.46	+23.5
11	OCP Répartition	Gr.Phar.	25.79	+6.3
12	Au Bon Marché	GM	25.15	–
13	Comptoirs Modernes	SM	22.57	+6.8

Source: *L'Expansion* No. 464, 10 November 1993, p. 79

Key: HM   – *hypermarché*
SM   – *supermarché*
GM   – *grand magasin*
MP   – *masgasin populaire*
VRC – *vente par correspopndance*

- low personnel costs (4.5–5 per cent of turnover against a 7–8 per cent norm);
- minimal levels of service;
- very low prices (–5 per cent in relation to the average of other types of supermarket for similar products).

Popular chains

These are in decline and suffer from a slightly 'old hat' and low quality image despite their making a vigorous effort to reposition themselves; Monoprix, for example, the sector leader, is modernising its shops and adapting its opening hours to the needs of city dwellers in full-time employment. It emphasises 'gourmet' prepared foods, guarantees the freshness of its fresh food, and concentrates on 'green' products and on younger more fashionable styles of clothes. However, all these initiatives did not prevent the group's turnover from declining by 5.7 per cent in the first half of 1993. The second leading chain, Prisunic, is following the same line.

Small chains and co-operatives

The decline of this type of network is even more marked than its predecessor and is affecting co-operatives more than classic chains. Both are reacting by closing smaller shops showing low profits and by opening supermarkets and hypermarkets with more floor space. For the more dynamic of the groups affected, such as Casino, Docks de France, Comptoirs Modernes or Franprix change has not meant decline. On the other hand some chains such as Viniprix and Radar have disappeared or have been taken over by other groups such as Félix Potin.

Large city centre shops (grands magasins)

These too are declining in France, as in most countries. For the 'crisis year' of 1992 for example, turnover in the retail sector fell by an average of 3.7 per cent. The large city centre outlets however fell by 8.9 per cent. Naturally, in order to stem the tide they have sought to reposition themselves in the market either by raising the levels of quality and prices and so becoming shops which focus on fashion or prestige brands or, like BHV, by specialising in household products and DIY.

Sale by correspondence

The leaders in the field are La Redoute, Les Trois Suisses and La Camif (a co-operative) which steadfastly maintains its 1 per cent market share of the retail sector. There is a growing tendency to order goods by telephone or Minitel.

Other retail sectors

This category is on the whole cutting back as much in market share as in sales outlets. Decline is particularly noteworthy for small independent retailers. Some sectors, however, are managing to do more than survive, in particular chemists who benefit from their monopoly and from the increasing health needs of an ageing population. Another sub-category which did not feature in Table 2.17 is that of the chains of supermarkets which specialise in the four areas of electrical goods (Darty), leisure and culture (FNAC, Virgin), furniture (Ikea, Conforama), DIY and gardening. The fact that they belong to large capitalist groups, their methods of working and their multiple outlets make them directly comparable with the large groups already referred to.

New tendencies in the distribution sector

The growing concentration in the infrastructure of trade and commerce is resulting in ever fiercer competition between the main groups. These groups can no longer be satisfied merely with taking the place of small traders in the marketplace. Their techniques of positioning are becoming sharper, their marketing strategies more sophisticated. Moreover, their management systems are developing as a result of technical progress. These developments include:

- **The centralisation of purchasing among the large distribution chains**
  As Gérard Gallo of the Monoprix group reminds, 'many firms, even those
  which used to be organised in a decentralised way in groups, are tending to
  concentrate their buying power as a means of strengthening their
  commercial strategy' (Gallo 1990).
- **Trade marketing**   Producers are becoming aware that distribution is the
  first obstacle to overcome in order to sell their products and that labelling or
  display on supermarket shelves is best achieved by co-operatives with
  distributors rather than by a 'hard sell' strategy based on massive investments
  in advertising which, as well as being extremely expensive, may not
  necessarily be effective. One of the outcomes of the crisis has been the
  realisation that advertising cannot achieve everything and that, in many cases,
  it should act as a support system rather than be the main driving force of a
  sales campaign. Indeed it has become clear that the real battle in the retail
  trade sector is at the level of distribution, hence the current growth of 'trade
  marketing', based on a new type of partnership between producer and
  distributor, which has replaced the traditional, and more antagonistic
  relationship between the two. Confronted by a fragmented retail trade sector,
  it was hardly surprising that industrialists who were more powerful and more
  advanced in merchandising techniques should seek to impose their own will.
  Now, the concentration within the wholesale trade has increased their power.
  They are developing independent marketing strategies to which producers are
  having to adapt, by cooperating instead of dominating as they used to. The
  growing influence of wholesalers is revealed in better logistical control of
  supply, which seeks to reduce costs and stocks. This is achieved by a tighter
  and more repressive control of firms, by fuller exchange of information and
  by collective agreement in the development of products, more suitable forms
  of packaging, pricing policy, promotional actions or merchandising. Nevertheless this new philosophy is only slowly breaking down the confrontational
  attitudes on both sides of the divide between producers and distributors.
- **New computer tools**   The growing computerisation of distribution has been
  another significant trend of the last few years. There has obviously been the
  rapid expansion of payment by credit card since the '*carte bleue*' has become
  generally recognised by banks. Barcodes on packages and scanners at
  checkouts are now universally used in shopping centres and are commonplace
  in supermarkets and shops. Computerised stock management has led to
  growing logistical analyses in the context of more tightly controlled
  movements of stock, sophistication in shelf layout, computerised databases
  and finally EDI, a data transfer system based on connections between
  computers of the shops of a chain and purchasing centres. This allows for
  immediate transfer of information on the state of stocks for and automatic
  updating of supply. The links with suppliers are less well developed in France,
  not for technical reasons but because they presuppose a high degree of mutual

confidence and the acceptance of a partnership relationship which, as we have suggested, is not yet fully developed in France. For these, as well as for technical reasons, distribution 'scanner panels' (based on the analysis of purchases at checkout points) are still being developed but should soon become operational.

The marketing of professional goods and services

Just as, in the public sector, cultural specificities tend to dominate, so, in the field of professional goods and services, cultural factors and the differences between countries are broken down. Response to calls to tender for a large-scale industrial project, the negotiation for a maintenance contract for a fleet of trade vehicles, the process for purchasing a machine tool or a computer for storing research data do not differ hugely from one country to another. General practices tend to predominate and it would be more appropriate to refer to similarities with other countries rather than to identify specifically French practices. Nevertheless there *are* differences. Some of these are at first sight subtle and low key. They are camouflaged by the niceties of social behaviour which derive from temperament and national character. Business lunches, traditional in France and, to a lesser extent in Britain, are rare in the Netherlands. Technical documents written in a foreign language would be rejected in Britain, accepted with reluctance in France but only if in English and, in the latter case, readily received in Scandinavian countries. These differences are significant. It is frequently only by respecting them that a contract may be obtained. Other differences apply to the national norms and regulations which the single market is a long way from having abolished. Precise knowledge of these norms and regulations is a pre-condition of successful negotiation in France as elsewhere.

Sales and commercial negotiation in France

As in all countries with a highly developed market economy, face to face selling and the management of sales personnel have an important part to play in the marketing mix of companies in France, particularly for professional goods and services; indeed for these, personal communication plays a key role, while wholesale products are more or less sold in advance through advertising. Here we deal exclusively with the problem of sales personnel visiting their clients which by definition rules out the special cases of shop assistants and telephone sales. Neither do we consider the problems presented by the management of a sales force since these are the same in France as in other countries. It can hardly be said that there is a specifically French way of motivating and monitoring the performance of sales personnel, of organising their work or of dividing their territory into zones. On the other hand, the question of choosing between different categories of sales personnel, regulated by quite different legal codes, is more important, as is the recommended approach for foreigners who wish to negotiate with French partners.

The legal status of sales personnel

One of the most notable characteristics of the commercial landscape in France is the importance given to the status of sales personnel. This corresponds to the large number of different levels at which they operate. They are outlined in Figure 2.1 according to each type's degree of integration into the company for which they work.

The intermediate status of the *VRP* ('*voyageurs-représentants-placiers*') applies to employees who have a particular status and various fiscal advantages such as free vehicle licences and an additional 30 per cent reduction in income tax. They may be 'exclusive', that is attached to a single company, in which case their links with the company and its degree of control over them are greater, or *multicartes*, that is to say working for several companies which are not in competition. This latter formula is worthwhile for small firms or for those which are setting up. The arrangement limits the costs of preliminary research and increases its impact if the *multicartes* taken on already have good contacts with clients. *VRP*s are generally paid on commission.

The status of the *VRP* is based on the laws of 18 July 1937 and 7 March 1957, which are part of the *Code du Travail* (Articles D751: 1–12, L751: 1–15 and R751: 1–5), and on the legal interpretation of these laws. Their main function is to guarantee the salesman a certain autonomy in his work. They also give the salesman certain rights over the clients which he has brought to the firm and give rise to compensation in the event of redundancy, retirement or change of sector. This compensation, the present level of which is equivalent on average to about twenty months worth of commission, represents a huge privilege to the extent that it is additional to other forms of entitlement under common law and is

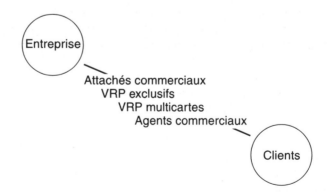

Figure 2.1 The relative status levels of different sales personnel

not subject to income tax. The benefit was established before the war of 1939–45 in order to allow *VRP*s a small pension. Now it is additional to the retirement benefits which form part of the standard compulsory social security provision for all. This has the disadvantage of making it expensive for companies to make changes in their sales force. However, in most cases, the level of compensation is based exclusively on income received in the form of commission and not on the fixed salary of the *VRP*.

The status enjoyed by *VRP*s is viewed as a public right in legal terms, that is to say that it applies automatically to all personnel whose main activity is to prospect for clients. Companies have an interest in establishing a detailed contract for their salesmen and frequently have recourse to a specialist for this purpose.

Attachés commerciaux, on the other hand, are more fully integrated into the firm which employs them. They have the legal status of employees and are euphemistically labelled '*inspecteurs de vente*', '*ingénieurs de vente*', '*ingénieurs technico-commerciaux*', '*chefs de clientèle*', etc. The only difference between *attachés commerciaux* and other staff is first the nature of their jobs – to obtain orders from clients – and, second, their mode of payment which is more flexible than that of 'normal' staff. The considerable development of this category of sales personnel over the last thirty years has been due to the fact that, having established a sales policy centrally, firms have become keener to direct the work of their sales staff and its outcome. However, as far as heavy equipment and highly technological goods are concerned, sales personnel, however highly qualified, no longer play an initial part in determining the outcome of the sale. Often they do not work alone but are supported by the technical, legal or financial departments. Equally with direct sales, the significance of face-to-face communication is diminishing and being overtaken by other jobs such as merchandising or the passing on of advice to distributors. Therefore the traditional autonomy of the *VRP* no longer matches firms' demands for the closer integration of their activities into company policy and for closer control over their sales territory.

By contrast, *agents commerciaux* have a status which brings them close to their clients and gives them a maximum of autonomy. *Agents commerciaux* are not paid individuals but entities. They are full agents, whose only constraint in their relationship with the firm for which they work is the outcome of their activity. Their status which is regulated by the law of the 23 December 1958 is as the holders of a franchise. They are free to recruit sub-agents or representatives, can trade on their own account, can accept new contracts without authorisation from the firms for whom they work and may be held responsible for overseeing payments for goods sold. In all these respects, they differ in status from *VRP*s. However, like *VRP*s, they have the right to indemnities for contracts which are independently negotiated with their contractor, rather than being based on the number of clients.

It is often economical for a company to be wholly represented by a commercial agent. In addition to taking responsibility for sales, the agent can manage warehousing and stock control, deal with delivery and invoicing, carry out market research, manage an advertising budget, etc. The agent can control the whole commercial operation. It is clearly essential if this formula is adopted to maintain regular contact with the agent, formally and informally, to keep track of his activities and to agree on the best commercial strategies for clearing any difficulties which may occur.

Habits of negotiation

It is a recognised fact that the French, perhaps more than any other European nation, lay store by cultural conventions which govern social behaviour and which directly affect the outcome of negotiations. Despite the spread over the last twenty years in the knowledge of English, it is still important to conduct negotiations in French or, at the least, to understand it. Respect for food and a basic knowledge of wine are real and valuable ingredients for maintaining social relationships in France, as are the commonplace rituals of courtesy such as the handshake, which opens and closes everyday interchanges. The French have a profound and genuine respect for clear argument, well-organised exposition and, if possible, for signs of brilliance in formal expression. This demands careful preparation and does not exclude the importance of an affective dimension. Contrary to Anglo-Saxon culture where the tendency is to proceed from the particular to the general, the French argue from general principles to specific examples. A sense of the concrete, popularly attributed to the British, is by no means absent from French people but the French feel the need to move from the specific to higher more abstract levels. Respect for a conceptual plan and periodic reminders of the manner in which an individual point relates to it are skills which are highly regarded when achieved with elegance and humour, as is the ability to sum up in a synthetic well-timed conclusion. The French also lay great stock by the written word which enjoys a higher status than the spoken language: '*verba volant, scripta manent*'. A command of written style and presentation in letters, reports and contracts is a vital ingredient of successful communication in France.

Advertising and promotion

In terms of expenditure, France is in an average position in relation to other advanced countries.

General trends

During the 1980s and up to 1991 there was an increase in investment in advertising of 8 per cent per annum against a 2 per cent rate of increase in GNP. However, this strong trend was not sustained in 1992 and 1993 as a consequence of the recession, the most severe since 1973 and the longest since the war. Apart

Table 2.18 Investment in advertising (in ECU) in different countries

Country/Area	1980	1989	% change
EU	47.2	139.3	+195
Belgium and Luxembourg	41.1	94.6	+130
Denmark	71.2	163.6	+130
Spain	22.3	126.7	+478
France	42.2	118.4	+180
Greece	7.5	31.8	+324
Ireland	27.0	65.3	+142
Italy	18.4	154.6	+740
Netherlands	87.1	150.7	+73
Portugal	3.9	24.8	+534
Germany	71.2	142.6	+100
UK	75.8	196.2	+159
Japan	47.3	202.0	+327
USA	111.9	288.0	+157

Source: *Tripartie Européenne de Publicité* – Comité de Statistiques

from these general economic factors, the *Loi Sapin* introduced in April 1993 forced the media to make their advertising rates public. Previously, little was known about these. Official rates were often reduced by 50 per cent or 60 per cent and sometimes more. Liberal pay-offs were frequent and led to the emergence of intermediaries who sold advertising space. These agents, who often worked for advertising agencies, would buy space cheaply on a large scale and would then sell it at a higher rate in individual lots to the advertisers.

The new law forces agents to publish their rates based on scaled down reductions agreed according to the amount of space involved and the possible savings (to professional agencies, exclusive advertisers, new clients, etc.). As for the agencies, the law now obliges them to show on their statements the extent of the reductions which have been allowed to them and to enable the client to benefit from these. This greater openness combined with the rationalisation of the market should in principle benefit advertisers and their subsidiaries. But some of the latter have sought to take advantage of the situation by increasing their prices and the new price scales still lack clarity and flexibility. However, the new law has undermined the role of the intermediaries – the agencies and the centres for purchasing space. Their role is changing and is likely to be more closely limited to creativity and counselling. The change which has been imposed on them has reduced the responsiveness of the market.

Finally, digressive tarification encourages advertisers to concentrate their purchasing of space on a restricted number of media and back-up agencies. The most powerful are the ones to benefit the most – television and above all the leading private station, TF1.

Development and breakdown of expenditure on advertising and promotion

Table 2.20 shows the development of investment in advertising in France between 1985 and 1992. It is certain that, up to 1990, the advertising market has consistently developed at a more rapid rate than the retail price index. There was a

Table 2.19 The main French dealers in advertising space

Ranking in 1992	Name	Owner of capital	Volume of purchases (in thousand million francs)* 1992	1991
1	Carat	Aegis (100%)	11.8	10.8
2	Publi Média Service (PMS)	Lintas, McCann, Publicis, Idémédia	9.0	9.4
3	Euro-RSCG	Havas (42%), Rouseca (8%), BNP (5%), Parthena Inv (10%)	9.0	7.8
4	The Media Partnership (TMS)	Ogilvy, DDB Needham, CLM/ BBDO, BDDP, Grey, JWT	7.5	7.5

Source: Centrales et *Marketing Mix* No. 74, July–August 1993
Note: *Figures are gross

Table 2.20 Advertising expenditure in France (1985–92)

	Advertising expenditure (in thousand million francs)	Change on previous year	Evolution of retail prices	% of GNP
1985	40.0	–	–	–
1986	44.8	+12	+2.7	1.06
1987	52.0	+16	+3.1	1.17
1988	58.3	+12	+2.7	1.12
1989	65.0	+11.5	+3.6	1.26
1990	70.2	+8	+3.4	1.28
1991	72.3	+3	+3.2	1.25
1992*	71.7	−0.8	+2.4	1.23

Source: IREP, *Le marché publicitaire français*, April 1993
Note: *Provisional figures

Table 2.21 The distribution of advertising income across the media in France (1984–92)

	1984	1986	1988	1990	1992*
Press	60	59.0	50.3	53.4	42.5
TV	16	18.5	24.8	25.4	26.3
Hoardings	13	12.5	11.5	11.2	11.0
Radio	9	8.5	12.4	9.2	9.5
Cinema	2	1.5	1.0	0.8	0.7

Source: IREP, *Le marché publicitaire français*, April 1993
Note: *Provisional figures

'catch up' phenomenon in relation to other advanced countries – up until the 1980s, France was behind its competitors in that the percentage of GNP spent on advertising was distinctly lower than that of other countries. Today, although it is not one of the very large 'consumers' of advertising (such as the United States and, to a lesser degree, Scandinavian countries and Great Britain), expenditure on advertising in France is average by comparison with that in Japan or Germany.

As far as the breakdown of expenditure is concerned, several major tendencies can be noted:

- The rise of television at the expense of the written press, hoardings and cinema where attendances are slowly but inexorably going down. Only radio advertising is keeping its head above water through its appeal to young people, housewives and the drivers of cars.
- As for distribution between sectors, that of food and drink remains in front (15.6 per cent of expenditure in 1992) although, relatively speaking, it is declining according to Engel's law which states that the share of household budgets spent on food goes down as prices rise. In second place is transport (11.3 per cent of expenditure), a sector which underwent the biggest increase in 1992 – seven car manufacturers are amongst the ten top advertisers. Next comes distribution with 10.7 per cent, a sector which is also in relative progression, leisure (10.5 per cent) and games and media publishing (9.1 per cent).
- Another basic tendency is the increase in non-media advertising – postal advertising, advertising at the place of sale, promotion, sponsoring, public relations (lobbying etc.) and the use of new media (telephone, minitel, fax), the import of which is still only slight. Non-media advertising absorbs 60 per cent of companies' communication budgets, against 40 per cent for media advertising, and its global share is constantly increasing. This trend worries the generalist advertising agencies which, for a long time, have been more interested by media based communication and now find themselves forced to broaden their portfolio of activities.

As far as promotion is concerned, its development is favoured by the recession which has forced companies to concentrate on the most profitable forms of communication. Postal advertising has also gained ground since it allows for a more highly targeted approach with results which are more easily measured. More restrictive laws on tobacco and alcohol advertising have put a brake on sponsoring, while lobbying and public relations are progressing strongly.

Investment in advertising

The recession has slowed down advertising investment which only went up by 1.1 per cent in 1992. However, most major advertisers have applied the principle that the winning strategy in a period of crisis consists in increasing one's market share which allows a firm to be in a strong position when growth picks up. In fact, in 1992, most large companies did increase their advertising effort – investment by the 130 most prominent advertisers went up by 8 per cent (Nielsen 1992).

Advertising agencies

One of the principal features of the advertising landscape in France as far as agencies are concerned is the fact that, contrary to the situation in other countries, it is not dominated by subsidiaries of the main American agencies. The latter hold approximately one-third of the market as against nearly 65 per cent for French groups. This is a situation which applies hardly anywhere outside Japan. It could be thought to provide evidence of nationalism; it is in fact more probably a sign of greater cultural autonomy from America. Another noteworthy characteristic is the relative concentration of the advertising sector. This concentration has once again been stressed by the merger in 1992 of Eurocom and RSCG. There are

Table 2.22 The main French investors in advertising

Top 20 groups			Top 20 companies		
Ranking			Total invest-ment 1992 (in million francs)	Ranking		Investment in 1992 (in million francs)
1992	1991	Group		1992	Company	
1	1	Nestlé	1,446.4	1	Renault	1,165.1
2	2	PSA-Peugeot Citroën	1,436.1	2	Peugeot Automobiles	753.0
3	4	L'Oréal	1,420.6	3	VAG	708.9
4	3	BSN	1,209.2	4	Citroën Automobiles	634.0
5	5	Renault	1,171.0	5	Proctor & Gamble France	594.7
6	6	Unilever	907.0	6	Ford France	485.0
7	7	Mulliez	842.2	7	Française des jeux	457.3
8	9	Proctor & Gamble France	783.2	8	SOPAD-Nestlé	450.9
9	8	VAG	708.9	9	Fiat-auto France	446.7
10	13	Fiat	671.6	10	General Motors France	398.7
11	15	Pinault	595.8	11	Henkel France	393.1
12	12	Philipp Morris	576.8	12	Lever	390.0
13	20	Ford	485.0	13	L'Oréal Parfumerie	381.1
14	14	Hachette	468.9	14	Colgate Palmolive	331.4
15	10	Philips	463.4	15	Carrefour	316.7
16	11	Française des jeux	459.0	16	France-Télécom	278.7
17	16	Mars	401.0	17	Auchan	272.8
18	24	General Motors	398.7	18	But international	272.5
19	17	Henkel	393.3	19	Conforama	264.3
20	25	L. Vuit.-Moët Henessy	340.8	20	Leclerc (GALEC)	257.8

Source: Pige Nielsen, 1993

Table 2.23 The main advertising agencies in France in 1992

Ranking	Group	Gross profit (in million francs)	% change on previous year	Number of personnel
1	Eurocom France	1,111.0	−0.9	−
2	Publicis	987.5	+4.5	1,336
3	BDDP	780.0	+1.6	1,250
4	RSCG France	723.5	−18.3	700
5	DDB Needham France	472.2	+9.3	480
6	Young & Rubicam	400.5	−1.2	−
7	France CCPM (Lintas)	344.7	−9.5	263
8	McCann-Erickson France	279.3	+6.6	268
9	La Compagnie/CLM/BBDO	266.0	+5.5	362
10	Ogilvy & Mather	262.6	−6.6	−
11	FCA!	244.8	−3.6	384
12	Saatchi & Saatchi France	236.0	+3.0	260
13	Grey Commission	161.6	−2.0	254
14	DMB & B	155.0	+20.1	157
15	FCB	149.2	−6.7	190
16	BSB France	146.2	+6.5	140
17	Bordelais Lemeunier/Leo Burnett	132.0	=	125
18	J. Walter Thomson France	104.0	−10.6	140
19	Business	102.0	+10.9	45
20	Groupe Ayer France	100.0	−9.1	100

Source: *Marketing Mix* No. 74, July–August 1993

approximately 600 agencies in France but most of these are extremely small and have less than ten employees each. The four leading groups represent 40 per cent of the gross profit margin for the profession as a whole.

As far as creation is concerned, some countries are marked by a particular style of presentation and discourse. American advertising, for example, is dominated by a marketing style which is strongly focused on selling. It seeks to emphasise a particular advantage or 'benefit' of the product. The strongest feature of British advertising on the other hand is its humour, that of Japan its concern with aesthetics. French creators are often more independent. They are kept on a less tight rein than their American counterparts and can allow freer expression to their fantasy and imagination. This relative freedom has unfortunately tended to diminish as a result of the recession. Advertisers have had to keep much more of an eye on their budget than in the past.

Specialised agencies: motivation, promoting, telemarketing and direct marketing

Motivation agencies are specialists in a particular type of communication – that focused on personnel (internal marketing) or, especially, on a sales force or retailers. It generally involves actions 'on the ground' which mix psychological initiatives of a qualitative kind with promotional initiatives in order to motivate a target group of personnel and to spur them on to greater efforts. Before the recession, this type of activity underwent rapid growth and has since somewhat slowed down (see Table 2.24).

The promotion agencies depend for the most part on larger organisations which have often created a subsidiary to handle their promotion so as to give themselves greater freedom and flexibility. For the last few years, there has been a tendency to give preference to promotional initiatives over media based advertising due to its more immediate and visible return. The recession has only increased this tendency. Thus, in 1992, the gross profit margin of promotional agencies increased by 6 per cent while media based advertising only grew by 1.1 per cent.

Table 2.24 The main French consulting agencies in the field of 'motivation' in 1992

Ranking	Agency	Gross profits (in million francs)	% change on previous year	Number of personnel
1	Everest Motivation	28.0	+16.7	35
2	Conseil Motivation	24.0	+14.3	30
3	Bernard Krief Motivation	20.0	−33.3	30
4	BPM Conseil (BLC)	19.0	+11.8	26
5	Ormès (Univers)	17.5	+6.1	22
6	Promostim	12.5	+4.2	9
7	Tir groupé	12.0	–	8
8	Euro-RSCG Motivation	11.0	+12.2	13

Source: *Marketing Mix* No. 74, July–August 1993

Table 2.25 The main promotion agencies in France in 1992

Ranking	Agency (Group)	Gross profits (in million francs)	% change on previous year	Number of personnel
1	Tequila (BDDP)	74.5	+11.4	120
2	Cato Johnson (Young & Rubicam)	71.4	+0.9	100
3	Eccla (Euro RSCG)	51.2	−12.8	104
4	Sogec Marketing	49.1	−31.7	239
5	Prosperyka (Euro RSCG)	40.7	+26.4	30
6	IPC	35.6	−22.4	136
7	AZ Promotion (IPC)	30.0	–	–
8	ID Marco Polo (FCA!)	23.6	−12.2	34
9	Impulsion (Europ RSCG)	21.6	−15.5	28
10	Doping (Saatchi & Saatchi)	21.2	+13.1	19
11	Procis (Publicis)	19.4	+32.3	26
12	Stag Ogilvy (Ogilvy & Mather)	18.0	+5.7	30
13	Proximité (La Compagnie/CLM/ BBDO)	17.0	+25.9	28
14	Sprint Promotion (Fr. CCPM Lintas)	14.7	+5.0	20
15	Go/Associés	13.7	+23.0	18

Source: *Marketing Mix* No. 74, July–August 1993

Table 2.26 The main telemarketing agencies in France in 1992

Ranking	Agency (Group)	Turnover (in million francs)	% change on previous year	Number of personnel
1	Téléperformance International (SRC)	190.0	+46.2	180
2	Pronytel Multicontact (GMF & France-Télécom)	131.0	+19.1	330
3	Matrix Phone Marketing (Cincinnati Bell Inc)	116.0	−12.1	−
4	Télémédia	82.5	+0.4	30
5	Phone Permanence	61.0	+8.9	62
6	MV2 Maxiphone	25.0	=	17
7	Téléobjectif-Belvédère (FCA!)	23.7	−0.4	18
8	Téléscore Dialogue (Dialogue International)	20.0	−20.0	47
9	Phone Communication (Adverbe)	18.2	+52.0	22
10	Interligne Bayard Presse (Bayard Presse)	14.7	−	90

Source: *Marketing Mix* No. 74, July–August 1993

Another tendency is the coming together of the three 'professions' (stimulation, promotion and direct marketing) which for a long time have been considered as distinct.

Among communication activities, telemarketing is one of three which have undergone the most rapid growth. This is a relatively recent development in France assisted by the fact that, during the last few years, France has regained lost ground in the field of telephonic equipment. Today almost all households have a telephone. A large number of agencies were created in the 1980s in order to benefit from this new market. Competition has become extremely fierce and the growing concentration which has recently taken place is a sign of the profession's maturity. The development of this market has been slowed down, however, by the restrictions imposed by government on 'telecopying' in which sales by telephone connected to a television enable products to be presented on the screen together with a telephone number which allows viewers to make an immediate order. Although this is standard practice in many other countries, it is regarded by the television broadcasting authority in France as infringing the very strict regulations which control the use of advertising by this medium.

Direct marketing is an older practice which has currently achieved a high degree of sophistication through the organisation of postal advertising, the use of files, the precise targeting of client groups, the computerised personalisation of managers and the management of accounts. Direct marketing grew by an average of more than 10 per cent over the fifteen years prior to 1992. Even if 1992–3 saw a substantial fall in business, it is taking off again since the sector benefits from the approval of advertisers who favour the trend towards personalisation and control.

The special character of French advertising design

As in other Western countries, advertising in France has acted as a mirror to social values. It is nevertheless interesting to raise the question of the particular character of French advertising discourse. This is influenced directly by the fact that culture expresses itself in both explicit and implicit registers of communication which can be defined as 'denotative' and 'connotative'.

- Denotative advertising is advertising that aims to represent the product by referring as closely as possible to its defining characteristics. This type of advertising generally relates to an aspect of daily life (e.g. at 100 km/h what makes the most noise in a Rolls Royce is the electric clock). This type of discourse, implicitly founded on behaviourist principles, frequently relies on the evidence of a photograph in order to give reality to the statement. Alternatively, it may consist of defining qualities of the product which speak for themselves, frequently through a direct statement or exclamation.
- Connotative advertising constructs a discourse around the product by emphasising its mythical qualities. The aim is to place the product in a

Table 2.27 The main direct marketing agencies in France in 1992

Ranking	Agency (Group)	Gross profits (in million francs)	% change on previous year	Number of personnel
1	Ogilvy Defrenois (Ogilvy & Mather)	49.5	+3.5	47
2	Rapp & Collins/Piment (R. & Col.-DDB-N)	39.0	+6.2	67
3	Bellanger Foucaucourt	38.9	−1.8	25
4	Répondances Nouveau Langage	38.2	+52.8	30
5	Manuel Noao (Publicis-FCB)	36.0	+9.1	50
6	Messages (BDDP)	32.7	+1.9	37
7	Groupe Directement (CLM/BBDO)	32.7	+37.9	30
8	Eurocom Direct (Euro RSCG)	26.8	+5.4	14
9	Lead Marketing (Groupe Lead)	26.4	+27.0	29
10	RSCG Génération Directe (Euro RSCG)	25.0	+71.9	38
11	Passion Directe (SRC)	24.7	+14.2	36
12	Directeam	23.0	+17.8	36
13	Directing	19.8	+2.2	40
14	Kobs & Draft (BSB)	19.0	−0.5	28
15	Publicis Direct (Publicis-FCB)	17.7	+17.9	21
16	Wunderman (Young & Rubicam)	16.9	−0.7	21
17	McCann Direct (McCann)	15.4	+27.9	18
18	Médiavente	15.2	−3.2	20
19	Cascades (Audour Soum Larue/ SMS)	15.0	+2.7	16
20	Grey Direct (Grey)	14.4	+19.0	20

Source: *Marketing Mix* No. 74, July–August 1993

fantastical context which eliminates its everyday context. The intrusive value of the product is limited and it is the task of the advertiser to give it a meaning through association. It is often a detached form of message which aims to provide a new approach to the product. It plays on the notion of connivance with the consumer who is required to decode the advertiser's discourse. Frequently the message is based on humour and irony. Comprehension is not immediate. This form of advertising demands a degree of lateral thinking and an effort of interpretation on the part of the receiver.

The French school of advertising can be distinguished mainly by its emphasis on an unbridled fantasy and imagination. One of its best-known proponents, Jacques Ségula (1983), has made much of the 'star strategy' in which communication cultivates the products' symbolic characteristics. As he put it, most of today's products do not differ from each other in respect of their objective features and performances. It would be artificial and even misleading to make promises which may be interchangeable between products. So his aim is to make products into stars in order to give them a personality, to build a myth around them and to remove their banal qualities. Thus he emphasises the imaginary, raising the description of the product to a higher level. The function of advertising is therefore to astonish, to tell a good story and to cause people to dream.

TOWARDS NEW VALUES

Paradoxical movements can be detected in a contemporary French society caught between the contradictory forces of globalisation and fragmentation (see also Chapter 1). Globalisation is the growing tendency towards homogeneity in habits of consumption, fashion, ideas and currents of thought. French society is one of sophisticated communication. The country is shrinking, distances are swallowed up by television, telephone, fax machines, aeroplanes and motor cars. Local differences such as patois dialects and regional accents are gradually fused by attendance at schools with standardised programmes taught by teachers recruited according to national criteria. This uniformisation is enhanced in the workplace, in factories and offices where there is a mix of people of different ages, regions and milieux. The employment market has become national with Bretons, Parisians and Marseillais competing for the same jobs. Interregional marriages have become the rule rather than the exception. Advertising evokes the same needs and leads to the same purchases in hypermarkets which resemble huge factories managed by national or, more frequently, international groups. The same beer cans are on sale from north to south, the same macaroni packets, the same Coca-Cola bottles, the same jeans and the same brands of television sets, deodorants or toilet soaps. The hierarchy of social classes has given way to a vast middle class reflected in the problems of recruitment encountered by the unions.

Yet we are still a long way from that homogeneous market which some economists and businessmen were apparently dreaming of, a single European market characterised by greater standardisation of consumers and products and realising substantial economies of scale. Instead there are signs of a greater fragmentation and breaking down of society into smaller elements. Is this the triumph of individualism which was heralded in the 1970s? It is certainly true that a reasoning rooted in individualism has been accompanied by a growing sense of freedom in all areas. 'The post-modern individual has extended his right to liberty in everyday life (hitherto constrained by economic, political and intellectual factors). This has generated a new style of managing behaviour which consists of escaping from the tyranny of detail, minimising constraints and maximising personal choice' (Lipovetsky 1983).

However, this surge of individualism has, for the time being, been halted by the economic crisis. The rise in marginal or pleasure-seeking lifestyles has been checked by the fear of unemployment. In 1993–4, unemployment was French people's major preoccupation – a justifiable fear in a country where there are more than three million out of work. There has been a retreat from the heady atmosphere of the 1980s into smaller groups such as the family, sports clubs, groups of friends, leisure, neighbourhood or work concerns. Club life has been growing as a means of avoiding a sense of ostracism and exclusion. A multicellular society has emerged in which each individual is at the centre of several groups or partnerships. These intersect in different ways at the crossroads of an individual's life and identity, influencing him/her in different ways.

The French are more and more diverse and divided in a society which has become fragmented in its cultural, ethnic and religious groupings. This is a new situation which raises fears for those who feel that there is not enough room for everybody. The increased antagonism towards immigrants bears witness to this attitude. The social climate does not lend itself to unanimity. Cleavages between groups are based less and less on the large traditional groupings – social class, church, region – but increasingly on numerous little groups built around age or shared interests, each having its own individual identity. This situation creates a difficult problem for market specialists confronted by micro-segmentation built around multiple interdependent criteria which, despite linguistic barriers, are beginning to transcend national boundaries. As Branzi (1985) puts it: 'Post-industrial society is characterised by the simultaneous presence of a large number of markets which correspond to different cultural groups. These recognise each other in the different behaviours, fashions, traditions and languages of each which has its own particular type of consumer preference.'

A symbolic precursor of the homogenisation of behaviours is the tendency towards the Americanisation of French society implied by the success of American films, the ubiquitous presence of McDonald's in France and the explosion in the consumption of colas which now represent 35 per cent of the consumption of soft drinks in 1991 against 16 per cent in 1982 (see also Chapter 1). Nevertheless, the consumption of soft drinks remains modest in France (39 litres per person in 1991 against 98 litres in Germany and 76 in the United Kingdom). Similarly, the annual personal consumption of cola is 12 litres against 70 in the US. The dominance of American cinema in France speaks for itself (see Table 2.28).

However, when seen in the context of other EU countries, the influence of American culture is perhaps less startling (see Table 2.29).

In fact, the French consumer maintains his/her specific characteristics and cannot readily be assimilated into the image of the 'Euroconsumer' as is revealed, for example, by perceptions of the watch Swatch in different countries (see Table 2.30).

Alongside a homogenisation in the behaviour of certain aspects of everyday life (cinema and music), it is possible, paradoxically, to uncover a new form of social fragmentation in which products are no longer perceived in the light of their use by small groups such as households but in relation to their consumption by individuals. Hence the shrinkage in the number of large-scale markets of which is reflected in the increase in the number of products developed around a strategy of narrow segmentation. The growth in methods of personal communication such as direct marketing illustrates the fact that companies see consumers more and more as individuals rather than as members of a social group. The growth in individuality is thus the corollary of a society in which the individual sees himself as the centre of gravity, a disturbing sign in a society which has tended to encourage exclusion and marginalisation – one French person in ten has insufficient income to live decently and for every ten people of working age one is out of a job.

Having lost firm reference points, the individual in modern French society is transformed into the uneasy role of spectator, observing a society in which speed and risk-taking have given way to uncertainty about the future and with which it is difficult to interact. It is as if French people feel a sense of fear at the coexistence of their historically charged past and an unstable modernity which attempts to build for the future by reconstructing the past. A characteristic

Table 2.28 American films in France as a percentage of spectators

1983	35%
1991	58%
1993	61.5%

Source: *La Croix L'Evénement* 23 September 1993

Table 2.29 Market share of American films in Europe

EU	73
France	58
Germany	80
UK	93

Source: *La Croix L'Evénement* 23 September 1993

Table 2.30 Perceptions of the qualities of Swatch watches in different countries

	France	GB	Germany	USA
Positive features:				
Pretty appearance	33.5	20.0	50.5	34.0
Amusing and original	31.5	28.0	46.0	9.0
Waterproof	29.5	29.5	17.0	37.5
Modern	30.5	24.0	36.0	7.5
Bright and varied colours	13.5	18.5	27.5	31.0
Strong	27.5	24.5	12.0	24.5
Adaptable	9.0	12.5	12.0	30.5
Quality	8.0	4.0	19.0	28.0
Inexpensive	32.0	5.0	17.5	3.5
Wearable anywhere	13.5	11.0	12.5	13.5
Negative features:				
Plastic bracelet	13.0	17.5	20.0	13.5
Too modern/fashionable	6.5	9.5	23.0	2.0
Looks too much like a gadget	10.0	8.5	17.5	3.5
Does not suit all types of clothes	4.0	14.0	14.5	1.0
Fragile	12.0	3.0	17.0	0.5
Dial too sophisticated	3.0	8.5	12.0	6.0
Too much plastic	7.5	–	18.0	1.0
Action too noisy	12.5	1.0	1.0	–

Source: Kimball Helen Chase, *Cas Swatch*, *INSEAD*, 1987

example is the feeling of anxiety created by the proliferation of non-places, that is places deprived of identity and history which work against the establishment of human relations such as supermarkets, cash points and airports; these places contrast with the progressive disappearance of the places which have together formed the fabric and character of French society – the cafés, parks and village squares where people exchange gossip, drinks and silence.

Moreover, the reduction in work hours has caused the basic elements of daily life to take on a different status. This has forced consumers to organise their free time differently. The increase in leisure hours has caused them to be regarded less as a recompense than as an activity like any other which has to be integrated into daily life. Free time has given freedom to the individual but it has also created the need to manage and save time, hence the emergence of easy-to-use products (over a quarter of households owned a microwave in 1992), the success of soup in cubes and the explosion of deep-frozen and ready-to-eat meals.

The turning in on oneself has been accompanied by a change in consumers' attitudes towards products – the product is sought after more for its basic utilitarian qualities than for its external or purely symbolic properties. There is therefore a recent tendency towards interiorisation of consumption in the sense that an object previously sought after for its ostentatious features, and whose value was frequently defined by the attitude of others towards it, now becomes an object in its own sake (the Renault slogan '*des voitures à vivre*' is very revealing in this respect). The consumer crisis is therefore also a crisis of the immaterial, the principal manifestation of which is the return to ecological products and the affirmation of more stable principles (see, for example, the success of the Renault Espace and the reassuring family values for which it stands). Advertising clearly illustrates this return to fundamental, substantive values. The era when the primary aim of advertising was to construct fantasy worlds through discourse appears to be over. Function and utility have regained pre-eminence. Price, which was formerly an instrument of product differentiation, now dominates every sector of the market.

In the 1990s, French consumers are distinguished less according to their professional milieu and to an ever-increasing extent by their patterns/forms of consumption. The co-existence of inconsistent behaviours is becoming more evident – the same individual may in a single shop buy basic products at a low price and then in the same moment purchase top of the range goods. The return of values such as naturalness, simplicity, and clarity is also clear. Clarity and purity of line can be seen in architecture. Recent trends favour glass surfaces such as in the *Pyramide du Louvre* as if to reflect a need for transparency in other areas such as politics, finance and art. Even the food and drinks sector has adopted a similar outlook as revealed by advertisements for mineral water. With transparency goes lightness, propagated through notions of 'fat free' and slimness, and the new materials used in the textile and car industries. It is even possible to detect a movement away from foods having a masculine symbolic value (red meat, sausages, paté, game, red wine) towards dishes which are 'feminine' in character (fish, white meats, milk products, mineral water).

The growth of leisure

In the same way leisure is losing its distinctive character by virtue of being accessible to greater numbers of people. The success of the *Club Méditerranée* has been due to its ability to provide multiple sources of satisfaction to the largest number while maintaining a sense of private space. The growth of free time has thus given rise to a new balance in the organisation of leisure activities. According to Mermet (1993), the amount of time devoted to watching television, reading magazines and eating at restaurants has increased significantly; every day, the average French person spends 3 hours 19 minutes watching television, 1 hour 59 minutes listening to the radio and 40 minutes reading newspapers and magazines. On the other hand, leisure consumption has decreased in terms of time spent reading, going to the theatre or visiting exhibitions or museums while the surge in leisure activities is linked to the astonishing growth in the purchase of audio-visual equipment and the inevitable transition towards markets based on the renewal and replacement of existing models.

Table 2.31 The French citizen's use of time

	Overall		Active	
	in minutes	%	in minutes	%
Sleep/Rest	552.6	38.4	475.8	33.0
Leisure/Interchange/Shopping/Reading	240.6	16.7	117.4	8.2
Media	153.5	10.7	97.6	6.8
Meals	150.0	10.2	119.9	8.3
Work	121.3	8.4	461.0	32.0
Children/Household	103.4	7.2	54.6	3.8
Mobility/Travel	73.6	5.1	76.4	5.3
Toilet	31.6	2.2	31.6	2.2
Other activities	13.4	0.9	5.6	0.4

Table 2.32 The exploitation of the media in different European countries as a percentage of an average working day

	TV	Radio	Newspapers and magazines	Total time (in minutes)
France	61	31	8	304
UK	64	27	8	360
Germany	46	38	16	419
Spain	71	22	7	277
Italy	76	16	8	261

Source: Euro Time Survey

CONCLUSION: THE EMERGENCE OF A NEW CONSUMER AESTHETIC

Consumer behaviour in the 1990s can be described as 'baroque' in the sense of following a curve subject to irregularity and interruptions. For the last few years it has no longer been possible to see behaviour in terms of homogeneity and continuity but rather in terms of changes arising from contradictory impulses. A model derived from television seems to have extended to many aspects of daily life – the individual shifts unpredictably from one shop to the next, from one brand to another, from one job to another, from one partner to another. Thus, society seems to suffer from the lack of a collective or even a revolutionary view of activities. The fall in union membership which has taken place in all Western countries has been particularly significant in France where it has gone down by two-thirds between 1974 and 1992. Some sectors are characterised by asyndicalism, particularly among SMEs. This decrease is reflected by behavioural indicators such as a fall in the number of demonstrations and in work days lost due to strike action. The middle class, which in the thirty years of post-war prosperity (*les trentes glorieuses*) could be recognised as an established

Encadré 7: The impact of social changes in France on new approaches to marketing

IDENTITY

- The growing awareness of the identity of the consumer and the company (e.g. the creation of products with a strong identity such as Swatch watches, Kookai clothes, etc.).
- The growing role of design as part of a global strategic approach (logo, interior architecture, product design, creation of 'ambiance' through sound, organisational design, etc.).

SEGMENTATION-DIFFERENTIATION

- Increased segmentation expressed through identifying narrow market niches and the linkage (packaging) of products and markets formerly viewed as distinct (e.g. linking yoghurt to children's products).
- An increased sense of differentiation leading to a growing awareness of perceptual positioning (e.g. the cosmetic market – L'Oréal, etc.).
- Conversely, the development of more simplified choices (e.g. the limited range of the Twingo).
- The shift from a product offer to a global marketing strategy linked to support services – after-sales support, associations, etc.
- The growth of 'brand' as a capital asset.

ADVERTISING AND PROMOTION

- Increased investment in promotional activities (direct marketing) and in expenditure on non-media activities.
- The refocusing of advertising discourse on the product and its utilitarian functions at the expense of its mythical and symbolic attributes.

PRICE

- The growing autonomy of the consumer in allocating the domestic budget so as to maximise the benefits gained from a judicious allocation of resources.
- The increasing importance attached to price as a determinant of consumer choice: the growth of distributor brand names and prices, the growth in the number of campaigns which emphasise the quality/price ratio as the principal selling point of the product.
- The tendency towards policies of penetration in lieu of appealing to the top segment of the market, an élitist tradition in French pricing policy.

Table 2.33 The possession of mass-produced electronic equipment in France

Type of equipment	Number of households	
	1988[a]	1992[b]
2 televisions	18.2	42.2
1 tape recorder	15.7	56.6
1 CD player	5.1	47.3
Minitel	9.8	31.7

Sources: [a] *INSEE: Enquête 'Loisirs'*, May 1987, May 1988
   [b] *CREDOC: Enquête de consommation*, November 1992

and relatively homogeneous group, now corresponds to a disparate and fragmented reality – a 'protectorate' which, outside the corporate sector, includes civil servants and managers, a neo-proletariat which lives independently of social and professional life, and a new bourgeoisie (lower and middle managers, owners of small companies and technical workers) which is responsive to changes in a developing marketplace. In this way, the individual seems to have lost his/her points of reference in a world in which integration into a set group is becoming rarer and more fragile. The restructuring of French society resembles the interaction of small tribes. It is like a process of miniaturisation in which microstructures are marked by emblems and small signs of federation which lend them legitimacy.

USEFUL ADDRESSES

ADETEM
221 rue Lafayette
75010 Paris
Tel. (1) 40.38.97.10.

Ecran Publicité
190 boulevard Haussmann
75008 Paris
Tel. (1) 44.95.99.90.

INSEE
195 rue de Bercy
75012 Paris
Tel. (1) 43.45.70.75.

CREDOC (Centre de Recherche, d'Etude et de Documentation sur les Conditions de Vie)
142 rue Chevaleret
75013 Paris Tel. (1) 40.77.85.00.

Dun & Bradstreet France
17 avenue de Choisy
75013 Paris
Tel. (1) 40.77.07.07.

Ministère du Commerce
207 rue de Bercy
75012 Paris
Tel. (1) 44.87.17.17.

Institut Proscop
25 rue Marbeuf
75008 Paris
Tel. (1) 47.23.56.26.

KOMPASS France
SNEI
66 quai du Maréchal Joffre
92415 Courbevoie-Cedex
Tel. (1) 41.16.51.00.

Lamy
187 quai de Valmy
75010 Paris
Tel. (1) 44.72.12.00.

Points de Vente
14 rue Chaptal
92300 Levallois-Perret
Tel. (1) 47.57.31.66.

Banque de France, Direction des Etudes
48 rue Croix des Petits Champs
75001 Paris
Tel. (1) 42.92.39.08.
Centre d'Etudes sur les Supports de Publicité (CESP)
32 avenue Georges Mandel
75006 Paris
Tel. (1) 45.53.22.10.

IREP
62 rue de la Boétie
75008 Paris
Tel. (1) 45.63.71.73.

Editions Tarif Media
5 rue la Boétie
75008 Paris
Tel. (1) 44.56.31.56.

SELECTED TEXTS

Baudrillard, J. (1968)
Floch, J-M (1990)
Fraisse, R. and Foucauld, J-B. de (eds) (1996)
Lipovetsky, G. (1983)
Mermet, G. (1996)
Rochefort, R. (1995)
Séguéla, J. (1982)

See Bibliography

3 Success and failure in research and technology

Joël Broustail and Frédéric Fréry

A TECHNOLOGICALLY RICH CULTURE

Whatever reproaches of superficial brilliance and abstraction are made against the French, they do not stand up to close analysis. France has, without any doubt, a tradition of cultural and scientific innovation as outstanding as that of any country in the world. And this reputation extends into the technological and industrial fields. However, it is true that France's research culture can be characterised by its taste for radical and grandiose inventions as opposed to the progressive refinement of existing paradigms and by its closed and elitist training system. One of the consequences of such a system is a certain imbalance between areas of excellence and gaps in expertise. As the above arguments suggest, France has a rich innovatory tradition but one which is marked by a clear predominance of fundamental over applied research. Pascal, Cuvier, Monge, Laplace, Lavoisier, Arago, Pasteur, Joliot-Curie, de Broglie, de Gennes and Thom are just a few of the names which have gained France her privileged place in the hall of fame of great scientific discoveries. Yet France's output in fundamental research might be thought surprising when set alongside the international statistics on the registration of industrial patents.

Although in a strictly quantitative sense, France is less innovatory than Japan or Germany, its industrial and technological production has also long been distinguished by its capacity for spectacular novelty. The example of the motor car is an instructive case in point. Mercedes, the most advanced German car manufacturer from a technological point of view, has always had a policy of progressive development in design and in engineering conception. In France, on the other hand, firms such as Citroën or Panhard have traditionally based their strategies on the shock presentation of radical new models which mark a complete break with classical concepts – the 'all steel' model of the late 1920s, the 'Traction' model of 1934 (front-wheel drive and the single body shell), the 2CV of 1948, the DS of 1955 (disc brakes and hydropneumatic suspension, power-assisted brakes and steering, aerodynamic body design), the Panhard Dyna (all aluminium body) of 1953 and the Citroën SM of 1970 have all represented turning points in the history of the automobile. The single frame design of the Renault Espace and the Twingo are in the same tradition.

For a long time, the same type of policy was also predominant in large scale public technological projects. This was most notoriously the case for the Concorde whose technological boldness in conception and design was substantially the product of French engineering which corresponded to the grandiose dreams of political decision-makers. Sadly the objectives ran counter to the financial viability of the project and the more pragmatic instincts of France's British partners. The same was true of the Aérotrain – a 'hovertrain' propelled by turbine engines – which was stillborn at the beginning of the 1970s and whose concrete railway is still visible near Orleans. French industry has sought to learn from these failures of former years which were often due to the country pursuing an exclusively technological vision at the expense of industrial and commercial priorities. Panhard went under, Citroën, after flirting with bankruptcy, was bought by Peugeot and Concorde's commercial viability was never realised.

Even if white elephants such as the electro-nuclear programme continue to exist, the three flagship achievements of contemporary French industry – the *TGV,* the Airbus and the Ariane rocket – represent firm indications of steady progress. The design technology of the *TGV* is more traditional than those of its German and Japanese competitors and is a far remove from the Aérotrain of fifteen years ago. Similarly the Airbus whose design was based on objectives determined by cost-effectiveness and commercial viability is diametrically opposed to Concorde. As for Ariane, it is based on classic rocket design and, as such, is clearly distinct from the radical concept of the American space shuttle.

It is worth analysing more closely the sources of France's reputation for innovation as well as the basis for its strength and durability. This can be explained firstly in cultural terms. There is a French historical tradition of radicalism and abstraction which is as present in the fields of politics and philosophy as it is in industry and science. Many French engineers and researchers find it easy to denigrate their American and particularly Japanese colleagues who concentrate more readily on applied research than on fundamental abstract issues. Much is made in French engineering circles of the Americans' ignorance in mathematics or Japanese lack of abstraction whilst all too readily forgetting that scientific purism is not necessarily a guarantee of economic success.

In contrast, this theoretical superiority complex is often linked to an inferiority complex when it comes to practical applications – above all when confronted by Japanese and American economic success. Sadly, the French are as ready to triumphalise the smallest success as they are to despise their greatest achievements, signs of an innate and typically French mixture of embarrassment and chauvinism which goes beyond the realms of engineering and scientific research.

A CLOSED AND ELITIST EDUCATION SYSTEM

The source of the technological and scientific originality of French engineers and researchers can also be explained by a training system which is peculiar to the French scientific *grandes écoles*. The legitimacy of the *grandes écoles* is based on highly selective recruitment, the cornerstone of which is an aptitude for mathematical abstraction. This is particularly true of the competition for entry to the celebrated *Ecole Polytechnique*, responsible for educating the leading engineers in public service, or the *Ecole Normale Supérieure* which trains researchers and teachers for the universities and the *CNRS* (*Centre National de la Recherche Scientifique*), the main institute for promoting publicly funded research together with the *Commissariat à l'Energie Atomique* and the *Institut National de Recherche Agronomique*. This system, which attracts and promotes students exceptionally gifted in abstract thought, has made an inestimable contribution to the quality of French research. Although the *Ecole Normale Supérieure* only admits fifty or so students per year, it has provided a greater number of Nobel prize-winners than Harvard, MIT or Oxford. Moreover, it is generally reckoned that France contributes approximately 5 per cent of the totality of world scientific publications representing major steps forward in fundamental research.

This elitist system explains in a dual sense the limits of applied research which have traditionally characterised France. Not only does the entry exam focus primarily on abstract forms of reasoning at the expense of the practical application of ideas, but, until recently, there has been a split between, on the one hand, universities and public research institutes and, on the other, the *grandes écoles*, the breeding ground for the senior executives and researchers in French companies (see also Chapter 1). For a long time there has been no structured link between research carried out in companies and that conducted in public research institutes and the universities. This gulf can be contrasted to the traditional osmosis in Germany between universities and private firms.

This strict separation between research-orientated institutions and those responsible for training technicians and engineers is nevertheless changing. Increasingly, engineering schools are engaging in research which is frequently linked to universities and the *CNRS*. Equally, contracts made with companies (currently totalling 3,700 with 900 companies) together with publications and research training are now criteria for assessing the performance of public laboratories. The total value of these contracts amounts to 1,600 million francs. At the same time, some twenty jointly run laboratories linking the *CNRS* to specific companies (including Elf, Saint-Gobain or Rhône-Poulenc) have been created. Finally, units within the *CNRS* such as the *FIST* (*France Innovation Scientifique et Transfert*) and the *ANVAR* (*Agence Nationale pour la Valorisation de la Recherche*) have specific responsibility for promoting the transfer and industrial exploitation of technologies.

More general developments in the system of training élites are also a reflection of the growing recognition of new forms of intelligence which are more 'pragmatic' and less abstract in form. In the public domain this has been the case for the *ENA* (*Ecole Nationale d'Administration*) for which general knowledge and personality are now significant recruitment criteria. This school now rivals the supremacy of the *Ecole Polytechnique* in the senior echelons of government. Similarly, in the private sector, the success of the *grandes écoles* in management, products of the chambers of commerce and industry rather than of the state – the *HEC* (*Hautes Etudes Commerciales*), the *ESCP* (*Ecole Supérieure de Commerce de Paris*), the *ESSEC* (*Ecole Supérieure des Sciences Economiques et Commerciales*) or the *ESC Lyon* (*Ecole Supérieure de Commerce de Lyon*) – has been marked. These schools have increasingly been developing research units whose objective is to carry out collaborative research with and on behalf of national and regional firms. The strengthening of these new élites at the head of the French companies to the detriment of the foremost engineering schools entails other dangers of which institutions of this kind should be aware. Technocratic or managerial 'slippage' may take place causing technological opportunities or major innovations to be overlooked. In seeking to protect themselves from the extremes of abstraction it is important that companies avoid becoming carried away by bureaucratic or cost-effective priorities.

STRENGTHS AND WEAKNESSES

As a consequence of its special innovatory traditions, France has a mixed profile as far as its technological competence is concerned. Both centres of excellence and surprising weaknesses go hand in hand. As a result of the extent of state support for research and engineering training, it is generally the sectors regarded as strategic for reasons of state interest (most often linked to national defence) which show the most startling success. This is particularly true of the aerospace industry which includes nationalised companies such as Dassault, Matra, Aérospatiale, Snecma (Société Nationale d'Etude et de Commercialisation de Moteurs d'Avions) or la SEP (Société Européenne de Propulsion). These companies, which are largely sustained by public orders, in particular from the army, have enabled France to achieve some spectacular technological successes (Mirage, Rafale, Airbus, Concorde, Ariane, CFM-56, Exocet, Hadès, etc.). The same is true of telecommunications, mainly due once again to state orders with the companies Alcatel, Matra and Thomson which have enabled France to develop the first public telematic network (Minitel), a number of telecommunications satellites and the *RNIS* (*Réseau Numérique à Intégration de Services*). On the same level of operation, mention should also be made of the nuclear industry which includes *EDF* (Electricité de France), the *CEA* (Commissariat à l'Energie Atomique) and, in particular, its subsidiary Cogema. Alsthom, for instance, which has been responsible for the reprocessing plant at the Hague, the high-speed reactor Super Phénix and the 56 GW series of power stations which together account for 73 per cent of national output in electricity.

French technology also leads the world in the field of transport, whether it be the export success of the *TGV* (built for the SNCF by Alsthom and subsequently exported to the USA and South Korea), urban trains (the metro locomotives and rolling stock designed by Alsthom or Matra and sold most notably to Mexico and Hong Kong), or motorised transport (Renault and Citroën produce 8 per cent of the world's cars and French engineers are responsible for technologies such as the four-cylinder engine, the turbocompressor, removable and radial tyres, front-wheel drive and hydropneumatic or automatic suspension). French research also excels in biology and medicine, with the work of the *INSERM* (*Institut National de la Santé et de la Recherche Médicale*) and of the Pasteur Institute (whose chief beneficiaries are Rhône-Poulenc and Elf), in mathematics (the applications of which underpin advances in software and micro-electronics), and in liquid state physics, benefiting companies such as Air Liquide – a world leader in its own sector. Equally, solid state physics has applications in Metallurgy benefiting Usinor Sacilor and Péchiney, and in the construction industry dominated by the giant Bouygues.

In general, technology linked to communication in the widest sense (transport telecommunications) is one of France's greatest strengths, along with the areas thought to be high priority by the state (medicine and the nuclear industry) and those where the level of abstraction is such that it attracts fundamental scientific researchers (mathematics, physics, chemistry, energy). In fact the real fields of excellence are those which combine those three criteria. The state encourages them through the massive scale of its orders. Virtually all the companies concerned are nationalised. If the research and development budgets of the main French sectors are compared, aeronautics and electronics (including tele-communications but not computing) are overall leaders with a 1991 budget of nearly 25,000 million francs. The automobile industry lies in second place (12,000 million francs), followed by chemistry (11,000 million), pharma-ceuticals (10,600 million) and energy (4,600 million).

On the other hand, France's technological prowess is extraordinarily weak in some areas either because they have not been judged to be strategic by the state or else because the scientific élites have not considered them to be sufficiently worthy of interest. This is particularly true in the field of industrial tools. The industrial tool was invented and perfected in France (most notably by Jacquard) between the seventeenth and nineteenth centuries. However, from 1914 onwards France was only in second place in the world ranking in machine tool production. The situation worsened significantly in the 1970s due to the strength of Japanese competition. The state attempted to establish a plan to promote the production of machine tools but it proved to be a failure. It seems that the technology of machine tools is too applied, too far removed from fundamental research to arouse the interest of the top French engineers. Thus there are three times fewer robots in France than in Germany.

Another example is the French computing industry symbolised by the tumultuous history of Bull, victim of a government policy which was at the same time too interventionist and insufficiently informed. Bull was founded in Norway in 1919 and set up in Paris in 1925. Since the state refused to finance the company's growth, Bull purchased a minority share in IBM. It was at that time an extremely prosperous company at the forefront of innovation in the world. It was responsible for designing and manufacturing the first keyboard printer in 1931 with fifteen years advance on the Americans. In 1951, when it brought out the first commercially manufactured computer, 50 per cent of its turnover was accounted for in exports to forty countries.

However, affected by a standard French malady, Bull encountered its first major setback in 1963. Its computer Gamma 60, despite being highly advanced technologically, only sold six models. In order to save the company, the state authorised its purchase by General Electric in 1964. In 1966, as a consequence of the White House veto on the delivery of a computer intended to lead to the creation of the French H-bomb, General de Gaulle decided within the framework of the '*plan calcul*' to create the Compagnie Internationale pour l'Informatique, a new firm which merged the specialist subsidiaries Schneider and CGE (Compagnie Générale d'Electricité, today Alcatel–Alsthom). Ten years later, following the failure of the Unidata project, an ambitious European consortium whose objective was to regroup CII, Siemens and Philips, the state undertook to merge CII and Bull, which had in the meantime been resold by General Electric to Honeywell, under the name CII-Honeywell-Bull.

In 1978, the government forced the CGE, which was still a minority shareholder, to withdraw in favour of Saint-Gobain. Shortly afterwards, Saint Gobain decided in its turn to merge Bull and Olivetti in which it had bought a 30 per cent holding. Once again it was a failure. Bull was unable to take advantage of the emergence of microcomputers despite, in 1978, having bought the French company R2E which had marketed the first microcomputer in the world in 1973, and since 1980 it has regularly made a loss. In 1983, Bull was nationalised forcing Honeywell to pull out with compensation totalling US$150 million.

In the wake of large-scale redundancies and considerable financial support, Bull made a profit in 1985 and, following the government's instructions, bought back Honeywell, its previous holding company in 1988 and then, in 1989, acquired Zenith Data Systems. But by 1990 the group was once again in debt to the tune of 6,700 million francs, mainly as a consequence of Zenith which was costing the firm 300 million francs per month. In the end the state was forced to allow the Japanese firm NEC and then IBM to purchase a minority holding. Between mid-92 and mid-93, three chief executives came and went. The latest holder of the post (in 1994) was given the responsibility of privatising Bull, which, having cost the French taxpayer 40,000 million francs, will in all likelihood be sold in bits, mostly to its old enemy IBM.

This example demonstrates some of the peculiar failings of French technology – excessive purism in innovation (the Gamma 60), a persistent fear of not being able to achieve world dominance (hence the multiple attempts at mergers) and, above all, repeated state intervention inspired either by the ideological notion of the greatness of France, which from Versailles to Concorde has swallowed up astronomical resources, or by a spirit of technocratic centralism worthy of Colbert, much cultivated by the senior civil servants in Paris. Whatever the causes, the shortcomings of French technology are reflected by the levels of certain R&D budgets – 3,800 million francs for computing in 1991, 1,000 million in precision tools but only 300 million in the textile industry.

Moreover, it should be noted that the geographical distribution of French research activities is particularly uneven. Almost 42 per cent of publicly funded research activities are concentrated in the Ile de France, far ahead of the Rhône-Alpes region (8.2 per cent) and Midi-Pyrénées (6.4 per cent). Equally, the Paris region monopolises 48 per cent of industrial research, 44 per cent of scientific publications and 54 per cent of partnerships between public laboratories and companies. In the Ile de France area, comprising Paris and the immediate area surrounding the capital, 21 out of every 1,000 inhabitants can be classified as a 'researcher', against 13.8 for the Pyrénées, 11.3 in Provence-Alpes-Côte d'Azur and 10.9 in Rhône-Alpes. Regional agencies expend considerable efforts in investment in order to compensate for this disequilibrium. Thus, in 1991, the twenty-two French regions invested 1,100 million francs in R&D, as against only 127 million in 1981. On the other hand, while the density of research activity in the Ile de France is comparable to that in California, it is lower than that in five other states in the USA. Another weakness of French research lies in the under-representation of small and medium-sized enterprises (SMEs). The main state programmes in nuclear energy, telecommunications, defence or the aerospace industry have little 'spread effect' outside their sectors and that of the main nationalised groups. Thus, while the SMEs represent 29 per cent of industrial production in France and 39 per cent in Germany, German SMEs absorbed 53 per cent of the industrial R&D effort against only 30 per cent in France.

THE STRUCTURE AND PROGRESSION OF THE FRENCH RESEARCH EFFORT

Having reviewed the state of French research and technological development from a historic, sociological and sectoral perspective, it is now appropriate to consider it in its wider economic context. Through a macro-economic analysis of the state of French research, it is possible to identify the following tendencies:

- overall progress in the research effort, particularly in companies;
- a reduced dependency on imported technological expertise;
- a level of research output at least comparable to that of other major industrialised countries but a shortfall in the number of patents registered and a high (if decreasing) level of state involvement.

Unless otherwise stated, all the findings quoted in this section are derived from data published by the *Ministère de la Recherche et de l'Enseignement Supérieur* (*MRES*), according to whose definition the French research effort can be analysed from two complementary perspectives:

- The *dépense nationale de recherche-développement* (*DNRD*) which brings together the finances allocated by national economic agencies. These accounted for 162,600 million francs in 1991.
- The *dépense intérieure de recherche-développement* (*DIRD*) which represents the totality of R&D expenditure undertaken by national and foreign economic agents. In 1991, this represented 164,000 million francs.

The difference between the *DNRD* which represents financial input and the *DIRD* which represents expenditure corresponds to the money flows between France and abroad. Among these, a notable item is the activity of European research organisations such as the *Centre Européen pour la Recherche Nucléaire* (*CERN*) or the European Space Agency. Given these circumstances, the situation in 1991 was as shown in Figure 3.1.

During the last fifteen years the *DNRD* has shown a steady increase over GNP, passing from 1.72 per cent in 1977 to 2.4 per cent in 1993. From 1980 to 1991 the *DIRD* increased in volume by 70 per cent while GNP only grew by 33 per cent. During this period, the most significant increases were recorded in 1981 and 1982 (+7.5 per cent and +7.8 per cent respectively) while the slackest years were 1986 and 1991 (+1.1 per cent and +0.7 per cent respectively). It is worth mentioning that during the previous decade (1970–80), the *DIRD* had only increased by 33 per cent, that is somewhat less than the rate of increase of GNP (38 per cent). Hence it is clear that France's research effort is increasing.

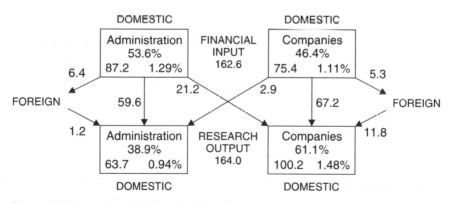

Figure 3.1 Domestic and foreign funding of research in France in 1991

Source: MRES

Note: Figures in thousand million francs or as a per cent of GNP

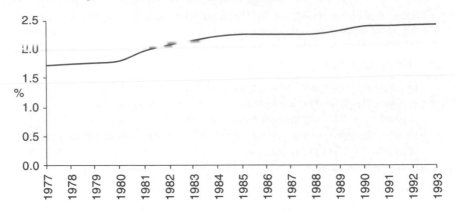

Figure 3.2 DNRD in France as a percentage of GNP (1977–93)
Source: *MRES*

Throughout the last fifteen years, the involvement of companies in the national research effort has increased in relation to that of the government, particularly as far as financing is concerned. To be more precise, the commitment of public finance to the DNRD decreased from 58 per cent in 1977 to 53.7 per cent in 1991. Between 1980 and 1991 the volume of R&D

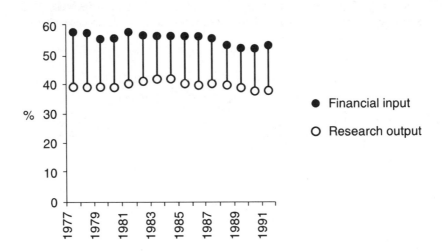

Figure 3.3 Public sector research in France: financial input and research output (1977–91)
Source: *MRES*

expenditure by companies grew by 72 per cent while that of the government was
only 66 per cent. These same figures were 45 per cent and 19 per cent for the
decade between 1970 and 1980. As far as the implementation of research is
concerned, however, the proportional balance between the public and private
sectors is more or less stable – around 40 per cent for state involvement against
60 per cent for the private sector.

The 1980s also witnessed a significant growth in the number of research
contracts carried out on behalf of companies by the state. These amounted to
2,000 million francs in 1991 which still only represents 3 per cent of the state
research budget (but 10 per cent of implementation costs excluding personnel).

The proportion of French R&D financed from abroad increased from 6 per
cent in 1980 to 11 per cent in 1991. It consists both of finance received from
foreign companies (frequently belonging to the same group as that carrying out
the research in France) and that received in the context of international
cooperation (e.g. the European Space Agency which represents one-third of the
total, Airbus and EU programmes). This growth on the part of foreign
investment underlines not only the growing internationalisation of research but
also that of the companies in which it is carried out.

Within industry alone, the development in the structure of R&D expenditure
between 1981 and 1991 was as shown in Figure 3.4.

As far as France itself is concerned, the balance of patents and production
licences is structurally in deficit. Thus in 1990, France received 7,500 million
francs from abroad but paid out 11,300 million, that is a deficit of 3,800 million
francs. Nevertheless, this deficit is being reduced year after year. While, in 1974,

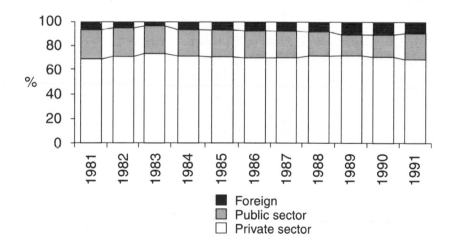

Figure 3.4 Sources of R&D expenditure in France (1981–91)

Source: MRES

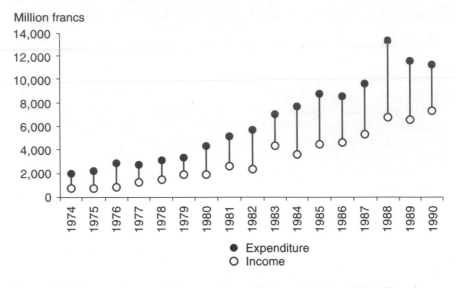

Figure 3.5 Balance of payments for patents and licences in France (1974–90)
Source: MRES

the income/expenditure ratio was 2.6, by 1990 it was only 0.7. France is therefore improving its balance on patents and licences. Even if the volume of deficit has more than tripled since 1974, income has multiplied by 10.1 against an expenditure of 5.8.

FRANCE'S RESEARCH PERFORMANCE COMPARED WITH THAT OF ITS PRINCIPAL PARTNERS

Most of the defining features of France referred to above are confirmed by the figures in Tables 3.1–3.4. The main macro-economic indicators are the total represented by the DIRD (the internal expenditure on R&D), the percentage of researchers in the working population, the number of requests made for patents and the weight of state funded research.

A comparison of France's national expenditure on research with that of its main partners reveals, interestingly, that, with the exception of Italy, the richer a country is, the higher is the ratio of its *DIRD* to GNP. It would not be right to deduce from this that there is a cause–effect relationship between the two. However, in either event, France's position is relatively predictable.

If the percentage of researchers in the working population in 1989 is considered, it is clear that, here too, France's position correlates closely with GNP.

Table 3.1 National expenditure on research in different countries in 1989

	GNP (in thousand million francs)	DIRD	DIRD (% of GNP)
USA	33,489.58	964.5	2.88
Japan	13,088.65	369.1	2.82
Germany	7,257.14	203.2	2.80
France	**6,136.75**	**143.6**	**2.34**
UK	5,909.09	130.0	2.20
Italy	5,798.39	71.9	1.24
Canada	3,251.85	43.9	1.35

Table 3.2 Researchers in different countries as a percentage of the working population in 1989

Unites States	7.7%
Japan	7.3%
Germany	5.9%
France	**5.0%**
UK	4.6%
Canada	4.6%
Italy	3.1%

The small number of patents registered by the French

French researchers register relatively few patents considering the extent of the national budget allocated to research. This figure is frequently used in order to demonstrate an apparent deficit in terms of innovation, especially in comparison with Germany or the United Kingdom (which registers twice as many patents as France relative to an equivalent number of researchers).

In fact, an enquiry by *INPI* (*Institut National de la Protection Industrielle*) has shown that only one invention in four is registered in France. These figures tend to suggest more a misunderstanding of industrial protection or a disaffection with it rather than a weak level of innovation. It should not, however, be forgotten that many French companies (the case of Michelin is well known) are secretive and do not wish to register patents for a proportion of the innovatory research in which they are engaged. It should also be noted that not all patents have the same scientific impact and that simply to aggregate a set of elements which are so disparate is not representative.

Finally, the attraction for fundamental research where few innovations can be patented (such as mathematical formulae or particle physics) and where reputation based on prestigious scientific publications is valued more highly than the commercial exploitation of a patent is undoubtedly a primary cause of the French deficit.

Table 3.3 Patterns in the registration of patents in different countries

	Patents registered in their country	Patents registered abroad	Patents registered by foreigners
Japan	317	115	40
USA	82	237	78
Germany	53	135	60
UK	24	62	66
France	12	55	60
Italy	3	25	50

Source: INPI

The extent of public research in France

The other original feature of research in France is the involvement of the state in its financing and execution. We have already mentioned this point, underlining the fact that the commitment of the State is tending to diminish. It is nevertheless significantly higher than in partner countries.

Publicly funded research in France with a budget in excess of 60,000 million francs brings together more than 67,000 researchers and engineers against only 57,000 in the corporate sector. The latter nevertheless allocates a budget (approximately 100,000 million francs) which is higher than that provided by the state. For the purposes of comparison, it is worth recalling that German companies include more than 110,000 researchers.

In a more global context, France is a relatively unusual case, a feature which it shares with Italy. It seems that in France the extent to which the state actually conducts research is still relatively high, particularly in relation to Japan and Germany. On the other hand, the proportion of public finance for research is slightly less than that in the USA as Figure 3.6 shows. It can be noted that only Japan is in a balanced position as regards the relationship between levels of public finance and the public implementation of research (approximately 25 per cent).

CONCLUSION: TRADITION AND FUTURE PERSPECTIVES

French research and technology have a specific national character. Their main features are a pronounced taste for fundamentalism and radical innovation, frequently at the expense of economic pragmatism, and the strong role of the state as a source of finance. These are essentially the expression of two traditional traits of 'Frenchness' which reflect both their qualities and excesses – abstract intellectualism and centralising rationalism. Thus the history of innovation in France is marked by outstanding scientific success, which has undoubtedly led to the spread of a national reputation of which every French citizen can justifiably feel proud. However, it is also accompanied by

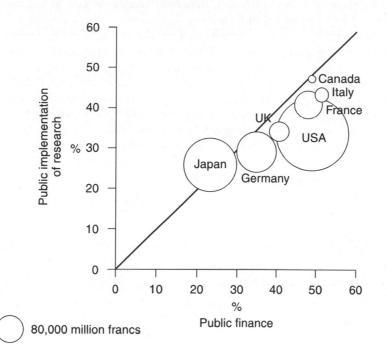

Figure 3.6 The international comparison between levels of state support for research and research output in 1991

commercial and industrial failures which are all the more regrettable for the fact that they indicate an inability to take advantage of real technological resources. For a long time, this paradox has been justified by value judgements which set the noble humanist inventor against the opportunistic tradesman. As a consequence, for engineers and even more for researchers, the world of the company was as often as not associated with a place which it was not worth frequenting, peopled with cynical individuals who had placed their talent at the behest of personal interest. The organisers of public research, on the other hand, were placed on a pedestal and symbolised material disinterest and a positivistic concern for collective progress.

Nevertheless, since the middle of the 1980s, particularly under the influence of Socialist governments forced by economic imperatives to refute their idealistic ideologies, the image of the company and even of private enterprise has become accepted as a worthy symbol of social success and the political and intellectual élites no longer hesitate to promote its material importance which they previously decried.

In short, the fundamentalist state-run tradition which underpins French research is being called into question. The signs of this change in attitude are quite clear. One such is the increasing attraction of studying management. Even in engineering schools, courses directly linked to management are now among the most highly sought after by students at the *Ecole Centrale*. Even the *Ecole Polytechnique* has now established a management research centre and a number of graduates from the *Ecole Normale Supérieure* complete their higher education with a diploma from a business school. Equally, many public research laboratories are now encouraged to collaborate with companies as part of an initiative to promote technology transfer. Finally, the privatisation of certain public companies which specialise in technology is a clear indication of the same will to break with a radical intellectual tradition.

SELECTED TEXTS

CREDOC (1995)
INSEE (1995)

See Bibliography

4 Capitalisation and company finance

Jean-Yves Eglem and Jyoti Gupta

The French financial system has undergone fundamental changes over the last few years as a result of deregulation and modernisation. France now has a highly sophisticated capital market with a diversified range of products, which includes pure equity and debt instruments, hybrid instruments and markets for derivative products such as futures and options. Its stock exchanges are among the most active in Europe and second only to London. In addition, the French banking system has been restructured and its major banks are among the biggest in the world. This explosive growth started in the early eighties with the liberalisation of both the banking sector and stock market. It is also due to the change in attitude of companies which shifted from bank borrowing to bonds as a result of the improved liquidity of the capital markets. With the creation of the *OPCVM* (*organismes de placement collectif de valeurs mobilières*), the French equivalent of unit trusts, there was also greatly increased activity on the part of investors. *OPCVM* assured diversified portfolios which have enabled investors to obtain higher returns while at the same time limiting their risk.

One important trend in terms of the financing of French companies has therefore been a move towards equity financing accompanied by a gradual reduction of debt. The debt to equity ratio has decreased from 64 per cent in 1985 to 38.8 per cent in 1991 reflecting this change of attitude. Traditionally, there was a strong link between French companies (particularly small and medium-sized enterprises) and the banks. The latter were reluctant to lose control of companies through the issue of new shares. In the last ten years, however, firms' greater openness towards equity has led to the need to create a second or 'junior' stock market (*second marché*). This was not sufficient to promote the growth of smaller size companies, particularly those with a strong potential for development accompanied by a high level of risk. The creation of yet another market known as the *nouveau marché* (which is comparable to the NASDAQ in the USA) therefore took place on 14 February 1996.

Another important characteristic of the French market has been the creation of new financial instruments which are hybrid in nature. Such instruments, which form a half-way house between equity and debt, include '*titres de participation*' and '*certificats d'investissements*', special types of shareholdings

---

Encadré 8: NASDAQ and SEAQ

The National Association of Security Dealers Automated Quotation (NASDAQ) is the agency which has been created on the New York stock exchange to facilitate investment in smaller companies with high growth potential. It is a profit-making institution which, as its title suggests, is linked to an automated trading system which avoids brokers buying and selling shares on the floor of the exchange. Its equivalent in London is the Stock Exchange Automated Quotations (SEAQ). NASDAQ has been criticised for setting prices too high and thus inhibiting the level of investment which it is designed to promote.

---

which are particularly suitable for nationalised corporations. Their main function has been to enable nationalised companies with a serious need for capital to raise funds from the public in the form of equity which allowed the government to retain control of the company concerned.

Developments in the French financial system since the early 1980s have inevitably been conditioned by French economic policy which went through three distinct phases linked to the economic philosophy of the political parties in power (see Chapter 1). In 1981, following the accession to power of the Socialist party, the government decided to nationalise the major corporations (Rhône Poulenc, Thomson, Pechiney, etc.) and also the major banks (BNP, Crédit Lyonnais, Société Générale, CCF, etc.). The new hybrid instruments mentioned above enabled these organisations to raise quasi-equity from the capital markets. The change of government in 1986 led to a reversal of socialist policy in which many of the banks (Société Générale, Paribas, Indo-Suez, CCF, etc.) were reprivatised, a development which had a further significant impact on the capitalisation of the Paris stock exchange. The final phase started in 1992 after the second major victory of the right-wing alliance over the Socialists. Since that time, the new government has undertaken a further programme of privatisation involving a number of state-owned companies including Renault, Elf Aquitaine and Air France. First estimates in 1993 gave a total flotation value for new shares of nearly 400 billion francs, marking a further stage in a continuing process which has progressively increased the capitalisation of the Paris stock market and modified considerably the roles of the different players.

THE FINANCIAL MARKETPLACE

Stock exchanges

The organised segment of the financial marketplace consists of the stock exchanges which deal with equity shares, bonds and other related instruments and the markets for derivatives, *MATIF* and *MONEP*.

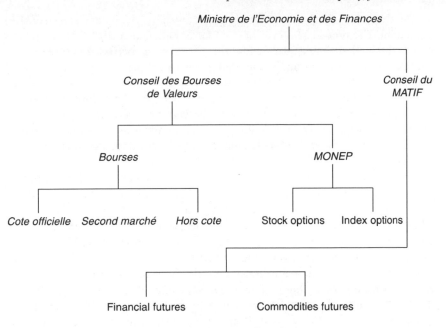

Figure 4.1 The organisation of the French financial market

The management of the organised markets is controlled by two new regulatory agencies, the *Conseil des Bourses de Valeurs* and the *Conseil du MATIF* which supervises the activities of the futures market. The stock exchanges, of which there are seven in France, trade in equities and bonds. They are located in Paris, Lyon, Marseille, Bordeaux, Lille, Nancy and Nantes. A company can have its securities traded in any one of the seven exchanges. Paris is by far the largest in terms of capitalisation and volume traded, and accounts for more than 95 per cent of the total transactions. The regional exchanges deal with the companies whose headquarters are in the same area. It is planned to connect the different exchanges through an on-line computer system.

Administrative structure

The Paris stock market or *bourse* is made up of four sections:

- *la cote officielle* – the main market;
- *le second marché* – the market for small companies and for new entrants to the stock market;
- *la hors cote* – the unofficial and unregulated 'over-the-counter' market;
- *le nouveau marché* – the market for new 'high-risk' companies with strong growth potential.

The *cote officielle* is reserved for larger companies which have an established reputation. The procedures for listing are fairly long and costly. Only companies which have distributed dividends for at least a period of three years consecutively can be formally admitted. At least 25 per cent of shares should be offered to the public. The companies can be listed in either the *marché comptant* or the *marché à règlement mensuel*. In the *marché comptant*, transactions are settled daily, whereas in the *marché à règlement mensuel* they are settled once every month. Trading volume is much higher in the *marché à règlement mensuel* and most large company stocks are traded on this section of the market.

The *second marché* was opened in 1983 to allow smaller companies to accede to the share market and to go public. The entry conditions are far less stringent than for the *cote officielle*. This market is particularly attractive for family firms whose owners were reluctant to go public because of the risk of losing control of the company, as only 10 per cent of the shares need to be offered on the open market. There are no restrictions regarding the minimum distributions. Furthermore, the requirements concerning the information to be published are far less limiting than those of the *cote officielle*. The *second marché* was designed for companies which were already established and of a certain size. Thus, in February 1996, as part of an attempt to rejuvenate the economy, the *nouveau marché* was created for newly founded, small companies which needed an infusion of venture capital.

The stock exchange was restructured during the 1980s and changes have continued in the subsequent decade. The renovation of the *bourse* started with the technical reforms undertaken in 1986 to improve the liquidity of the market. A computerised system of quotation (*système informatisé d'aide à la cotation*) was introduced in that year. The continuous quotation system was followed by the appointment of a new regulatory structure to improve the organisation and control of the financial market. These new agencies are the *Conseil des Bourses de Valeurs* (*CBV*), the *Société des Bourses Françaises* (*SBF*) and the *Association Française des Sociétés de Bourse* (*AFSB*). The reforms in market practices were intended to improve stockholders' security while increasing the liquidity and the efficiency of the market. As well as introducing a computerised quotation system, it was made mandatory for the delivery and payment of transactions to conform to international standards.

The *Conseil des Bourses de Valeurs* (*CBV*), whose members are representatives of the *Sociétés des Bourses Françaises* (*SBF*), is responsible for maintaining the procedures and practices of the French financial market. The members of the *CBV* are mainly concerned with the nomination of intermediaries, the principles of quotations, the listing of new companies and the delisting of firms, while the *SBF* is the body responsible for implementing the *CBV*'s decisions. The equity of the *SBF* is held by the *Sociétés des Bourse* and by the financial institutions (banks, insurance companies, *Caisse des Dépôts*) which are the major investors in the market, while the *Association*

Française des Sociétés de Bourse (*AFSB*) is the representative body which defends the interests of the *Sociétés de Bourse*.

Some of the above functions were originally fulfilled by the *Commission des Opérations de Bourse* (*COB*) which now has a broader remit. The *COB* is a state-appointed body which is modelled on the US Securities and Exchange Commission (SEC). Its role is to ensure the smooth functioning of the stock exchange. The *COB* analyses prospectuses and other documents issued by companies wishing to raise money on the markets and is responsible for investigating any irregularities in the functioning of the market. It has the legal power to pursue any company or individual who is involved in illegal operations on the stock exchange such as insider trading.

Equity market

The equity capitalisation of the Paris stock market evolved favourably between 1987 and 1992, increasing from 830.8 billion francs in 1987 to 2,415 billion francs in 1994. After a rapid increase, market capitalisation stagnated in the year 1992 and increased again in 1993. The increase during the early years was linked to the privatisation programme introduced by the Chirac government in 1986, and the growth was maintained by the dynamic economies of France and her major industrialised trading partners. The year 1992 was characterised by two events, first the September 1992 crash in the stock market and second the monetary turbulence in the European Monetary System (EMS) which followed the 1991 ratification of the Maastricht Treaty. The market was boosted again in 1993 following the renewal of privatisation under the government of Alain Madelin and subsequently that of Alain Juppé. Clearly, the future performance of the equity market will depend upon economic conditions in France and abroad, bearing in mind the general principle that share prices rise when interest rates are low.

Table 4.1 The number of companies listed on the French stock market (1988–94)

	1988	1989	1990	1991	1992	1993	1994
Cote officielle	608	606	578	547	513	472	459
Paris *bourse*	459	462	444	412	–	–	–
Regional *bourses*	149	144	134	135	–	–	–
Second marché	286	298	297	288	271	254	265
Paris *bourse*	180	186	186	186	–	–	–
Regional *bourses*	106	112	111	102	–	–	–

Source: *COB Annual Report* 1994

Table 4.2 Market capitalisation* (in billions of francs) (1987–92)

	1987	1988	1989	1990	1991	1992
Capitalisation of shares	330.1	1,330.1	1,911.9	1,761.0	1,803.1	1,000.7
Transactions	477.7	390.4	640.3	626.3	614.9	644.5

Source: COB Annual Report 1992 and 1994

Note: *End of year figures

The bond market

The growth in the bond market has been more pronounced than that of the equity market such that, in 1992, its market capitalisation stood at 3,185.4 billion francs.

Government and state entreprises are the major issuers of bonds and, in 1992, the latter accounted for 82.5 per cent of their capitalisation. The public status of the state owned companies, which included amongst others such corporations as Renault, Air France, EDF, GDF and Bull, meant that they could not raise equity capital because of budgetary restrictions. The bond market was therefore their only means of increasing their available funds. This led to a deterioration in their debt/equity ratio and put enormous constraints on their capacity to raise money outside France. Their ratings were adversely affected, which further limited their capacity to borrow, both in quantitative and qualitative terms. It was these constraints which forced the government to introduce new financial instruments which were hybrid in nature, in other words instruments which had the characteristics of equity without limiting government control.

Among the new instruments, two in particular – *certificats d'investissement* and *titres participatifs* were largely used during the mid-1980s by state-owned companies to reinforce their equity base. The dividends derived from these instruments are based in part on companies' performance. Yet at the same time there is no obligation for the company to pay back the amount borrowed. In other words, they are a permanent source of funds, while the subscribers to these

Table 4.3 Market capitalisation of French bonds listed on the Paris Stock exchange (1989–92)

	1989		1990		1991		1992	
	billion francs	%	billion francs	%	billion francs	%	billion francs	%
Government bonds	778.4	33.1	825.8	33.5	965.7	33.3	1,137.2	35.7
Public sector bonds	1,116.3	47.5	1,182.6	47.9	1,388.4	47.9	1,489.4	46.8
Private sector bonds	450.6	19.2	457.0	18.6	545.4	18.8	558.8	17.5
Total	**2,346.3**	**100.0**	**2,467.4**	**100.0**	**2,899.5**	**100.0**	**3,185.4**	**100.0**

Source: SBF

securities have no voting rights. The major investors in the bond market are banks and institutional investors such as insurance companies and pension funds. In fact, the banks are obliged to hold a minimum portfolio of French bonds to satisfy the prudential criteria imposed by the monetary authorities. The favourable development of the stock index during the eighties and in 1990–91 also enabled companies to raise funds by using convertible bonds and OBSA (*obligations avec bons de souscription – actions*) which further enabled companies to reinforce their equity base. The dependency of major French companies on bonds purchased by institutional investors is a particular characteristic of the French economy which is closely linked to central government control. It carries with it serious dangers of inbreeding which are often associated with centralised mixed economies of the French type. The more or less closed system protects companies which may be in difficulties and puts pressure on major institutional investors to place their money in large national corporations rather than in smaller companies whose need for capital investment may be just as great. In this way, it masks investment problems at the national level and limits the economy's potential for growth.

Given that the inflation rate in France has stabilised at around 2–3 per cent, it is highly likely that the above trend will continue. Although certain events could always counteract this tendency, long term rates should remain at about 3 per cent above inflation, i.e. at about 6 per cent. Amongst the new compulsory or hybrid products, none has really undergone a steady growth. Despite its relative flexibility, OBSA for example appears today to have declined. The same has been the case for hybrid stock. On the other hand, the issuing of bonds at variable rates has grown steadily. Investors' interest in this form of placement has increased considerably, particularly on the part of fund managers for the SICAV and public investment companies. In 1980, only 19 loans at variable interest rates were allowed on the market, representing 16.8 per cent of the total loans issued. At the end of 1990, there were a total of 126 representing 50 per cent of the borrowing undertaken in that year.

Derived capital markets

France has two derived capital markets:

- the *MATIF* (*Marché à terme international de France*),
- the *MONEP* (*Marché des options négociables de Paris*).

The uncertainty and volatility of the financial markets have been to the benefit of both the *MATIF* and the *MONEP* whose volume of trading has increased strongly. Between 1993 and 1994, the number of contracts established by the *MATIF* increased from 71 million to more than 93 million, while the *MONEP* increased its volume by 26 per cent, reaching 8.8 million francs by the end of 1994.

Encadré 9: The MATIF

The MATIF opened in Paris on 20 February 1986 under the name '*marché à terme d'instruments financiers*' which was changed in January 1988 to '*marché à terme international de France*'. It is a financial futures exchange which deals in standardised 'off the shelf' contracts and covers both financial instruments and commodities. The *MATIF* is organised by the Paris stock exchange and is placed under the control of the *COB*. The *Conseil du Marché à Terme* (*CMT*) is responsible for the general regulation of the *MATIF* and for the two offices which handle compensation, MATIF SA for financial instruments and the BCC (Banque Centrale de Compensation) for commodities. *MATIF* is linked to the GLOBEX system which brings together a number of stock exchanges representing 60 per cent of futures and options activities worldwide. Its membership of the executive committee of GLOBEX has made it possible for MATIF's activities to be widely recognised and promoted abroad.

Encadré 10: THE MONEP

The *MONEP* opened in Paris on 10 September 1987 and the shares of three major French companies were chosen as the main reference points for options trading – Lafarge Coppée, Paribas and Peugeot SA. This limited selection of companies has progressively been extended to cover a total of thirty-four French firms and now includes other types of monthly settlement as well as the CAC40 index which acts as a benchmark for two types of options contract, a short-term American style option and a long-term European option. The *MONEP* is controlled by the *CBV* (*Conseil des Bourses de Valeurs*). Under the *CBV*'s authority, the *Société des Bourses Françaises* (SBF) has delegated the responsibility for running the *MONEP* to its subsidiary, the *Société de Compensation des Marchés Conditionnels* (*SCMC*). The *MONEP*'s business is conducted on the floor of the Paris *bourse* with the two types of option contract linked to the CAC40 index representing by far the largest proportion of transactions.

MONEY MARKETS

Until the reforms of 1985, the French monetary market was a closed system controlled by merchant banks. Financial institutions only intervened in order to exchange money for public or private goods. Other economic agents (companies in particular) were excluded from such transactions. The 1985 company reform was aimed at restructuring the two sides of the capital market (money/bonds), the principal innovations involved being to identify two areas of activity:

- trading limited exclusively to banks;
- an open market dealing in negotiable stock.

The second of the two types of activity, the objective of which was to open the money market to agents other than financial institutions, covers five different types of financial instrument:

- *certificats de dépôt (CD)* – units issued by banks;
- *billets de trésorerie (BT)* – bonds issued by companies and foreign banks;
- *bons des institutions et sociétés financières (BISF)*;
- *bons du trésor (BTN)* – government bonds;
- *bons à moyen terme négociables (BMTN)* – bonds issued collectively by all the above agents together.

The creation of this additional range of bonds gave companies possibilities for short-term financing other than those offered by the banking sector. Moreover, the opening up of the markets improved the management of the total amount of money available in the system by introducing flexible rates which were subject to negotiation. The key factor in facilitating negotiation in a less segmented marketplace is the yield on maturation which varies according to the rates agreed and the degree of risk associated with the signature of the issuing agent. Since treasury bonds have been made available for purchase on current accounts, it has been possible for private individuals and companies to make use of this facility. Thus, a secondary financial market has been created, one whose liquidity has been improved through the creation of a group of specialists in the values of treasury bonds (*spécialistes en valeurs du trésor – SVT*), the most active stock being treasury bonds which are issued annually (*bons de trésor annuel normalisé – BTAN*). Meanwhile, bank loans remain the principal source of support for SMEs.

THE BANKING MARKET

The only participants in this market are those recognised under banking law as authorised financial trading agencies. These include the *Banque de France*, the *Trésor Public* and the *Caisse des Dépôts et Consignations*. Insurance agencies, pension fund organisations and the investment companies (*société d'investissement à capital variable – SICAV*) are excluded from this market on which funds emanating from the central bank – the *Banque de France* – are lent and borrowed. As has already been seen, the development of the markets dealing in negotiable credit (*TCN*) has had a considerable influence on the development of the banking market, being accessible to all economic agents and offering opportunities for short and medium-term placements. This stock, most notably treasury bonds, has therefore become a supplementary currency of exchange between central financial trading agencies. In respect of their size and standing on the merchant banking market, a number of lending agencies have been approved by the *Banque de France* as 'main traders' (*opérateurs principaux du marché – OPM*). The OPM are required to provide regular quotations and to keep the *Banque de France* informed as to the nature and volume of their activity, their rates and the duration of their loans, etc.

Institutional investors

The best-known institutional investors on the French market are:

- insurance companies;
- pension funds;
- the *Caisse des Dépôts et Consignation* (*CDC*);
- the *organismes de placement collectif en valeurs mobilières* (*OPCVM*).

The acronym *OPCVM* covers seven different vehicles for collective placement:

- *SICAV* (*sociétés d'investissement à capital variable*);
- *FCP* (*fonds communs de placement*);
- *SICAF* (*sociétés d'investissement à capital fixe*);
- *FCPE* (*fonds communs de placement d'entreprise*);
- *FCPR* (*fonds communs de placement à risque*);
- *FIMAT* (*fonds communs d'intervention sur les marchés à terme*);
- *FCC* (*fonds communs de créances*).

OPCVM are open products. They are easy to buy and sell, their value being calculated according to the levels of trading on the stock exchange. Of these, the *SICAV* and the *FCP* are general products which are by far the most significant in terms of the overall sums involved. They have undergone an astonishing growth (see Table 4.4).

Table 4.4 The growth of institutional investment (in thousand million francs) in France (1988–92)

	1987	1988	1989	1990	1991	1992
SICAV						
Net annual subscriptions	151.7	174.5	141.8	154.8	82.9	22.9
Total volume of funds managed on 31/12 of each year	821.6	1,074.5	1,269.6	1,447.3	1,661.4	1,803.9
Number of *SICAV* on 31/12 of each year	634	772	872	916	949	983
FCP						
Net annual subscriptions	22.9	81.8	95.1	136.0	42.6	87.4
Total volume of funds managed on 31/12 of each year	269.8	357.6	441.6	495.8	563.7	708.4
Number of *FCP* on 31/12 of each year	3,029	3,659	4,048	3,872	3,566	3,693

Source: COB Annual Report

The banking system

Like the financial market itself, the banking system is involved in an extremely far-reaching set of changes. These affect as much the nature of operations as the ways of approaching customers, the conditions of employment of staff and the organisation of institutions. As a result of progressive deregulation, French banks have had to adapt from a centrally controlled system to highly competitive conditions in which many of the boundaries limiting the freedom of capital movements have been abolished. Thus, since 1984, French banks have been regulated by legislation which sought to rationalise the statutes governing what was then an excessively diverse range of institutions. At the same time, it was necessary to bring French banking practice into line with European law.

The powers of the new law extended to all French banking institutions which were known from then on as *établissements de crédit*. Hence, the distinction between customer banks and merchant banks was abolished and the majority of institutions offering credit facilities have been brought together under a single legal umbrella. Agencies which are not covered by the framework of the 1984 banking law include *Chèques Postaux*, the *Caisses d'Epargne* run by the Poste Télégraphe et Télécommunications (PTT), the *Trésor Public*, the *Banque de France* and the *Caisse des Dépôts et Consignations* (*CDC*). Control over lending institutions is exercised by the *Commission Bancaire* which has replaced the *Commission de Contrôle des Banques* (*CCB*), while professional representation is run by a single organisation the AFEC (*Association Française des Etablissements de Crédit*). At the end of 1991, there were 1,869 lending institutions in France, 426 of which were banks.

Institutions formally recognised as banks constitute the largest sector (40 per cent) of the French banking system. At the beginning of 1992, they employed around 240,000 people and represented a network comprising more than 10,000 branches.

Institutions belonging to centrally coordinated networks

Alongside the banks in the strict sense of the word, the second most significant grouping which can be identified within the French banking system is made up by institutions belonging to networks run by central agencies. These institutions own more than 15,000 branches, that is 60 per cent of the total number of outlets. They receive 29 per cent of the total of sums deposited in francs and hold 24 per cent of the volume of credit within the internal economy. These establishments have a special social status, being cooperative or mutualist in character. This is the case for example with the *Banques Populaires*, the *Caisses de Crédit Agricole* or *Crédit Mutuel*. Alternatively, they may be non-profit-making institutions (e.g. the *Caisses d'Epargne et de Prévoyance*) or state run (*Caisse de Crédit Municipal*).

Encadré 11: The main types of bank in France

The national banks   The three great banks described as 'national' are the Banque Nationale de Paris (BNP), the Crédit Lyonnais (CL) and the Société Génerale (SG). These three are among the 15 leading banks in the world in terms of their total assets. The three institutions have an extended network of branches in France, a diverse range of activities and an international profile. Having more than 5,500 branches between them, they distribute approximately 23 per cent of their overall funds to customers on terms agreed with associated institutions and claim 27 per cent of the amounts deposited with these institutions. Moreover, each of these banks is the holding company for diversified groups comprising numerous branches in France and abroad. Each engages in activities in the fields of banking and finance (portfolio management, mortgages, investment banking, trading arbitrage) as well as in insurance and even in non-financial sectors such as real estate and software.

The great merchant banks   Certain of these, such as the Banque Indo Suez and the Banque Paribas, deal mainly with corporate clients' market operations and international activities, or with the banks CCF, CIC and the Crédit du Nord which have a large number of private customers and SMEs/SMIs on their books.

Local and regional banks   These focus, as their name suggests, on a particular locality. Their customers consist essentially of private customers and SMEs/SMIs. More than half of these banks belong to larger banking groups.

Banks dealing in specialist financing   These are characterised by activities which are focused essentially on the distribution of certain types of credit (building loans, hire purchase, etc.). There are approximately forty banks of this type, of which a number belong to larger scale groups.

Specialised merchant banks   These deal with placements, booking and portfolio management in the different sectors of the financial markets (banking, *TCN, MATIF, MONEP,* the exchange market, and so on). Several of these merchant banks are officially recognised by the *Banque de France* as institutional dealers (*opérateurs principaux du marché – OPM*) or by the treasury as *spécialistes correspondants en valeur du trésor* (*SVT* or *CVT*).

Banking groups   These number about forty and are characterised by the fact that the majority of their capital is held by non-banking agents, most notably industrial firms and insurance companies. These institutions carry out a significant proportion of their trade in collaboration with the group to which they belong (treasury stock, risk insurance, currency dealing, bonds).

Foreign banks in France The deregulation of banking and finance activities which has taken place over the last few years has encouraged new foreign banks to establish themselves in France. The number is steadily increasing. According to figures published by the *Commission des Etablissements de Crédit* there were apparently 181 foreign banks in France at the end of 1991 of which seventy-eight were from the EU. Taken together, foreign banks represented 8.5 per cent of branches in 1991. Since 1985, their increase in numbers has been rapid and the recent period has been marked by a significant strengthening in the position of European banks. The 1960s and 1970s had seen a widespread growth of American influence, the Japanese arrived on the scene in the 1980s, but over a five-year period there has been a substantial effort on the part of a few European banks to develop networks in France. In 1993 there were scarcely more than ten banks with a network of more than ten branches. The largest of these, Barclays International, has seventy branches, while the second largest, a Spanish bank, the CAIXA, whose establishment in France is much more recent than that of Barclays, has forty-eight.

Encadré 12: Centrally coordinated networks

The *Crédit Agricole Mutuel* The *Crédit Agricole* is organised on three levels – local agencies (of which there are approximately 3,000), regional agencies (which numbered ninety-one in the year 1991) and the *Caisse Nationale de Crédit Agricole*, whose capital has been held since 1987 by the regional centres (*caisses*). The *Caisse Nationale* has a highly diverse range of activities, in particular the management of the funds available in the regional centres, investment on the money markets and overseas operations.

The *Banques Populaires* The *Banques Populaires* receive deposits from a wide variety of sources and exist principally to support industrial companies, small businesses and artisans. An ever-greater proportion of the activities of the *Banques Populaires* deals with the funding of businesses and individuals within the region for which the bank is responsible. The organisation of a group of *Banques Populaires* is on two levels:

- local banks having responsibility for a given geographical region;
- two central organisations, one concerned with administration, including collective human resource management issues (*la chambre syndicale*), the other with financial affairs (*la caisse centrale*).

The *Crédit Mutuel* The *Crédit Mutuel* is subdivided into two sectors, agricultural and general. The agricultural sector includes the centres (*caisses*) which depend on the *Fédération Centrale du Crédit Agricole*

Mutuel. The general sector has a three-level hierarchy (local centres, regional groups and a national confederation) and is most active in Alsace. Its resources derive for the most part from *comptes sur livrets exonérés or livrets bleus.* The main clients are individuals or professional organisations and it has more than 3,200 outlets.

The *Caisses d'Epargne et de Prévoyance* These are non-profit-making institutions. Their main income derives from a special category of investment (*livret A*) which is tax free and on which interest is fixed by the financial authorities. The network as a whole employs 34,000 people, has more than 4,300 outlets and sets aside 15.6 per cent of clients' deposits received by approved institutions.

Specialised financial institutions (*institutions financières spécialisées* – IFS)   At the present time, there are thirty-two specialised financial institutions whose activities are extremely diverse. The *Crédit National* and the *Crédit Foncier de France* (*CFF*) are only two of the most important!

The main objective of the *Crédit National* is to provide medium to long-term financial support for companies. In this sense it acts as a banker. It is in direct contact with companies and makes funds available to them in the form of loans which can vary in duration from two to twenty years. Many different arrangements including fixed or differential rates of interest are offered to companies and, in order to finance these loans, the *Crédit National* itself offers loans on the financial markets. It is extending the range of its financial dealings notably in the international field. An analogous agency, the *Crédit d'Equipement des Petites et Moyennes Entreprises* (*CEPME*), was created in 1980 to finance the investments of SMEs. If appropriate, it is also authorised to allocate special loans at favourable rates.

The *Crédit Foncier de France* provides investment for building projects and acts as an agent for the state in promoting state development. The decision taken by the government in 1984 to reduce the volume of special loans and to abolish certain categories of finance linked to state aid has caused a number of *IFS*, particularly those specialising in the financing of development companies, to undergo a substantial change. They have sought to adapt their loan activities to the conditions of the market and to diversify the nature of their interventions (currency loans, *apports de fonds propres,* financial consultancy, etc.). To this end, they have created new branches or have taken control of existing institutions (banks, stockbroking firms etc.).

VENTURE CAPITAL IN FRANCE

Venture capital was introduced to France in 1955 by the creation of *SDRs* (*sociétés de développement régional*). The *SDR* are specialised financial institutions. For 25 years, venture capital activities remained very marginal for the *SDR*. In order to respond to companies' need for capital, the public authorities created three structures – in 1972, the law on the creation of firms promoting financial innovation, the establishment in 1977 of the *Instituts Régionaux de Participation* and in 1979 the establishment of the *Institut de Développement Industriel* (*IDI*). The real development of private venture capital took place from the middle of the 1980s thanks to incentives from the public authorities. The main measures taken were the laws of 3 January 1985 on the creation of the common venture capital fund (*fonds commun de placement à risque – FCPR*) and that of 11 July 1985 on the creation of venture capital companies (*sociétés de capital-risque – SCR*). The establishment of the second market in 1983 also helped the development of this activity. The funds, which were intended for investment in companies, were provided by institutional and individual contributions supported by tax relief. They were conditional on funds being held for five years so as to allow the dividends to be reinvested. These funds are kept by the *FCPR* or the *SCR*. At the end of 1992, there were 138 *FCPR* in France, of which eighty-four were managed by credit-lending institutions. The total funds being managed amounted to 1.16 thousand million francs.

PARIS AS AN INTERNATIONAL FINANCIAL TRADING CENTRE

The opening up of the European marketplace and the state of the global economy have enhanced the competitive relationship between the major cities of the world. As has been seen in this chapter. Paris has undergone a complete overhaul over the last ten years as a financial trading centre. France now possesses a banking system which is open and modernised. The four main types of capital markets have been progressively upgraded. International financial exchange has been enhanced by the exploitation of external information networks such as Reuter and Télérate, while trading operations use the channel provided by SWIFT. However, the volume of transactions at Paris remains distinctly lower than that at London. Meantime, as a consequence of having introduced the *MATIF* and the *MONEP*, Paris has become one of the top markets in the world for derivatives.

It is the progressive computerisation of the different phases of financial trading – negotiating, establishing and disseminating rates, compensation and closure – which has given the Paris exchange its international status. Its strong points can be summed up as follows:

- the 'dematerialisation' of shares;
- the simplification and increased security of the trading process;

- the introduction of continuous trading;
- the fact of being networked by satellite with other major trading centres;
- the reduction in the time of settlement of transactions;
- improved access to the market and a greater facility in issuing shares (the creation of the *second marché*);
- the increased availability of venture capital which has enhanced the financing of young companies;
- the strengthening of the derivatives market (*MATIF, MONEP*);
- an increasingly competitive and efficient banking system.

Despite the remarkable progress of the last few years, Paris has some way to go before it can claim to rival London as a world financial trading centre. However, without the greater flexibility and variety of the financial instruments which have been created in the last ten years, it is difficult to imagine that the growth of the 1980s in terms of investment and the creation of new businesses could have taken place. France now has a more responsive set of instruments for raising credit than any country in Europe.

SELECTED TEXTS

Commission de Opérations de Bourse (COB)
Conseil National du Crédit (CNC)
Delpit, B. and Schwartz, M. (1993)

See Bibliography

USEFUL ADDRESSES

Association Française des Banques
18 rue Lafayette
75009 Paris
Tel. (1) 48.00.52.52.

Centre de Recherche et de Documentation des Experts-Comptables et des Commissions aux Comptes
88 rue de Courcelles
75008 Paris
Tel (1) 42.27.02.90.

Commission Bancaire
73 rue de Richelieu
75002 Paris
Tel. (1) 42.92.42.92.

Commission des Opérations de Bourse (COB)
39–43 quai André Citroën
75739 Paris Cedex 15
Tel. (1) 40.58.65.65.

Comité de la Réglementation Bancaire
BP 140–01
75049 Paris Cedex 01
Tel. (1) 42.92.42.92.
Conseil National du Crédit (CNC)
1 rue de la Vrillière
75001 Paris
Tel. (1) 42.92.27.10.

Conseil des Bourses de Valeurs
39 rue Cambon
75001 Paris
Tel. (1) 49.27.10.00.

Conseil des Marchés à Terme
176 rue Montmartre
75002 Paris
Tel. (1) 40.28.82.82.

5 Financial management and accounting procedures

John Kennedy

As foreign corporations began to set up in France in the post-1945 era, their management encountered a number of cultural barriers, including language, which restricted effective business practice. The social unrest in 1968 gave rise to a political commitment to modernise French society, particularly the education system. In parallel with these social initiatives, a series of business reforms which have impacted on financial and accounting management procedures were enacted during the 1960s and 1970s. These included in particular:

- revisions of company law relating to the content and form of annual accounts, and the requirements to disclose more information for employees and shareholders;
- reforms in the capital markets, including, in 1967, the creation of a stock exchange regulatory authority, the *Commission des Opérations de Bourse* (*COB*).

These reforms established a basis for the 1980s, when French accounting procedures were substantially modified in order to implement the European Directives on financial statements. To a large extent, change has been the result of European market forces and their effect on different governments of France. Since the first Socialist president under the Fifth Republic was elected in 1981, both left-wing and right-wing governments have exercised power and, while different governments have given contrasting emphases to policy, the long-term 'vision' on strategic development has remained consistent. During these years, France has enjoyed financial stability and growth to become the second largest economy within Western Europe. Its environmental and social infrastructures have been financed by a complex tax system. Financial reporting procedures have been radically transformed and foreign practices have been adopted and adapted to the French environment. Finally, educational policies and development funds have focused on international exchanges which have given the younger French generation a more global view of business practices.

Any country's reporting procedures must be seen within their cultural and historical evolution. The French traditions are based on the Roman and

Napoleonic models of codified and detailed regulations with a strong influence of government. While these traditions are strong in countries such as Belgium, Germany, Italy, Portugal, Spain, etc., they run counter to Anglo-Saxon practices and those prevalent in countries like the Netherlands. Other factors have influenced the French reporting environment – the nature of corporate owners (traditionally banks, governments and families), the tax system, and the size and development of the auditing and accountancy professions. Such factors certainly held back the development of modern auditing and accountancy as seen in the UK and USA in the 1960s and 1970s, particularly on such issues as accounting policies, presentation of financial reports, disclosure of information and the preparation of financial statements. However, with the development of the European Community and the publication of new Directives, countries like France have evolved and adapted their reporting procedures. As a result, and as described below, France has developed 'parallel' reporting systems, for individual company units and for consolidated groups.

Thus, while controlling or regulatory bodies have remained intact, the professional bodies have quickly developed and now occupy a position equivalent to the older Anglo-Saxon professional institutes. (In recent years two French accountants have presided over the International Accounting Standards Committee (IASC) and the *Fédération Européenne des Experts-Comptables* (*FEE*). In short, the French mechanisms for regulating companies' traditional accounting procedures are still firmly established, but their approach is now more in line with international financial market requirements.

INTERNAL PROCEDURES

Books and records

The French Commercial Code (*Code de Commerce*) requires enterprises to keep records in which all accounting movements affecting the rights and obligations of the company are recorded. The main records required are as follows:

- a general journal (*livre-journal*) in which all transactions are recorded on a daily basis;
- a general ledger (*grand livre*) summarising the transactions of the general journal;
- a balance sheet book (*livre d'inventaire*) recording the assets and liabilities of the company which need only be written up on an annual basis;
- a payroll book (*livre de paie*);
- a starters and leavers book (*livre d'entrées et sorties*) containing the dates employees commence and terminate their employment with the company.

These records must be conserved for a period of ten years from the date of the last entry. During this period the documents must remain in the original form and cannot, therefore, be transferred onto microfilm or magnetic tape. Original records may be held on computer or other readable forms, but must also be available on hard copy. All these books must be maintained in the French language. The *livre journal* and *livre d'inventaire* are considered special registers, every page of which the commercial courts must sign, annually.

Related to computerised and complex accounting procedures is the requirement to prepare and maintain a comprehensive procedures manual which defines and describes the following:

- employees' duties and functions;
- supervisory and authorisation procedures;
- detailed accounting plan used;
- accounting information circuit (i.e. computerised systems description, audit trail, program security, etc.).

Statutory matters

In addition to the above records required by the Commercial Code, statutory books must be maintained under commercial law. The main registers required are the following:

- board meeting information (attendances and minutes);
- shareholders' meetings information (attendances, voting records and minutes);
- share register (details on movements);
- share register (information on shares bought/sold by the company itself or by the employees).

SOURCES OF FRENCH ACCOUNTING LAW

The European context

Since its foundation, the European Community, known officially since 1994 as the European Union (EU), has been making efforts to reduce the differences in accounting and auditing law in member states. The main mechanism used to achieve this is the issuing of Directives which are drafted by the Commission, adopted by the European Council of Ministers and implemented by the parliaments of the member states. The intention of Directives is to harmonise the laws in member states concerning corporations, how they conduct business and how they account for their actions. In many cases, the Directives define only minimum legal requirements or, in other cases, provide options. If they so desire, member states may add more restrictive requirements or legislate more specific treatments for their own countries. Therefore, in an overview such as that provided in this chapter, reference must still be made to the legislation of individual member states for information on applicable accounting practices.

Notwithstanding these differences, the EU Directives constitute useful benchmarks for comparing accounting practices in Europe.

The French context

French accounting practices are set out in national legislation and various regulatory texts, which are clarified and supplemented by authoritative pronouncements. The main sources of these practices are:

- **Business Code** (*Code de Commerce*) The text of the Business Code is derived from the accounting law of 30 April 1983 and Articles 1–27 of the decree dated 29 November 1983. Collectively, these enactments implement the terms of the EC Fourth Directive relating to the format and general accounting rules for annual accounts.
- **General Accounting Plan** (*Plan Comptable Général – PCG*) The 1982 *PCG* lays down general principles and provides definitions of terms, a list of accounts to be used, rules relating to valuation methods and the presentation of a typical set of financial statements. The plan was updated in December 1986.

Application of the general principles outlined in the *Plan Comptable* should lead to the accounts' showing a true and fair view. The financial statements must also satisfy, with due consideration of the rule of prudence, the obligations of compliance with accounting regulations (*régularité*) and fairness (*sincérité*). The general accounting charter together with any additional provisions rendered necessary by the legal, economic, social and technical environment within which the company operates, constitute the framework of generally accepted

Table 5.1 Main EC/EU Directives relating to accounting and auditing

Directives on company law	Subjects
First	*Ultra vires* rules
Second	Separation of public companies, minimum capital, distributions
Third	Mergers
Fourth	Formats and rules of accounting
Fifth	Structure and audit of public companies
Sixth	Demergers
Seventh	Consolidated accounting
Eighth	Qualifications and work of auditors
Ninth	Links between public company groups
Tenth	International mergers of public companies
Eleventh	Disclosures relating to branches
Twelfth	Single member companies
Thirteenth	Takeovers
Fourteenth	Employee information and consultation

Source: Treaty of Rome Article 54-3g

accounting principles. The accounting charter used by each company should be established with reference to the general charter which exists at national level.

Those business activities which relate to specialised sectors (e.g. banking, insurance) have a more highly 'tailored' accounting charter but within each sector the charter remains uniform and standard.

GENERALLY ACCEPTED ACCOUNTING PRINCIPLES

The legislative and professional sources outlined above effectively recognise two parallel sets of accounting principles, one set designed for a single company's statutory reporting (the *Code de Commerce*) and the set of principles involved when the accounts of several statutory entities are brought together in group accounts (see the consolidation law of 1985, a revision of the Companies' Act of 24 July 1966). When preparing a single entity's annual accounts, French accounting policies are still influenced by tax considerations (i.e. there are few differences of substance between accounting policies and tax rules). Tax regulations have always had a strong influence on accounting doctrine in continental Europe, particularly on such matters as depreciation rates and provisions to reduce asset values. The predominance of tax rules is at its most extreme in Germany, where the *Maßgeblichkeitsprinzip* requires a company's

---

Encadré 13: Sources of national accounting regulation in France

- **Pronouncements and recommendations** issued by the National Accounting Board (*Conseil National de la Comptabilité*), a consultative body attached to the Ministry of the Economy.
- **Consolidation accounting principles** are set out in the law of 24 July 1966 (Articles L357–1 to L357–10) and the decree of 23 March 1967 (Articles D248 to D248–13). The consolidation principles are based on the EU's Seventh Directive.
- **The Institute of Public Accountants and Authorised Accountants** (*Ordre des Experts Comptables et des Comptables Agréés*) which issues recommendations designed to assist members in the application of accounting legislation and regulations.
- **The Stock Exchange Commission** (*Commission des Opérations de Bourse* – known as the *COB*) which participates in the development of accounting doctrine by publishing recommendations and opinions designed to encourage public companies and their auditors to adopt good accounting and auditing practices. The *COB* was set up in 1967 on the lines of the Securities and Exchange Commission (SEC) in the United States and, while it lacks the full power of the SEC, it is nevertheless a powerful and influential body for the 'surveillance' of quoted or listed companies.

annual accounts to be prepared on the same basis as its tax return. This practice is almost unknown in countries like the UK and the Netherlands where a company's annual accounts and tax return are prepared separately according to different sets of principles.

The French approach to preparing annual accounts seems to take a 'middle road'. There are few significant differences between accounting and tax rules and, where differences do exist, they are disclosed in the notes to the annual accounts. In addition, differences are also recorded in the annual tax return, including a reconciliation between 'accounting results' and 'taxable results' derived from applying the two sets of policies or rules. French practice does not extend to the calculation of deferred taxation (i.e. calculating the tax effect on the differences between the two sets of rules) as is done in the UK and the Netherlands.

As indicated earlier, when consolidated accounts are prepared, alternative accounting policies may be applied which give rise to more significant differences between 'accounting results' and 'taxable results'. The alternative accounting policies can relate to asset values, leasing transactions, certain interest expenses on borrowings to finance investments and foreign exchange differences. In addition to these alternative accounting policies, the principles of deferred taxation are applied and the tax effect on the differences between accounting rules/tax rules is included in the consolidated results. The application of these accounting policies enables French groups to present consolidated financial statements that are in accordance with international accounting standards.

Valuation of assets

Under the Fourth Directive, there is a three-tier approach to accounting principles which have a direct impact on the valuation of assets.

First tier: 'true and fair' (image fidèle)

In France (and most continental European countries, excluding the Netherlands), the 'true and fair view', which relies heavily on professional judgement and the interpretation of the 'substance' of a transaction, is relatively new. Prior to 1984, French law assumed that compliance with detailed rules ensured correct financial statements (form over substance). When French accounting legislation was enacted to implement the Fourth Directive, the development of accounting principles – as distinct from tax regulations – quickly took off. The notions of 'true and fair' and 'substance over form' gradually became the basis for the preparation of annual accounts.

Second tier: 'basic accounting principles'

The second tier approach of the Fourth Directive established the basic accounting principles for preparing annual accounts. These included 'prudence' and the 'accruals concept', that is the principles that accounts are prepared on the basis that a company is a 'going concern' and that asset valuation rules are specifically applied. To a great extent, post-1984 French legislation has implemented these concepts of the EC's Fourth Directive. However, the historical tradition of conservatism in countries like France (and Germany) has remained. For example, it is still a legal requirement to allocate 5 per cent of annual profits to 'legal reserves' (*réserve légale*), which is designed to protect creditors.

Third tier: 'detailed valuation rules'

Such rules have always existed in countries like France and Germany but were absent from the laws of the UK and the Netherlands before the 1980s.

For tax accounts and individual company accounts, there are often tax-deductible provisions recorded for rises in the price of stocks (*hausse des prix*) or fluctuations in the prices of commodity stocks (*fluctuation des cours*). While disclosure of such tax provisions are made in the notes to the accounts (*l'annexe*), they are not included for deferred tax purposes in an individual company's accounts. Deferred tax is, however, calculated for consolidated accounts.

The general principle of prudence underlies the valuation of receivables. Assets are valued against anticipated receipts (i.e. net of any doubtful debt provisions – estimates of future losses or expenses). Provisions for specific and general doubtful debts are deducted from debtors and charged as an expense. However, the tax rules on provisions in France are strict and narrowly defined, with the result that companies tend not to account for general provisions. In this respect, French practice may be contrasted with that in Germany. Beyond the Rhine, even general provisions (i.e. provisions not specifically identified) are tax-deductible. It is therefore common for German management to assess general provisions at a higher level than would normally be considered commercially realistic.

Measurement of profit

The three tiers outlined above with respect to company valuation also apply to profit measurement. While the Fourth Directive gives no detailed rules on profit calculation (except to state turnover net of tax), the asset valuation rules have a logical impact on a company's results. The effects of asset valuation rules on profits may be grouped under the following three factors – depreciation rules, provisions and deferred taxation.

Depreciation

In France, the driving force behind the calculation of depreciation is taxation regulations. This 'tax culture' puts France close to Germany and in direct

Encadré 14: Valuation rules applicable in France

Tangible fixed assets

Fixed assets are shown in the accounts at their historic cost which is represented either by their acquisition cost or their cost of construction. Acquisition costs are those costs related directly or indirectly to the purchase. A revaluation can be effected either in accordance with a legal revaluation (the last permitted legal revaluation was in 1976) or by a decision of management. In the latter case, the revaluation surplus is treated as taxable income, consequently while revaluations are not forbidden, they are rare. The norm of historical cost (also followed in Germany) can be contrasted to the UK, where revaluations are common, and to the Netherlands, where the replacement cost concepts are often applied.

Intangible assets

While the Fourth Directive allows companies to record intangibles as assets at their purchase cost (the practice in France), some member states (e.g. the UK) record such assets at current cost. In addition, member states may allow companies to capitalise training expenses, and research and development. This is the case in France, subject to their being depreciated over five years (training expenses) or over their useful economic life. The recent practice in the UK of creating balance sheet values for 'brand names' (i.e. establishing a fair value for a brand name under which a company markets its products) is not common in France, although, when purchased, the brands (*marques*) are included as intangible assets.

Investments

Generally, investments (*titres de participation*) are valued at cost in individual company accounts, unless they have permanently lost value.

Stocks

The principle of prudence and the valuation of stock at cost or market value are the main issues covered under the Fourth Directive. However, the definitions of 'cost', the options on costing 'methods', the treatment of 'overheads' and the influence of tax regulations often give rise to different practices in European countries. The 'lower of cost or market' is used in France, and 'cost' must be calculated using the first in first out (FIFO) or 'weighted' average methods. (The weighted average method is more common, referred to as the *PMP* or *prix moyen pondéré*). Last in first out (LIFO) is not permitted.

Encadré 15: The FIFO and LIFO principles

FIFO

The 'first in first out principle' is based on the artificial assumption that the first goods bought are the first sold. This means that in effect the stock held at the year end is assumed to be that purchased more recently.

LIFO

The 'last in first out' principle is based on the assumption that the last goods bought are the first sold. It therefore charges the latest price from suppliers against the revenue.

Average cost

This is a compromise between the FIFO/LIFO principles. It makes no assumptions about the way in which goods flow through the business. For the purposes of arriving at the profit and loss charges, calculate the average cost per unit of stock and multiply that by the number of units sold. Similarly, the closing stock is arrived at by taking the number of units left in stock multiplied by the average cost per unit.

---

contrast to the UK and Dutch cultures which follow professionally set accounting standards. In France, it is not necessary to estimate an asset's life or residual value, since accounting depreciation is based on the tax tables or rates. Often the asset lives implied by the tax depreciation rates are broadly in line with commercial rates. However, accelerated tax depreciation is fairly common for certain assets such as computer equipment and related software.

Provisions

The distinction between provisions and reserves is broadly similar throughout the EU member states, but the occasions on which provisions are used differ, hence the direct effect on profits. Provisions are estimates of future losses or expenses and are created by a charge against profit. Reserves are an allocation of profit. While the Fourth Directive (and hence European accounting) generally recognises that provisions for future losses or expenses must be specifically identifiable and do not depend upon the level of profits, there is a tradition – in France and Germany – of setting them against profits and thus reducing the level of profits declared.

Deferred tax

Deferred taxation represents the effect on tax levels arising from the application of different rules for the accounting of a transaction (tax rules and accounting rules). It is a major issue in 'accounting-based cultures' like the UK and the Netherlands, but traditionally unimportant in individual company accounts in France, Germany, Spain, Italy, etc., where accounting and tax are closely related. In France, deferred tax is not normally calculated at an individual company level though it is more common in group consolidated accounts.

Group accounting

In contrast to the UK and USA, consolidation is relatively new in most European countries since, historically, it tended to be American and British multinationals that established overseas subsidiaries. The need for French or German parent companies to consolidate subsidiaries' activities into an economic group evolved in parallel with the economic growth of these two countries in the 1970s. With the implementation of the EC's Seventh Directive on consolidation accounting (1984), national legislation began to be enacted in member states. In France, the requirement to consolidate groups began in 1985 (for quoted or listed companies) and in 1990 for all companies. As indicated earlier in this chapter, two sets of accounting principles exist in France — those which apply at the level of the individual company and those which apply to consolidated groups. At the level of the individual company, the accounting and tax rules are closely linked and are in most cases the same. At group consolidation level, 'complementary' or 'optional' accounting rules may be applied and, by modifying national practice, effectively bring French group accounts into line with international accounting principles.

Requirements to consolidate

Consolidation is the process of adjusting and combining financial information from the individual financial statements of a parent company and its subsidiary undertakings. Its outcome is a consolidated financial statement that presents financial information for the group as a single economic entity. The consolidation methods used in France, as detailed in the law on consolidations (January 1985 and decree in February 1986), respect the main requirements of the Seventh Directive. However, certain variations are allowed in member states' legislation. These variations cover such matters as the calculation and treatment of goodwill, the use of merger accounting and proportional accounting, the exclusion of certain types of subsidiary and exemption for 'small' groups.

Exempt parent companies

The Seventh Directive permits non-listed parents which are themselves wholly owned subsidiaries to be exempted from preparing group accounts as long as the parent's holding company is in the EU and prepares proper group accounts. However, the conditions under which exemption can apply are often confusing, as may be gauged by an overview of the differences between national legislations.

Exempt groups

The Seventh Directive allows member states to exempt 'small' and 'medium' groups from preparing consolidated accounts. The size criteria for exemption can be expressed in national laws either gross for the whole group or net of consolidation adjustments. The exemption is allowed where groups fall below two of three levels, which, as applied in France, are:

- sales – 200 million francs gross
- balance sheet totals – 100 million francs gross
- number of employees – 500

Encadré 16: Exemptions from preparing group accounts applicable in different countries of the EU

France   Exemption extended to subsidiaries holding less than 90 per cent as long as this is not opposed by shareholders holding 10 per cent or more of the capital. Exemption is also extended for sub-groups of non-EU parents that prepare equivalent group accounts.

UK   Exemption irrespective of the size of holdings as long as there is no opposition by more than 50 per cent of the remaining shareholders or by holders of 5 per cent of the total assets.

Netherlands   Exemption extended to sub-groups who have parents outside the EU that prepare group accounts equivalent to those required under the Seventh Directive.

Germany   Exemption extended to subsidiaries holding less than 90 per cent as long as there is no objection from 10 per cent of shareholders (*AG* companies) or 20 per cent (*GmbH* companies). The government may further exempt sub-groups of non-EU parents that prepare equivalent group accounts.

Subsidiary companies excluded from consolidation

Certain subsidiaries may be excluded from consolidation. This applies where subsidiaries:

- are below a certain size relative to the group as a whole;
- operate under severe long-term restrictions that hinder control over assets or management;
- would incur significant delays and expense in submitting information to the parent company;
- are held exclusively with a view to subsequent resale.

In addition, subsidiaries 'must' be excluded where they are so different from the rest of the group that their inclusion in the group accounts would not give a true and fair view. This last provision is obviously very subjective and its application in member states is not very consistent. In the French context, the practice of 'strategic alliances' between companies in different sectors of activity (banks and insurance) and the definition of 'dissimilar activities', are often given a wider interpretation than is usual in the UK.

Consolidation techniques

While under the Seventh Directive four consolidation techniques are permitted. French consolidation law makes no reference to the merger accounting method (or pooling of interests). This is far more common in the UK. Conversely, the proportional method is frequently applied in France but is rarely used in the UK. Equity accounting (*mise en équivalence*) is used in all member states when 'significant influence' but not majority ownership exists over the company in which investment is taking place. Significant influence over the management and financial policies of the company is usually presumed to exist when the investor holds 20 per cent or more of the voting shares.

COMPANY REPORTING PROCEDURES

General

According to French legislation, all limited companies (*SAs*) and all limited partnerships with share capital ('*sociétés en commandite par actions*') are required to appoint auditors who are responsible for ensuring that the annual financial statements have been properly prepared. The same applies to private companies (*SARLs*) and to ordinary partnerships that meet any two of the following criteria:

- total assets in excess of 10 million francs;
- total assets in excess of 20 million francs;
- employees, in excess of 50.

Encadré 17: Consolidation techniques permitted under the Seventh EC Directive

Acquisition or purchase method

The financial statements of the parent and its subsidiaries are combined on a line-by-line basis by adding together like items of assets, liabilities, equity, income and expenses. In order that the consolidated financial statements present financial information about the group as that of a single enterprise, inter-company transactions are eliminated and minority interests are disclosed.

Merger accounting method

In applying the pooling of interests method, the financial statement items of the merging enterprises are simply 'combined' – with minimal changes or eliminating adjustments. The condition for a merger of interests is that no acquisition should have occurred and the businesses should continue to be mutually shared.

Proportional method

This is normally used in joint ventures whereby two or more parties undertake an economic activity which is subject to joint control. A venturer's share of each of the assets, liabilities, income and expenses is combined on a line-by-line basis with similar items in the venturer's financial statements or reported as a separate line item.

The equity method

The investment is initially recorded at cost and the carrying amount is increased or decreased to recognise the investor's share of the profits or losses of the investee after the date of acquisition.

While the contents and presentation of annual accounts may vary depending on the size of a company, the reporting dates for their submission are the same (and perhaps, more strict compared to other European countries). All companies must submit their annual tax return within three months of the financial year end and the annual accounts within six months (since the shareholders' annual general meeting must be held no later than six months after the year end).

The actual contents of the annual financial statements are dependent on the company's size and on whether or not the entity is reporting as an individual unit or as a consolidated group. Moreover, reporting requirements can be affected by the number of employees employed (i.e. the social balance sheet or *bilan social*) and whether or not the company is listed (i.e. half-yearly accounts or *comptes prévisionnels* in addition to the quarterly reporting of turnover). Current French

---

Encadré 18: Goodwill

'Goodwill' is the excess of the consideration paid over the fair value of net assets acquired. It can also be seen as a premium paid to acquire control over another company. The predominant consolidation method used in France and Europe is the purchase acquisition method (*l'intégration globale*). When using this consolidation method, goodwill (or *l'écart d'acquisition*) usually arises at the date of acquisition of a subsidiary. Goodwill is either calculated on the basis of 'fair values' of net assets (the normal practice in the UK and the Netherlands) or initially on the basis of 'book values' (the normal practice in France and Germany). Under the latter method, the difference between the purchase price of the acquisition and the underlying net assets at the date of acquisition, is allocated as far as possible among identifiable assets and liabilities. The unallocated balance is recorded as goodwill. In practice, the initial goodwill is allocated primarily among non-current assets, including intangibles and long term debt. Allocations of the initial goodwill to assets and liabilities effectively restates the net assets at fair values, but these adjustments to asset values cannot exceed the goodwill to be allocated. The French practice of dealing with goodwill consists of two distinct steps:

1 calculate the difference between the purchase price and net assets acquired = *l'écart de première consolidation*;
2 allocate goodwill difference to assets and liabilities purchased.

Thus the final difference (*l'écart d'acquisition*) could be positive or negative.

---

legislation affecting reporting procedures respects the EC's Fourth and Seventh Directives and, as explained earlier, the disclosure, presentation and choice of accounting policy depend essentially on whether the annual financial statements are being prepared for an individual company or group.

Contents of financial statements

In France, as in most countries, there is a basic requirement under law to prepare an income statement and balance sheet showing comparative figures. However, there is no legal requirement to prepare 'changes in shareholders' equity' and 'changes in financial position'. While these latter requirements are not compulsory, most groups include some form of these details in the notes to consolidated financial statements. Given the non-requirement for changes in financial position statements, the move towards preparing 'cash flow statements' is slow, particularly compared to the UK requirements.

Encadré 19: The annual financial statement

The following documents are legally required for inclusion in the annual financial statements:

- directors' report
- the annual accounts (income statement, balance sheet and notes to the accounts)
- a five-year summary of results
- auditor's report

A 'source and application of funds statement' or a 'cash flow statement' is not a legal requirement, but such statements are strongly recommended for consolidated accounts. While all companies are required to include 'notes to the accounts', smaller companies do not have to disclose all the information required by larger companies (i.e. details on numbers employed, director's remuneration, turnover analyses, differences arising from applying certain accounting policies compared to the tax rules, etc.). The presentation of the income statement and balance sheet is also in a simpler format for smaller companies and, in most cases, these companies make use of their annual tax return – the tax return being attached to the other documents noted above. As shown above, a 'small' company is one that does not exceed two of the following three criteria – balance sheet totals of 10 million francs, a turnover of 20 million francs and a total of fifty employees.

In addition to the above documents, a 'social balance sheet' is required when companies employ more than 300 persons. The *bilan social* became a requirement in 1977. The document must be submitted to the company's staff committee (*comité d'entreprise*) and to the Ministry of Employment. It covers:

- analysis of employment, employee remuneration and related costs;
- statistics on health, safety and working conditions;
- staff training facilities and expenditures;
- industrial relations;
- living conditions of employees, insofar as they are affected by company policies.

Format of financial statements

All companies are required to present their balance sheet and income statement according to a standard format, which may be simplified for small businesses. French accounting regulations also specify the method of calculating each balance sheet and income and expense item based on the accounts contained in the General Accounting Plan. Assets and liabilities, income and expenses may not be offset. Assets and liabilities are not segregated between current and non-current, but this classification is required in the notes. Balance sheet items are classified on the basis of their purpose of origin, income statement items being presented by type of income and expense. However, as a departure from this rule, the consolidated income statement can be presented by function, provided that certain minimum requirements concerning content are met. In respect of the physical layout of financial statements, individual companies normally follow the two-sided format for the profit and loss account and balance sheet presentation, the vertical presentation (more commonly used in the UK) being used for consolidated accounts. Notwithstanding this last comment, a vertical format balance sheet and income statement are presented in Figures 5.1 and 5.2, in order to illustrate the standard headings used in French financial statements.

THE AUDIT AND ACCOUNTING PROFESSION

Annual audit requirements

Not all French companies are required to have an annual audit. The necessity for audit depends on the size and legal structure of the company. All *SA*s must be audited by a statutory auditor (*commissaire aux comptes*), and, where consolidated accounts are prepared, two statutory auditors must be appointed. Recently the *COB* and the *Compagnie des Commissaires aux Comptes* have clarified this requirement in declaring that the two statutory auditors must be appointed from different firms.

Since the accounting law of March 1984 relating to the prevention of financial difficulties in companies (*la prevention et le règlement amiable des difficultés des entreprises*), the statutory audit obligations were extended to *SARL*s, *SNC*s and *SCA*s when two of the following three criteria are met:

- balance sheet totals exceed 10 million francs;
- turnover exceeds 20 million francs;
- average number of employees is 50.

With the exception of the UK, all other EU member states exempt 'small' companies from annual audit requirements. However, French law does permit 'small' companies to be audited when a company's statutes call for one and/or when shareholders holding 10 per cent of a company's capital request the nomination of an auditor.

Professional duties of statutory auditors

Auditors are appointed for six years, renewable without limitation for successive six-year terms. Companies are also required to appoint a replacement *commissaire* (*suppléant*) for the same period, although the *suppléant* only acts in the event of the death, incapacity or resignation of the primary auditor. The six-year appointment term (or 'mandate') is designed to give the auditor more security and independence from a company's board of directors, in return for which the auditor is strictly limited to auditing the accounts and cannot therefore carry out any consulting, accountancy or tax work.

The *commissaire aux comptes* issues two reports and one certificate subsequent to the annual audit. The first report gives the opinion on the financial statements according to the principles of the Fourth Directive which stipulates that the statement should represent a 'true and fair view', that it should comply with accounting principles and that the application of these principles should be consistent. In addition, the report (*le rapport général*) certifies that the auditor has checked all the information given in the directors' report (*rapport de gestion*) and all information provided to the company's shareholders. These 'explicit' confirmations distinguish the French auditor's report from the more 'implicit' confirmations contained in the UK audit reports. The second report issued by the *commissaire aux comptes* is called *le rapport spécial*, which reports on the '*conventions*' or contracts between directors and the company as well as those with other companies of the same group. This form of report deals with related party transactions and directors' interests and specifies whether such contracts have been formally approved by the board. The third document issued by the auditor is the certificate of remuneration paid to the top five or ten officials of the company.

In addition to these annual reports, the statutory auditor has a legal duty to report on any changes to the company's financial structure or to the time when interim dividends are declared. These 'special' interventions by the statutory auditor reflect the 'permanent' nature of the auditor's role in the life of the company. For example, the auditor must report to the board and shareholders on any factors or circumstances which might compromise the company's ability to trade. This procedure is seen as 'preventive medicine' or an early warning system for companies in financial difficulty.

The statutory audit profession is supervised by the Ministry of Justice which lends a 'legal' nature to the work carried out by the *commissaire aux comptes*. To be eligible for appointment, the auditor must be registered on a list kept by the regional *cours d'appel* or commercial tribunals. The auditor's legal responsibilities (both civil and penal) are very clearly defined and, compared to the Anglo-Saxon profession, could be considered rather heavy. For example, the auditor has a penal responsibility to report to the public prosecutor any serious infractions of company law, tax law, etc., committed by a company's directors. In extreme cases, failure to do so could lead to a jail sentence.

Encadré 20: *Le bilan – L'actif*

Bilan	Balance sheet
Actif	**Assets**
Immobilisations incorporelles	Intangible assets
Terrains	Land
Constructions	Buildings
Installations techniques	Industrial plant and machinery
Autres	Other
Immobilisations en cours	Construction in progress
Immobilisations corporelles	Tangible assets
Participations	Long-term investments
Créances rattachées à des participations*	Debtors related to long-term investments*
Autres titres immobilisés	Other long-term investments
Prêts*	Loans*
Autres*	Other*
Immobilisations financières	Investments
Total I	**Total I**
Avances et acomptes versés	Payments on account to suppliers
Créances clients et comptes rattachés	Trade debtors and related accounts
Autres créances	Other debtors
TSDI à recevoir	Perpetual notes (TSDI)
Créances	Debtors
Valeurs mobilières de placement	Short-term investments
Disponibilités	Cash at bank and in hand
Charges constatées d'avance	Prepaid expenses
Total II	**Total II**
Charges à répartir sur plusieurs exercices **III**	Deferred expenses **III**
Primes de remboursement des obligations **IV**	Bond redemption premium **IV**
Ecart de conversion actif **V**	Deferred translation difference **V**
Total général (I+II+III+IV+V)	**Grand total (I+II+III+IV+V)**
*Dont à moins d'un an	*Including amount due in less than one year
Engagements reçus	Commitments received

Encadré 21: *Le bilan – le passif*

Bilan	Balance sheet
Passif	**Liabilities and shareholders' equity**
Capital	Share capital
Primes d'émission de fusion d'apport	Share premium account
Ecart de réévaluation	Revaluation surplus
Réserves	Reserves
Réserves légales	Legal reserve
Réserves réglementées	Tax-related reserves
Autres réserves	Other reserves
Report à nouveau	Retained earnings
Résultat de l'exercice	Profit for the year attributable to shareholders
Provisions réglementées	Tax-related provisions
Total I	**Total I**
Titres subordonnés à durée indéterminée	Perpetual notes
Provisions pour risques	Provisions for risks
Provisions pour charges	Provisions for losses
Total II	**Total II**
Emprunts obligataires convertibles*	Convertible bonds*
Autres emprunts obligataires*	Other bonds*
Emprunts et dettes auprès des éts. de crédit**	Bank borrowings**
Emprunts et dettes financières divers*	Other borrowings*
Total des dettes financières	Total borrowings
Dettes fournisseurs	Trade creditors and related accounts
Dettes fiscales et sociales	Taxes and social security creditors
Dettes sur immobilisation et comptes rattachés	Amounts owed for fixed assets and investments
Autres dettes	Other liabilities
Total des autres dettes	Total other liabilities
Total III	**Total III**
Produits constatés d'avance **IV**	Deferred income **IV**
Ecart de conversion passif **V**	Deferred translation difference **V**
Total général (I+II+III+IV+V)	**Grand total (I+II+III+IV+V)**
*Dont à moins d'un an	*Including amount due in less than one year
**Dont concours bancaires courants et soldes créditeurs de banques	**Including short-term bank advances and overdrafts
Engagements donnés	Commitments given

Encadré 22: *Le Compte de résultat*

Compte de résultat	Profit and loss account
Produits d'exploitation:	Operating income:
Montant net du chiffre d'affaires	Net turnover
Reprises des provisions	Provisions written back
Autres produits	Other income
Total I	**Total I**
Charges d'exploitation:	Operating expenses:
Achats d'approvisionnements	Purchases of materials
Autres achats et charges externes	Other purchases and expenses
Impôts, taxes et versements assimilés	Taxes other than on income
Salaires, traitements	Wages, salaries and other costs
Charges sociales	Social security costs
Dotations aux amortissements et aux provisions	**Depreciation and movement on provisions**
Sur immobilisations: dotation aux amortissements	On long-term assets: depreciation charge
Autres charges	Other expenses
Total II	**Total II**
Résultat d'exploitation (I–II)	**Operating results I–II**
Produits financiers:	Financial income:
De participations	Income from investments in subsidiaries and associates
Autres intérêts et produits assimilés	Other interest and similar income
Produits nets sur cession de valeurs mobilières de placement	Net gain on sales of short-term investments
Reprises de provisions et transfert de charges	Write back of provisions and deferral of financial charges
Différences positives de change	Foreign exchange gains
Total III	**Total III**
Charges financières	**Financial charges**
Dotations aux amortissements et provisions	Depreciation and amortisation
Intérêts et charges assimilées	Interest and similar expenses
Différences négatives de change	Foreign exchange losses
Charges nettes sur cession de valeurs mobilières de placement	Net losses on sales of short-term investments
Total IV	**Total IV**
Résultat financier III–IV	**Net financial income III–IV**
Résultat courant avant impôts	**Results on ordinary activities before tax**

Encadré 22: Continued

Produits exceptionnels	Exceptional income
Sur opérations de gestion	On ordinary activities
Sur opérations en capital	On capital transactions
Reprise sur provisions et transferts de charges	Write back of provisions and expenses deferred

Total V	**Total V**

Charges exceptionnelles	Exceptional charges
Sur opérations de gestion	On ordinary activities
Sur opérations en capital	On capital transactions
Dotations aux amortissement et provisions	Amortisation, depreciation and provisions

Total VI	**Total VI**

Résultat exceptionnel V–VI	**Net exceptional results V–VI**

Impôt sur les bénéfices	Income tax

Résultat de l'exercice	**Results for the year attributable to shareholders**

The accounting profession

As indicated above, accounting and auditing are organised as two separate professions and no one may act as both statutory auditor and public accountant to the same company. The accounting profession is organised by the Institute of Public Accountants and Authorised Accountants (*Ordre des Experts-Comptables et des Comptables Agréés*) under the supervision of the Ministry of Finance. The *experts-comptables* provide accountancy services – submission of periodic returns, taxation services consultancy services, and any general advisory services. The *experts-comptables* may 'audit' the accounts of their clients but may not replace the statutory auditor. Any audit work undertaken by the *expert-comptable* is requested not by the shareholders but by the management or any third party who is interested in the financial position of a company. This type of audit is of a 'contractual' nature as opposed to the 'legal' requirements applicable to accounts carried out by a *commissaire*.

While the French system of two separate professional bodies may seem complex or too 'legalistic' to the Anglo-Saxon (particularly since both professional bodies are supervised by government ministries), most other European countries maintain separate professions for auditing and accountancy. Belgium, for example, is organised according to the same principles as the French system, while Germany has three professional bodies, each with its own responsibilities. Table 5.2 gives an outline of the professional bodies in the major EU countries.

Table 5.2 Professional accounting bodies in different European countries

Country	Institutes	Members
France	Conseil Supérieur de l'Ordre des Experts-Comptables Agréés	11,000
	Compagnie Nationale des Commissaires aux Comptes	9,000
Germany	Wirtschaftsprüfer	6,000
	Vereidigte Buchprufer	not available
	Steuerberater	40,000
Italy	Dottori Commercialisti	20,000
	Ragioneri e Periti Commercialisti	20,000
	Sociétés de Révision Légale	28
Netherlands	Neederlands Instituut van Registeraccountants	7,000
Spain	Censores Jurados de Cuentas	4,000
United Kingdom	Institute of Chartered Accountants in England and Wales	90,000
	Institute of Chartered Accountants in Scotland	15,000
	The Chartered Association of Certified Accountants	33,000

Duties of auditors/accountants

Notwithstanding the existence in France of two separate professional bodies, there are certain *missions* which can be carried out either by *commissaires aux comptes* or *experts-comptables* if they are registered as *experts judiciaires* (legal experts) with the regional commercial tribunals. These activities are described as *commissariat aux apports*, the *apports* being a capital injection to a company in any form other than cash. The main responsibility of a *commissaire aux apports* is to certify the valuation of any capital injection and to report to the shareholders on the reasons and methods used for any change in the company's financial structure.

Endcadré 23: Duties of auditors and accountants
Commissaire aux apports

Transactions certifiable by a *commissaire aux apports* include:

- constitution of a company with public funds;
- capital increases other than by cash;
- mergers and takeovers;
- sell-offs and disposals;
- calculation of assets contributed by shareholders.

TAXATION

General

French resident companies are subject to corporation tax (*impôts sur les sociétés* or *IS*) on income from French and overseas sources where the latter is regulated by tax treaty. The trading profits are taxed at a rate of 33.33 per cent for financial years starting on or after 1 January 1993. The tax is paid on account in four instalments per annum with any late payments resulting in a penalty which is not deductible for tax purposes. The taxable profits are based on the accounts after specific adjustments provided by French tax law (*Code Général des Impôts – CGI*). Short-term capital gains (assets held for less than two years) are subject to the standard rate of tax and long-term gains are subject to a reduced rate of 18 per cent.

Encadré 24: Companies subject to tax

Entities are subject to corporation tax by reason of:

- legal form (share capital companies – *SAs* and *SARLs*);
- profitable activity (civil associations engaged in profitable activities);
- choice (partnerships electing for *IS* assessment).

The taxation on 'group entities' became optional in 1988. In order to be able to elect for a group assessment basis certain conditions must be met:

- the holding company must own directly or indirectly 95 per cent of the consolidated subsidiaries;
- the holding company should be not owned more than 95 per cent by another company;
- the election for group taxation assessment remains effective for a five-year period.

In addition to the above standard forms of taxation on companies, and excluding various property and residence taxes, France has a number of other taxes which are assessed on companies and which are designed to finance construction, infrastructure investment and training. For example:

- Business licence tax (*taxe professionnelle*) is assessed on all persons or entities carrying out industrial, commercial or professional activities. The rate varies according to the location of the business activity and is based on the rental value of the business premises and the salaries paid.
- Compulsory construction levy (*l'effort de construction*) is assessed on all firms that employ ten employees or more.
- Apprenticeship and training taxes (*taxe d'apprentissage* and *formation professionnelle*) are levied on the basis of the salaries. The apprenticeship tax is levied at the rate of 0.6 per cent and the training tax is levied only on businesses employing at least ten persons at a rate of 1.5 per cent.

Encadré 25: Calculating company tax

Some of the main factors that affect the taxable results of corporations are:

- depreciation of property – buildings, equipment, patents, vehicles, etc.;
- start-up expenses (*frais d'établissement*) which may be deducted from taxable income or capitalised and amortised over a maximum period of five years;
- dividends – a company's dividend distribution to either an individual or company resident in France is not taxed where the profits have already been subject to corporate tax at the normal rates;
- withholding taxes which are assessed on the net profits of foreign branches as it is deemed that these profits will be distributed abroad;
- relief for trading losses which can be offset against other income;
- value added tax (18.6 per cent standard and 5.5 per cent reduced) is charged on most supplies of goods and services made in France by a taxable person in a course of business but deliveries of goods occurring in the EU transported from France to another state of the EU are expressly VAT exempt.

- Payroll tax (*taxe sur les salaires*) is assessable on companies which are not assessable for VAT on their sales (mainly banks and insurance companies). The payroll tax rates range from 4.25 per cent to 13.60 per cent depending on the level of annual salaries.

The above taxes indicate the complexities of the French business environment and, bearing in mind that the overview does not represent a complete list of French taxes on business activities, the costs to the employer in money and administrative time are quite considerable. The rationale of the system, however, is to force companies to contribute to infrastructure development costs (housing, transport, etc.) and training. In comparing France to the other EU members states, it seems that only France assesses employers for the construction levy, the apprenticeship tax and the general training taxes indicated above.

FORM AND SUBSTANCE OF FINANCIAL STATEMENTS

For many years, accountants, auditors, professional bodies and academics have been engaged in a grand debate on the structure and contents of financial statements. Traditionally, the process has been characterised as a 'culture debate' between the Anglo-Saxon and Franco-Germanic worlds whereby, in recording and presenting transactions, the former put more emphasis on economic substance and the latter on legalistic form. These 'cultural determinants' are reflected in the financial statements of each group in the sense that generally accepted accounting principles are given more emphasis in Anglo-Saxon financial statements while uniform presentations (based on a standard accounting charter) predominate in countries such as France. The language of this debate often refers to the 'flexibility' of Anglo-Saxon accounting and the 'rigidity' in countries like France and Germany. Flexibility is often the result of having to select and interpret the generally accepted accounting principles, whereas rigidity comes from the requirement to standardise the format of financial statements.

In practice, these cultural differences have been reduced over the past ten years, particularly as the French have moved towards more 'economic' accounting and the application of accounting policies which are separate from fiscal regulations. As noted earlier in this chapter, the main driving force of change in France has been the EC/EU Directives, especially the Fourth and the Seventh. However, notwithstanding the trend in France towards more substantive and selective accounting policies, for the sake of economy and convenience some bankers and financial analysts are arguing for more standardised forms of presentation. In this way, computer-based reviews and ratio analyses could be performed more quickly. Thus, the trend towards flexibility and pragmatism and that towards efficiency are in many ways running counter to each other.

REPORTING PROCEDURES

The French reporting procedures may be seen as a 'multi-menu' computer package which serves all interested parties or users of financial statements. The 'database' is the general accounting charter or *'Plan Comptable'* which facilitates the collection of national statistics, reduces the development costs for accounting software and enables checks, controls and audits to be effected more quickly. Given that the accounting charter is developed by mixed teams of experts (drawn from the auditing and accountancy profession both in practice and in private business) who work with the government's national accounting committee (*Conseil National de la Comptabilité*), a reasonable consensus emerges on reporting requirements.

Once transaction data is 'plugged in' to these uniform databases, the production of reporting statements becomes almost routine. The basic accounting records can automatically produce the required reports – the annual tax return, the annual accounts, and the special reports required by the banking and insurance commissions.

Since auditors must be registered with the commercial tribunals (also with the *COB* for listed companies and with the Banking Commission for banking clients), the surveillance of companies' financial positions follows an integrated procedure. External controls and checks are numerous and frequent – on the auditors in the form of 'peer reviews', on banking and insurance companies by the relevant commissions, on listed companies by the *COB* and on all companies by the fiscal and social security authorities.

CURRENT DEVELOPMENTS

As has just been suggested, accounting and reporting procedures are being directly affected by the internationalisation of business and the growing complexities of computer-based information systems. Decentralised operations are forcing companies to implement computer networks, expert systems and other EDI (electronic data interchange) processes, all of which impact on traditional accounting and reporting systems. For example, the French tax return or returns for banking and insurance corporations are prepared directly from the accounting records – by means of computer software – and can be transmitted automatically to the relevant authorities via computer modems or magnetic tape.

These advances in information technology require codification of accounting data, standardised formats and software programs, the bases for which can be found in the French accounting charter. Current developments in French accounting software suggest that the profession is moving towards an approach requiring more integrated accounting and reporting systems. The guiding principle behind an integrated system is that a common database (in which the source transactions are stored) can be assessed by multiple users of financial information. For example, the same data from a source transaction, suitably codified, can be used for a range of different purposes – financial and management accounts, treasury reports, returns to governmental authorities, etc. It is inevitable that changes in technology represent the main force which will determine the nature and direction of developments in French accounting and reporting procedures in the foreseeable future. Moreover, the changes will call for updated legislation on all aspects of computer-generated data. Some legislation has already been enacted to allow for the use of records held in computerised form. However, in most European countries, it has not been possible to keep abreast of new technological developments and their effects on common business practices. The disappearance of paper documentation and handwritten signatures has already called traditional legal concepts into question, while the EC's 1988 initiative in creating a common programme for trade electronic data interchange systems (TEDIS) will undoubtedly have far-reaching implications for the European accounting practices of the future.

SELECTED TEXTS

Alexander, D. and Archer, G.S.H. (1992)
Blake, J. and Amat, O. (1993)
Scheid, J.-C. and Walton, P. (1992)

See Bibliography

USEFUL ADDRESSES

Centrale des Bilans de la Banque de France
BP 140–01
75049 Paris Cedex 01
Tel. (1) 42.92.36.10.

Centre de Documentation de la Comptabilité Publique
Pièce 29, 4 rue Lobau
75004 Paris
Tel. (1) 42.76.44.58.

Centre de Recherche et de Documentation des Experts-Comptables et des Commissaires
aux Comptes.
88 rue de Courcelles
75008 Paris
Tel. (1) 42.12.85.55.

Commission des Communautés Européennes
61 rue des Belles-Feuilles
75116 Paris
Tel. (1) 45.01.58.85.

Commission Bancaire
c/o Banque de France
73 rue de Richelieu
75002 Paris
Tel. (1) 42.92.59.31.

Commission de Opérations de Bourse (COB)
Tour Mirabeau
39–43 Quai André Citroën
75015 Paris
Tel. (1) 40.58.65.65.

Compagnie Nationale des Commissaires aux Comptes (CNCC)
8 rue de l'Amiral-de-Coligny
75001 Paris
Tel. (1) 44.77.82.82.

Conseil National de la Compatibilité
6 rue Louise Weiss
75013 Paris
Tel. (1) 44.87.17.77.

Fédération des Experts-Comptables Européens (FEE)
rue de la Loi 83
1040 Brussels
Belgium
Tel. (32) (2) 231.05.05.

Ordre des Experts-Comptables et des Comptables Agréés (OECCA)
153 rue de Courcelles
75017 Paris
Tel. (1) 44.15.60.00.

6 Law, business and the workplace

Marie-Pierre Fénoll-Trousseau, Sylvie Hébert and Annie Médina

BUSINESS AND THE STATUS OF LEGAL CONTROL

Any entrepreneur wishing to engage in commercial activity is obliged to take account of the legal context in which his/her company is to operate. This is especially true of France. The growing role of law in French business life is now so significant that it is questionable to what extent it is possible to speak of 'free enterprise' in a literal sense. The extent of state intervention in private affairs is yet another echo of the French notion of 'citizenship' which seeks to reconcile the seemingly opposite aspirations of individual liberty and collective responsibility. This balance becomes all the harder to strike in times of economic difficulty when there are increased pressures to protect the less well-off citizens of the Republic, whilst at the same time allowing companies free rein to conduct their affairs as cheaply and efficiently as possible. In providing a general introduction to the fundamental legal processes which are at work in business operations, the aim of this chapter is therefore to give the non-specialist a superficial insight into the legal status of companies in France and an acquaintance with the laws governing managerial processes, particularly on the social side. In so doing, it has omitted to consider taxation law, despite its importance, as an area to which it would be impossible to do justice without going into excessive technical detail. For this and for any more in-depth study of the topic, the reader is referred to the selected text reading at the end of the chapter and to the summary of company tax liabilities in Chapter 5.

Although, in France, the number of individual firms (*entreprises individuelles*) – 1.7 million – presently exceeds that of companies proper (*sociétés*), the disproportion between the two is largely insignificant. Statistics show that, beyond a minimal level of turnover or of staff, the vast majority of commercial enterprises in France can be classified as '*sociétés*'. The purpose of '*sociétés*' is to bring together people and capital with a view to conducting commercial transactions. For a long time, the basic classification of companies in France was between civil and commercial firms. Since the law of 4 January 1978, however, this distinction has become blurred, while the essential difference relating to commercial companies is between those based on an association between people and those based on capital. In the first case, the associates carry full responsibility for their personal investment while, in the second, the risks undertaken are limited to their financial contribution. The legal statutes which regulate company practice are spread among several sources. Principally, however, they are to be found in the *Code Civil* and the *Code de Commerce*. Two texts – the law of 24 July 1966 and the decree of 23 March 1967 – bring together the majority of legislation governing the conduct of commercial companies.

THE DIFFERENT TYPES OF FRENCH FIRM

Société en nom collectif (SNC)

*SNC*s are relatively few in number in France (approximately 30,000). An *SNC* is built entirely around the persons of the associates who make it up and who have the status of traders (*commerçants*). The associates carry complete collective responsibility for each other's personal assets and no transfer of assets can take place without their unanimous consent. The death of an associate terminates the company unless there is a special clause allowing for its continuation. No minimal level of capital input is required. The associates are collectively responsible for managing the firm. Outsiders who are ascribed managerial responsibility do so under contract and have the status of employees. From a fiscal point of view, *SNC*s are transparent organisations. The associates are personally responsible for paying tax. This allows them to accumulate deficits and to set these against their personal income. Profits, on the other hand, are taxed under the category of 'industrial and commercial profits' – *bénéfices industriels et commerciaux (BIC)*.

Société en commandite simple (SCS)

An *SCS* functions according to virtually the same principles as an *SNC*. It is composed of associates who share the risk entailed in the firm's performance but some of these are co-opted (*commandités*) as unpaid associates. *Commandités* cannot play an active role in the management of the firm. There are less than 1,500 *SCS*s in France and they are diminishing in number in favour of *sociétés anonymes (SAs)* and *sociétés à responsabilité limitée (SARLs)*. There are good reasons for this. *SCS*s are complex to run because of the different status, rights and obligations of the two types of associate and because each is subject to different forms of taxation.

Société anonyme (SA)

A *société anonyme* brings together associates who are unknown to each other and whose participation in the company is based on their personal investment in the firm. *SA*s of different kinds may be family firms or multinationals. They can invite public investment and can even be quoted on the stock exchange. In the latter case, they are subject to strict controls exercised by the *Commission des Opérations de Bourse* (*COB*). Board members of *SA*s are invested with social responsibility and are not employees in the conventional sense. They are not insured by the firm but are obliged to take out policies of their own. The profits of *SA*s are subject to company tax with the salaries of board members being deducted in advance.

Société en commandite par actions (SCA)

*SCA*s consist of a group of not less than three associates which can co-opt other members. As a structure, it has met with considerable success even though the number of *SCA*s is relatively limited. It has been adopted by such firms as Casino, Michelin and Hermès and offers administrative flexibility, opportunities for cooperation between owners and investors and effective protection against takeovers. From a legal point of view, *SCA*s are hybrid organisations which share the characteristics of capital and human foundation.

Société à responsabilité limitée (SARL)

*SARL*s are the most successful form of company in France and numbered at least 560,000 in 1996. It is a form which is well suited to small and medium-sized enterprises (SMEs). It is easier to administer than an SA and the associates are in a more secure situation than those of an *SNC* since their responsibility is limited to the amount of their investment. From a legal perspective, a *SARL* is the only type of company which can consist of a single associate from the day of its creation. In this case, it is known as an *entreprise unipersonnelle à responsabilité limitée* (*EURL*). Moreover, it is the only type of company where there is a legal limit to the total number of associates.

SETTING UP A FIRM IN FRANCE: THE INSTITUTIONAL FRAMEWORK

Two contradictory principles govern the legal right of an individual in France who wishes to found a business:

- Any private person has the right under French law to engage in economic activity.
- This right is restricted by certain legal principles and procedures as defined in the constitutional decision 132-DC: JO January 1982 p. 299.

These basic principles are regulated by a number of key agencies which play a central role in the process of setting up a firm:

- **The Ministry of Finance and, at the local level, the** *préfet*   These agents are involved in decisions concerning the availability of land and its appropriate exploitation as well as of determining the allocation of eligible financial provision (see the reform of 1982 and 1984: *Décret* No. 82-762, 6 September 1982; *Décret* No. 84-621, 5 July 1984).
- **The regional, departmental and communal agencies**   These act both as regulators and as promoters of commercial and industrial activity (see Law No. 82-213, 2 March 1982; Law No. 88-13, 5 January 1988; *Décret* No. 88-139, 10 February 1988; *Décret* No. 88-366, 18 April 1988). Financial support for setting up a company which is provided mainly by regional authorities is granted on three conditions:

  1   that due recognition is given to the role of the state;
  2   that due respect is shown towards the principles of equality and freedom of commercial and industrial exchange;
  3   that state funds may not be used for private capital investment in a firm.

  Regional authorities may also provide collatoral against loans raised from private financial agencies.
- **Local business representatives and national agencies representing the state**   The public institutions which represent local business are composed essentially of the chambers of commerce and trade institutions. These two institutions consist of members elected from among the business community. However, as well as representing regional business interests, the *chambres de commerce et d'industrie* (*CCIs*) are state institutions which offer a public service and raise a tax which supplements those raised directly by the state.

  Chambres de commerce play an important role in the field of professional training by supporting business and technical schools (*Ecoles de Commerce, Ecoles Techniques*) and by offering assistance and advice. In particular, they manage the *Centres de Formalités des Entreprises* (*CFE*). These centres keep a record of each firm in the region which is used to establish the official register of firms (*registre du commerce et des sociétés*), the company inspectorate (*L'Inspection du Travail*) and *INSEE* (*Institut National des Statistiques et des Etudes Economiques*). The *CCIs* are also directly responsible for a range of key infrastructures such as industrial parks, transport and distribution centres, air and seaports. There are 162 *CCIs* in France. For artisans and the self-employed, the equivalent organisation to the *CCI* is the *chambre des métiers* which is also a source of financial support for creating companies.

  At the national level, the institutions whose mission is to support companies are:

- the *CFCE* (*Centre Français du Commerce Extérieur*) which provides information on foreign students and promotes French firms abroad;

- the *ANVAR* (*Agence Nationale de Valorisation de la Recherche*), a public institution which has the objective of assisting researchers to exploit their inventions and also offers grants for innovation and new ideas;
- the *INPI* (*Institut National pour la Protection Industrielle*) which manages the registration of patents, brand names and designs.

Purchase and location

Different legal constraints apply according to whether a purchase refers to a site alone or else to buildings already in place.

Site purchase

Virtually all buildings require planning permission which forms part of planning law. Certain developments fall outside this category and these are spelled out in Article R421-1 of the planning code. These include:

- infrastructural projects involving communications, ports and airports and underground construction;
- temporary buildings for fairs and exhibitions;
- signs and other forms of advertising;
- internal alterations to buildings.

The allocation of building permits is governed by Articles L421-2 and 421-1-1 of the planning code. Since Law No. 77-2, 3 January 1977, was passed, requests for building permits can only be approved if they are presented by an architect or a legally recognised chartered surveyor. Requests for planning permission are submitted to the *Mairie*. The mayor issues the building permit either in the name of the *commune* or of the state, depending on whether or not the request includes a *plan d'occupation des Sols* (Article R421-31 of the planning code). There are also special forms of authorisation such as those relating to requests which represent a threat to persons or the environment, and those which come under the framework of commercial planning law. These include activities which carry a high level of technological risk such as the transport of dangerous materials, dams, tunnels and those accompanied by dangers of industrial or nuclear contamination. Such requests are the subject of special studies and the regulations governing their approval are contained in Law No. 76-663 of 19 July 1976.

An EU Directive dating from 24 June 1982 and followed up by two similar texts of 19 March 1987 and 27 November 1988 also aims at preventing and controlling risks arising from the application of new technologies. Excluded from its field of application are nuclear, military and mining installations and those relating to the manufacture or storage of explosives and munitions. French law was already in line with this Directive in virtue of the law of 19 July 1976 just mentioned but this has been added to by circulars of which the most recent (No. 90-88, 13 July 1990) defines for the benefit of the *préfets* the obligations which derive from the text of 24 November 1988. As far as supermarkets are concerned, the *Loi Royer* (1973) requires that any new installations conform to the prescribed dimensions of a special authorisation. This authorisation, which has been declared to be compatible with EU law has been amended by the law of 13 July 1991 and *Décret* No. 92-150 of 17 February 1992. The decision to authorise commercial development is taken by the planning board of the *département* (*La Commission Départementale d'Urbanisme Commercial*) which is composed of twenty locally elected members who are representatives of trade and industry and consumers in the area.

The purchase of buildings

The major problems which confront a business seeking to purchase a building are the cost and the lack of tax relief, though state grants may be available for companies wishing to set themselves up outside the Paris region. The cost of renting premises, however, is tax-deductible. It is therefore standard practice for companies to arrange for prospective premises to be purchased by a legally independent developer who is responsible for managing the building and who then rents it to the firm. It is quite common for the individuals who make up the property development company to be themselves the owners of the firm seeking to use the building. It is thereby possible to avoid the danger of the lease expiring.

THE ROLE OF LAW IN COMPANY AFFAIRS

The company and its employees

The role of law in the workplace is defined by Lyon-Caen (1985) as 'the collection of rules applicable to individual and collective relationships which emerge between private employees and those who work under their authority against payment of a financial recompense or salary'. Labour law (*le droit du travail*) does not therefore apply to the liberal professions or to self-employed traders or artisans. Among state employees, a distinction is made between *titulaires*, who are formally employed on a permanent basis, and *auxiliaires* who are employed under independent contracts which may themselves be governed by the principles of *le droit du travail*.

Labour law in France has its origins in the claims of workers. It is they who laid its foundations and, until recently, it was hard to imagine that labour law could have any other objective than that of promoting progress in what can be referred to as the 'social sphere'. At the same time, of course, conditions of employment are inseparable from the principle of profit and depend on the organisation of companies. They are inescapably linked to pressures on the national economy. The economic difficulties which companies are experiencing today are inevitably running counter to the social objectives of the law. In a period of crisis, there is a natural tendency for employment law to protect companies which, whatever the social pressures, remain the only secure basis for future employment. Moreover, to the extent that employment law imposes constraints on companies' ability to operate freely and has become more and more intricate in recent times, French firms have become adept at circumventing it and have thereby reduced its status.

The law is caught between two opposing pressures. On the one hand, there is the need to allow companies the greatest possible freedom of action – for economic reasons and out of traditional, quasi-feudal respect for the right of the *patron* to be 'master in his own house'. On the other, there is the equally French tradition of social protection which has been intensified by the political – and economic – pressure to reduce unemployment and, in particular, to provide young people with an adequate range of opportunities to gain training and work experience – a conflict of objectives which is common to all West European countries.

The background to the development of labour law in France

Three main stages can be identified in the development of French labour law:

- the period from 1791 to the establishment of the *Code du Travail* in 1973;
- the period between 1973 and 1982 when the *Code du Travail* was reformed;
- the period since 1982.

The real foundation of labour law in France dates from the enactment of the *Décret d'Allarde* in March 1791. The *Décret d'Allarde* asserted both the right to conditions of employment which respected the freedom of the individual and the right to engage freely in commercial activity. This seminal law was followed in 1842 by the law forbidding companies with a labour force of more than twenty to employ children of less than eight years old and limiting the hours of work of children as a whole. Other laws prescribing different forms of social protection followed: the protection of women and children in the workplace (1893), support for the victims of industrial accidents (1898), the introduction of weekly rest from work (1906) and the law regulating meetings and conventions (1919). Contrary to certain claims, the foundations of modern employment law were laid in the early days of the French Republic and have been progressively reinforced ever since.

The year 1936 saw the signature of the *Accords de Matignon*, the first agreement signed at the national level between a privately run organisation and the representative of an employers' union – the *Confédération Générale du Travail* (CGT). Under Léon Blum's *Front Populaire* government a number of laws were passed, including that on weekly hours, paid leave and the collective settlement of work disputes. There were also substantial changes in the law governing collective meetings and the recognition of employees' representatives.

In the post-war period, the major upheaval in industrial relations was the wave of strikes which shook France during the 'events' of May 1968. Under the premiership of Georges Pompidou, the government instigated negotiations between management and workers which led to the *Accords de Grenelle*. The most significant measures which could be said to have arisen from the *Accords de Grenelle* are:

- development of trade union law;
- the introduction of a minimum wage (*SMIC*) in January 1970;
- the establishment in 1973 of a *Code du Travail*.

In the aftermath of the sharp increase in unemployment which followed the first oil crisis of 1973, laws were passed in 1975 which obliged all reductions in personnel to be subject to official inspection. Although these were subsequently rescinded, the period following the election of François Mitterrand to the presidency in 1981 saw a significant increase in the state's involvement in the workplace. These were presented under the names of the ministers responsible – the *Ordonnances Mauroy* and the *Lois Auroux* (1982). The areas of employment which were covered included:

- the reduction and control of hours of work (*Ordonnances* 82-40 and 82-41 of 16 January 1982);
- the regulation of fixed-term and temporary employment (*Ordonnances* 82-130 and 82-131 of 5 February 1982);
- the liberty of workers within the company (the law of 4 August 1982) in the areas of disciplinary procedures and freedom of expression;
- the maintenance of institutions representing personnel (union organisation, the administration of delegations and work committees);
- the regulations governing collective negotiation (the law of 13 November 1982);
- the establishment of safety and hygiene councils (the law of 23 December 1982).

The main outcome of this series of laws was to view the worker as having the rights of a 'citizen' in the workplace. This meant providing him/her with the right of direct negotiation of salary and conditions of work (the laws of 4 August and 13 November 1982) and protecting the principle of equality between workers on standard and fixed-term contracts (laws of 5 February and 28 March 1982).

However, despite the introduction of these new legal mechanisms, their effect has been limited. There are two main reasons for this. First, the type of worker whose rights the 1982 laws were designed to protect is no longer the model of the 'average' employee. He/she is now equally likely to be a member of a small or medium-sized enterprise, probably does not belong to a union and does not represent a sufficiently substantial pressure group within the firm. Companies below a certain size do not, in any case, fall within the terms of the law. Second, because of the constraints imposed by the law, companies have sought to take on part-time employees on an extra-legal basis or have franchised ('outsourced') a large number of functions which were formerly carried out within the firm.

The focus of legal provision has therefore shifted from protecting the rights of workers in confrontations between labour and employees to safeguarding companies' potential for growth. Thus certain of the 1982 laws governing hours of work and redundancies have been relaxed in order to allow companies greater flexibility.

Encadré 26: Disputes in the workplace

Most disagreements at the place of work are not brought before a judge, partly for reasons of expense and partly because of the potential consequences for the employee concerned. Such conflicts are subject to the judgement of four legal institutions:

- the *Tribunal de Grande Instance* for cases of major litigation (strikes, lock-outs, etc.);
- the *Juge d'Instance* who rules on cases concerned with personal representation;
- the *Juge Pénal* (*Tribunal Correctionnel* and *Tribunal de Police*) who adjudicates on criminal offences;
- the *Conseil des Prud'hommes*, a 'lay council' composed of representatives of employers and employees which deals with 90 per cent of disputes in the workplace. Judges for the *Conseil des Prud'hommes* are elected every five years. The elections are based on lists of union and employers' representatives which form two colleges. The employers' college includes a number of managers who have official status as senior executives. Members of the employees' college must be allowed time under law to fulfil their function as representatives and have the same rights of protection against compulsory redundancy as other personnel (Article L514-2 of the *Code du Travail*).

Disputes which come before the *Prud'hommes* (95 per cent of which are brought by monthly paid employees) are dealt with in two phases – conciliation and, if conciliation fails, judgement. Today, less than 10 per cent of disputes are resolved at the conciliation stage. Judgement is conducted by four judges – two from among the employers and two from the employees – and is based on majority decision. It takes on average twelve months for the *Prud'hommes* to reach a decision.

THE COMPANY AND ITS CONTRACTUAL PARTNERS

General principles governing contracts

Under French law, contracts are of two types – public (*administratif*) and private (*privé*). Contracts of the first type (*privé*) are governed by common law. Those of

Encadré 27: The source of French employment law

Laws which are externally imposed

1 The French Constitution (1946; 1958)

- conduct in the workplace;
- trade union law;
- the right to strike;
- the right to non-discrimination;
- the right to participation in company management.

2 International Treaties

- UN Law of 1979 (Articles 1186 and 1189);
- EC law, notably the Single Act of 1986 and the Maastricht Treaty of 1992.

3 French Law
Governed by the *Code du Travail* (3,800 articles) which is divided into three parts:

- legislative;
- regulatory (*Conseil d'Etat*);
- *décrets simples.*

Laws which are negotiated (conventions collectives)

Articles 131-1, 131-2, 132-2, 132-5 of the *Code du Travail* define respectively:

- the fields within which negotiation is permitted under the law (131-1);
- the types of company allowed to negotiate collective agreements (131-2);
- the categories of individual parties entitled to sign *conventions* or collective agreements (132-2);
- the fields within which agreements can be drawn up (132-5).

Established practice

Established practice is only legally binding in fields not covered by other parts of the law in circumstances perceived by both parties to constitute an obligation.

The individual work contract

In accordance with the above principles, the personal contract cannot contain stipulations which are less favourable to the individual employee than the texts already described.

the second type (*administratif*) conform to an independently codified set of rules which is referred to in cases of litigation. These include contracts which:

- relate to 'public markets';
- involve occupation or exploitation of publicly owned land;
- entail the sale or purchase of public property;
- apply to an individual holding public office;
- relate to the administration of public services (health, environment, utilities, local services, etc.).

Although there are many instances where it is difficult to determine whether contracts fall under public or private jurisdiction, it can be said that the majority of contracts between companies are private, that is governed by common law (*droit commun*).

French law is based on the principle of establishing a balance between private and public interests. It is founded first and foremost on the respect of individual autonomy. This means in philosophical terms that, despite being a member of society, every individual should be free to exercise his/her will and should only be held to his/her commitments to others if he/she has entered into those commitments freely. This principle has three main implications:

- The law should have an essentially supplementary function, that is it should only intervene in circumstances which have not been anticipated by the parties.
- There should be consensus between the parties to any legal agreement (*le principe du consensualisme*). The form of the agreement is therefore less important than the evidence of the agreement having been entered into freely. Only in exceptional cases – such as marriage – are there prescribed formalities which must be followed for an agreement to be legally binding.
- There are no external or independent criteria which have to be respected for agreements to be legally binding provided that the terms of the agreement are clear and precise (*clairs et précis*).

Nevertheless, the implementation of these principles which originate in the revolutionary (or 'Rousseauvian') conception of human rights (*les droits de l'homme*) are tempered by the economic imperatives which demand that the weaker party be protected against the stronger. Thus, legal conventions (*conventions*) regulate certain types of private contract such as:

- leasing accommodation;
- work contracts;
- insurance contracts;
- credit agreements.

Certain other principles such as the respect for public order may also override the principle of individual autonomy or at least serve to define the boundaries of its application. This development has been accentuated by the primacy of EU Directives in such areas as consumer rights or the protection of the environment.

The outcome of the above developments is that French business law is tending to become a law based on negotiation rather than on imposition. The government encourages agencies and associations which represent individuals to formulate their own contractually binding regulations or, where necessary, to apply existing laws. Such agencies (*commissions, conseils, chapitres*, etc.) are formally recognised by government and are free within the framework of national jurisdiction to establish rules which govern the conduct of their members. Thus the principle of individual autonomy has of late been extended to imply the collective freedom of groups which represent the shared interests of a given sector or field of activity. Such developments serve to mitigate the reproach that common law in France is too concerned with protecting the rights of the individual.

Contractual validity

The conditions which regulate the validity of a contract relate either to its form or its substance. As far as the form of contracts is concerned, the mere fact of agreement (*consensualisme*) is sufficient. It is not necessary in principle that the contract be in writing, though in practice – as under German or English law – this is normally required in order to provide concrete evidence that agreement has been reached and formalised. For example, written contracts are demanded under law in the case of leases and fixed-term or part-time work contracts. As regards substance, there are four prior conditions which serve first to protect the contractor and second to safeguard public order and civic morality:

- The contractor must be capable of entering into an agreement and is assumed to be so unless proven otherwise under law (namely minors or those deemed not to be in possession of their faculties).
- The consent of the contractor must be given freely, in an 'open, and honest manner' and on the basis of 'adequate information' (*éclairé et exempt de vices*). No deception or obligation must be involved if the contract is to be valid.
- The object of the contract, that is its content, should relate to a 'tangible reality'. For example, in contracts of sale, the object should be identifiable as a good which is subject to commercial exchange.
- The contract should respect principles of civic morality. These are inevitably relative and subject to the individual judgement of a legal representative. For example, a contract involving a prostitute purchasing an apartment for 'commercial' purposes could be declared invalid under law.

The application of civil responsibility in the field of competition

As in other member states of the EU, the combination of national and European competition law is based on Articles 85 and 86 of the Treaty of Rome and on

Regulation CEE 4064/89 of 2 December 1989 concerning monopolies. Like the law in Germany and England, French law includes rulings relative to:

- the control of monopolies;
- the limitation of abuses of power (*Ordonnance* 86-1243 and *Décret* No. 86-1309 of December 1986);
- discriminatory practices (*ordonnance* of December 1986 and Law No. 92-1442 of December 1992).

In addition, Articles 1382 and 1383 of the *Code Civil* control 'unfair competition' (*'concurrence déloyale'*) in respect, *inter alia*, of the following practices:

- 'engineering' the resignation of a competitor's staff (*débauchage de salariés*), though, in this complex area, it is not considered malpractice to recruit or 'headhunt' personnel employed by other companies;
- 'denigration' (e.g. advertisements stating that washing powder without phosphates poisons rivers);
- 'putting off' competitors' clients;
- 'false advertising' or imitating existing advertisements;
- 'copying' a competitor's products.

In cases such as the above, the consequences of malpractice must be proven and must lead to a demonstrable loss of clientele. There must also be a causal link between the malpractice and the blame attaching to the instigator (e.g. an increase in the turnover of the instigator's business simultaneous to a fall in that of the 'victim' in the immediate aftermath of blameworthy actions on the part of the instigator).

LAW AND THE INDIVIDUAL IN THE WORKPLACE

The work contract

As in other countries of the EU, the main distinction between types of work contracts is that between contracts of indefinite duration (*contrats à durée indéterminée*) and fixed-term contracts (*contrats à durée limitée/déterminée* – CDD) which are the main support for what is known as *le travail précaire*. Despite recent developments, the law is based on the assumption that long-term contracts are the norm within firms.

In order to make fixed-term contracts less attractive, French legislation applies the following conditions:

- Fixed-term contracts can only be applied in specific instances laid down by law. These include the sudden replacement of a salaried employee, a temporary increase in the firm's level of activity, a contract for a job which, of its nature, is limited in duration, etc.

- It is forbidden to have recourse to this form of contract in order to replace a person laid off as a result of a work dispute, in cases of work officially described as 'dangerous' or where it has arisen as a result of redundancies due to 'economic' factors during the previous six months.
- Fixed-term contracts cannot exceed twenty-four months and can only be renewed once. The total of two periods cannot exceed the maximum duration allowed under law (L122-1-2 and L124-2-2 of the *Code du Travail*).
- Fixed-term contracts cannot be ended before their agreed term. This rule applies to both employee and employer (Article L122-3-13 *contrats à durée déterminée* and Article L124-7 *travail temporaire*).

General principles governing the establishment of work contracts

As with Section 38 of the UK's Sex Discrimination Act (1973) and Section 29 of The Race Relations Act (1976), Article L122-45 of the *Code du Travail* stipulates in its most recent form (No. 92–1446, December 1992) that:

> No person can be excluded from the employment process and no employee sanctioned or made redundant for reasons of sex, customs, domestic situation, ethnic, national or racial origin or religious conviction (. . .) nor for reasons of handicap or state of health (. . .). Any ruling contrary to the above principles is declared invalid under the law.

These principles are protected by the penal sanctions expressed in Articles, 225-1 and 225-2 of the new penal code drawn up on 1 March 1994, the punishment for contravening the law being two years' imprisonment or a fine of 200,000 francs.

The conditions of substance governing the validity of contracts are similar to those already described above and include:

- the legal right to engage in a contract;
- freedom of consent;
- the moral purpose to which the contract is directed.

The principal formal condition of work contracts is that they be drawn up in writing (*cf.* comments above on the validity of contracts under French law). This principle is the direct outcome of the EU Directive of 14 October 1991 under the terms of the Maastricht Treaty. Under French law (No. 91–1383, 31 December 1991), a written document is stipulated as a means of protecting the employee but its absence does not render the contract null and void. Thus, the EU Directive, which came into operation on 1 July 1993, goes further than French law and lays down that the contract should include:

- the identity of the parties;
- the date of commencement of the contract;
- the level of remuneration and the frequency of pay;

- the hours of work;
- the title and description of the post.

However, the text of the Directive does not stipulate what sanctions should be undertaken in the absence of such a document or in cases where individual elements are omitted.

Hours of work

In contrast with the UK where employers and employees are free to agree their hours of work, the period is fixed under French law at thirty-nine hours per week. Any hours worked beyond this limit are considered supplementary (*heures supplémentaires*) and, on an average calculated over a period of twelve consecutive weeks, the number of work hours should not exceed forty-six and, in any single week, should not be more than forty-eight (Article L212-7 al 2).

In any given year, the maximum number of *heures supplémentaires* which may be carried out by an employee is limited to 130. This limit may be raised by collective agreement (Article L212-6) with the authorisation of the *Ministre du Travail*, the *Directeur Régional du Travail* or, in the case of the annual 130-hour limit, of the *Inspecteur du Travail*.

Interruption of work

As in other European countries, work may be interrupted without the contract being suspended in cases of illness, strike action, accidents at work and maternity leave. It is illegal to make a person redundant during the period of recuperation following illness or an accident at work or during pregnancy (Article L122-32-2 al 1er; Article L122-25-2 of the *Code du Travail*). In contrast with UK law, French employees have a statutory right to five weeks paid holiday per year, that is two and a half working days a month up to a total of thirty days (Article L223-2 of the *Code du Travail*).

CONCLUDING REMARKS

From this brief overview, it can be seen that the regulation of business practice in France aims to provide satisfactory social protection for employees and is statutorily controlled at every level of government. There is also a well-developed and effective institutional infrastructure which helps firms to set themselves up and which supports regional provision for training and recruitment. Yet, as in other areas of constraint on individual behaviour, French firms are adroit at ignoring or circumventing the law. During the final years of the Mitterrand presidency, France was rocked by a series of damaging corruption scandals (*affaires*) due essentially to the illegal use of public funds for private gain at the regional and national level (see Chapter 1). Thus a new scrupulousness has entered the management of business. This does not prevent companies from making use of part-time employment in a period of uncertainty or from paying employees below the minimum wage. The huge deficit on the social security budget makes it increasingly hard for France to afford the level of social protection which the country has traditionally allowed itself, yet the need to control the levels of unemployment means that the barriers to cost cutting can only partly be removed.

SELECTED TEXTS

Dekenwerr-Defossez (1990)
Bertrel, J-P (1996)
Guéry, G. (1994)
Lyon-Caen, G. (1985)
Ray, J.F. (1993)
Ripert, G. and Roblot, R. (1993)
Teyssié, B. (1993)

See Bibliography

7 Tradition and transition: the implementation of organisational principles

Loïc Cadin and Carla Mendoza

As the previous chapters have shown, French companies, like those elsewhere in Europe, have been confronted by an increasingly turbulent and competitive environment. Whilst coping with financial pressures, other factors of competitiveness have also been at the forefront of managerial thinking – the quality of products and services, timescales and deadlines, responsiveness to client demand, etc. The main issue facing those responsible for human resource management in the widest sense has therefore been how to make firms more flexible in their production systems and responsive to changes in the attitudes and behaviour of employees. In an attempt to come to terms with this new environment, French companies have introduced a number of organisational practices as well as a range of instruments designed to motivate personnel. These practices should be seen in the context of the legal principles described in Chapter 6 and against the development of organisational sociology in France over the last twenty years.

The creation in 1973 of the *Agence Nationale des Conditions de Travail* (*ANACT*) marked the implementation of a proposal made by Jacques Delors in 1972 when he was labour adviser to Jacques Chaban-Delmas, Prime Minister under the presidency of Georges Pompidou (1969–74). The principle behind his proposal was to provide 'a basis for improving work conditions and for developing participation in the workplace'. The report was intended to herald a new departure for French organisations in a 'post-Taylorist' age inspired by the research of such 'philosophers' of behaviour and motivation as Maslow (1970) and Herzberg (1966) from North America, the principles of 'industrial democracy' developed in Scandinavia by pioneers such as Thorsrud and the explorations of group psychology undertaken by the Tavistock Institute in London.

Taylor's vision of organisations was based essentially on two key concepts, operation and 'post' or function. A job or 'post' was defined according to the precise characteristics of the tasks involved – their procedural character (a series of operations) and the prescriptive principle that there was 'one best way' of carrying them out. As well as serving as a backdrop to political initiatives, the idea that these concepts were ill-suited to the new industrial environment found expression in a number of important sociological reviews in France between the years 1974 and 1988. During the 1970s attention focused primarily on the various forms of human dysfunction to which Tayloristic systems of production appeared to give rise – absenteeism, boredom and frustration at the repetitive nature of work, etc. Thus, the concern of researchers and government was with conditions of work especially as these were experienced by workers themselves. In 1974, for example, the journal *Sociologie du Travail* published a special number entitled *Le Taylorisme en question* while in 1977, *Le Taylorisme à l'envers*, a monograph produced by the *Institut de l'Entreprise*, enjoyed wide circulation. Seminars and experiments took place in leading companies such as Rhône-Poulenc, Leroy-Sommer and Poclain and these and other similar experiences were publicised in a conference organised in October 1977 by the *Conseil National du Patronat Français* (CNPF) and subsequently published under the enticing slogan *Portes ouvertes sur l'Entreprise, l'Amélioration des conditions de vie dans l'Entreprise*.

The problem behind these experiments, the 'social-democrat' spirit of which had been taken up by the new president, Giscard d'Estaing, following his election in 1974, was that their economic efficiency could not be demonstrated in the aftermath of the first oil crisis of 1973. Moves to encourage greater freedom of expression among working people championed by Antoine Riboud of BSN (since merged with the food giant, Danone) led to experiments by a number of major French companies. The implementation of these innovations was consolidated by the enactment of the *Lois Auroux* in 1982 (see Chapter 6). They certainly increased the number of meetings and multiplied the reports and questionnaires which circulated within French firms. They instilled a climate which was in line with the spirit of the times and created a legal basis for a general improvement in the quality of working conditions.

It was a response on the part of management as much to the climate of enhanced participation within companies as to the example set by Japan which led in the 1980s to a shift in emphasis towards quality circles, mission statements and the fuller integration of technological innovation. This meant in practice hastening the introduction of technological processes and demanding higher levels of qualification as a precondition of recruitment. A debate ensued in 1987 between the then newly elected right-wing government and leaders of industry as to how quickly such changes could reasonably take place. Companies had after all to adapt to innovation. New skills or 'competencies' would be required of employees. It was concluded that employees already in post would be able to adapt to meet the new challenges, provided that appropriate training was made available. Excessively radical or uniform programmes would be unlikely to succeed. Companies should be allowed to determine their own needs and to develop their personnel accordingly. Despite the widespread integration of Japanese principles into existing practices, research carried out in the late 1980s showed that organisational innovations such as quality circles were in fact being very unevenly applied. An *INSEE* study (Gollac 1989) suggested, not surprisingly, that the extent of individual autonomy in work practices was inversely related to the scale of production and that Tayloristic principles were far from dead.

While efforts were being made to improve conditions for the workforce, the management was interested not only by the quality of output but also by enhanced – and assessable – performance. The focus on quality was therefore matched by the widespread application of 'Direction by objectives' (*direction par objectifs* also known as *direction participative par objectifs – DPO*) in which individualised performance objectives could be set, measured and periodically evaluated. However, as d'Iribarne (1989) argued, these were peculiarly difficult to apply in France because of the respect for the security of status accorded to a given stratum within the hierarchy of the organisation.

While the popular concept of 'Taylorism' has remained the benchmark against which change has been set, the 1990s have been marked by a continuation of the debate concerning new models against the background of recession and 'downsizing'. As elsewhere in Europe, the main themes in the discussions surrounding organisational change have focused on:

- teamwork;
- greater autonomy linked to responsibility for achieving performance objectives measured in terms of improved quality and cost-effectiveness, output and timescales;
- integration of the tasks of marketing, quality and technical maintenance, financial management and supply;
- reducing the number of hierarchical levels, i.e. the transition towards 'flatter' organisations;
- closer cooperation between functions.

Clearly, in any organisation there is a tension between a functional logic based on predetermined roles and a human logic founded on individual needs, qualities and capabilities. A successful organisation is one which is able to achieve a satisfactory balance between the two. As we have seen, the trend within France as much as elsewhere has been to emphasise the human dimension by identifying the 'competencies' required to accomplish particular tasks and matching available human resources to these. In an agreement drawn up by the steel industry in January 1991 (*Accord ACAP 2000 de la Sidérurgie*), pay was related to the attainment of goals based not on the status of the post but on the proven acquisition of personal skills. This was formally agreed and regularly updated in the negotiation and evaluation of individual career paths. Such agreements could be said to represent new forms of 'social contract' within the firm. They went beyond the simple fact of creating structures to improve conditions of work which had been the main characteristic of the agreements of the 1970s.

These developments have been taking place alongside the measures referred to earlier. As already suggested, one of the most influential of these has been the growth in fashion of the mission statement (*projet d'entreprise*) which takes on the status of a charter (*charte*) within the organisation. As a statement, the *projet d'entreprise* seeks not simply to be a blueprint for action but to represent the principles, values, beliefs and ambitions around which the 'culture' of the organisation can be built. As such it aims to act as an inspirational symbol which motivates personnel by enhancing their corporate loyalty and sense of belonging to the organisation as a human group. The leitmotifs of such discourses are slogans such as 'the pleasure of performance', 'the value of facing challenges', 'a passion for quality', 'the importance of winning', etc. Inevitably perhaps, the integrity of such statements has given rise to scepticism on the part of employees since they immediately highlight the mismatch between words and deeds, between statements of intent and lived experience at the organisational grassroots.

Nevertheless, the '*projet d'entreprise*' is in accord with certain aspects of French culture. As has been shown elsewhere in this book (notably Chapter 2), the French attach value to words and concepts, particularly when they are expressed in well-formulated and rhetorical terms. They prefer to operate within the framework of an internally coherent plan which precedes action, if only so that they can criticise the culture in power. Such conceptual schema represent part of the machinery of state which is integral to a certain view of citizenship and to the principle of codified law. This ambivalence of attitude differs, however, from the manner in which mission statements are traditionally perceived in Japan where the sentiment of corporate loyalty translated from the traditional bond between son and father is normally understood to be much stronger and different in kind (*cf.* de Maricourt 1996).

In the aftermath of twenty years' debate over the most effective form of organisation which should characterise the post-Taylorist era, the emphasis has shifted in the latter half of the 1990s from the company itself to the effects of downsizing on the wider community. Productivity alone is no longer a sufficient objective if it means swelling the ranks of the unemployed. Employees can hardly be expected to apply 'new' principles if these are likely to put them out of work, above all in a climate in which growth appears to be stagnating. As has been frequently been stated in this book, the outcome has been to place still further pressure on French firms not only to maintain if not increase levels of production but also to become an instrument of socialisation and training. It is the company which has become the main agency in the fight against marginalisation and exclusion.

In a context such as the above, it is instructive to compare the approach to education and training taken by French and German companies, especially since the latter are often seen to be in advance of their European competitors in the educational sphere. In comparing the impacts of salaries offered by French and German firms from a variety of perspectives – sector, technological resources, size, number of employees, age, etc. – researchers of the *Laboratoire d'Economie et de Sociologie du Travail* (*LEST*) established that the salaries offered differed considerably, that the hierarchies of salaries contrasted with each other and also that the qualifications of staff varied widely.

In order to understand salary distribution, it is not sufficient to consider the operations of the labour market. It is a matter of reconstituting the manner in which behaviours originate and establish themselves taking account of the competencies which are implied by production processes. Clearly, each country has its own way of expressing its educational, organisational and industrial relationships. It is this conjugation of relationships or 'spaces' (*espaces*) which we refer to as 'the social effect' (*l'effet sociétal*). There is insufficient space in this chapter to describe each of the systems in detail but we aim to show how they interact and, in doing so, to understand better the impact of this background on the management of human resources in French companies.

Salary structures are a valuable indicator of social relationships. Table 7.1 shows that the disparity between salaries is greater in France than in Germany, that in France senior executive staff (*cadres*) are privileged in relation to middle management, white-collar in relation to blue-collar workers and specialists (*ouvriers qualifiés*) in relation to the rest of the workforce.

The information relative to pay policy is complemented by data relating to the number of staff. This data, shown in Table 7.1, reveals the economic paradox that the French tend to employ resources which are more rather than less expensive.

Table 7.1 Differentials in the structure of salaries and wages in industry

	France	*Germany*
Variable coefficient of monthly salaries	55%	31.5%
Relationship between the average salary of employees to that of workers	1.70	1.28
Relationship between the average salary of managers to that of other non-workers	1.91	1.39
Relationship between the average salary of qualified workers and that of normal workers	1.45	1.23

Source: *LEST* 'Productions de la hierarchie dans l'entreprise. Recherche d'un effet societal Allemagne-France', *Article paru dans Travail et Emploi*, No. 2, September 1979.

Table 7.2 Categories of staff as a percentage of the total workforce in France and Germany

	France *%*	*Germany* *%*
Non-manual staff	21.0	17.0
Non-manual and non-management staff	24.6	17.9
Foremen (companies having a staff of more than 1,000) in relation to the overall number of workers	6.4	3.5

Source: *LEST* 'Productions de la hierarchie dans l'entreprise. Recherche d'un effet societal Allemagne-France', *Article paru dans Travail et Emploi*, No. 2, September 1979.

Table 7.3 Calculation of overall salary relative to the structure of employment represented in public statements of accounts (*Plan Comptable*)

	France %	Germany %
Proportion of overall national salary allocated to staff classified as		
'non-workers'	42	32
Major firms	45	33

Source: LEST Productions de la hierarchie dans l'entreprise. Recherche d'un effet societal Allemagne-France', *Article paru dans Travail et Emploi*, No. 2, September 1979.

It is in the most concentrated sectors and those which are technologically most advanced (chemicals, cement, non-ferrous metals, artificial fibres) that the gap between employment structures in the two countries is the most clear-cut (see Table 7.3).

These pay structures clearly have an impact on the distribution of salaries within organisations. French companies are marked by a preponderance of senior managerial staff, a characteristic to which we shall return. In the meantime, it should be noted that three key dimensions lie at the heart of the employment system.

THE EDUCATIONAL DIMENSION

A comparison of the profiles of French and German staff reveals that, taking account of variations in level, the system in Germany for calculating pay scales is generally based on level of training, while in France it tends to be founded on length of service. In both countries, however, the level of education reached is a powerful determinant of the career followed with each grade of responsibility corresponding to a particular type of educational background. It should also be noted that in France professional training is on the whole less highly valued than general education and is aimed at those who have not succeeded in that field. Considerable efforts have been made to enhance the status of vocational training in France. Despite the initiatives taken in the 1970s under the presidency of Giscard d'Estaing and, more recently (1991–2) during Edith Cresson's period of office as Prime Minister, the results have so far been modest. Yet the implications are serious. Each year 100,000 young people in France leave school without a qualification, considerably more than in Germany. The manner in which competencies are developed has a direct impact on the upward mobility of staff. The dual system in Germany combines theoretical and practical apprenticeship and facilitates flexibility. In France, training takes place in the workplace within a specialised operational field and thus limits employees' potential mobility.

These two models of education and training also impact on the selection of directorial elites. Two *grandes écoles* (*Polytechnique* and *ENA*) alone train 45 per cent of the chief executives of the country's leading firms. As is widely recognised, French industry therefore relies on a small selection of élite schools as a source of training and recruitment of its senior managers. Moreover a significant proportion of these are educated in state-funded institutions. While in Germany, 25 per cent of the directors of the main firms began their professional careers as apprentices, with the main emphasis being on internal systems of promotion, in French firms there is a tradition of franchising the training of managerial élites to outside agents. As Albert (1991) points out, these different patterns of education and training directly influence company strategy in the two countries. While German managers develop medium-term growth strategies for firms, the system of grafting in senior executives from outside, which tends to dominate in France, favours externally orientated patterns of growth based on mergers and takeovers. Bauer and Bertin-Mourot's (1993) reference to the 'tyranny of diplomas' is therefore not out of place and may be said to derive directly from the stability which governs the prestige-based hierarchy of schools in France, and determines in advance a French manager's lifetime career path.

THE ORGANISATIONAL DIMENSION

The organisation of French companies can be described as burcaucratic (both mechanical and administrative) by comparison with German firms which appear both more organic and professionalised in their management style. Another oversimplified way of explaining this consists in emphasising the functional and horizontal character of the German firm as opposed to the vertical character of its French counterpart. As has already been mentioned, the vertical structure of French firms is emphasised by many analyses among which the most notable are those of Philippe d'Iribarne (1989) who sees features in the organisation of French companies which can be traced to the *ancien régime*. According to 'honour's logic' (*la logique de l'honneur*), an employee does not merely carry out a job or exercise a function, he occupies a 'state' (*état*) which is an indelible part of his identity. The action of 'senior manager' (*cadre*) which is specifically French does not refer to a function but to an essence (*cf.* Encadré 3 'Hierarchy and Honour's Logic'). It is interesting to analyse the paths to promotion within the echelons of senior management (*encadrement*). They aim less to enhance the person's qualifications than to reduce social distance. As Bourdieu (1989) explains, 'the further down the social hierarchy you go, the more individuals are defined by what they do, whereas the higher you ascend, the more they are defined by who they are'.

In his international comparison of management styles, Bollinger and Hofstede (1987) place France in the category of cultures marked by hierarchical distance which they define according to criteria similar to those given above. D'Iribarne reveals the day-to-day organisational consequences of this definition. Each professional group has a strong sense of the rights and duties implied by his position. It is mutually understood that the excessive desire to involve oneself in a subordinate's job is an attack on his/her dignity. As has already been pointed out in this chapter, it is not hard to imagine how difficult it is to evaluate performance in French firms. It should be remembered, nevertheless, that despite the tendency of French companies to organise themselves feudally, 'servile' obedience brings dishonour. A baron who does not react against being ordered about by a king loses both legitimacy and the capacity to mobilise resources.

THE INDUSTRIAL DIMENSION AND THE CRISIS IN MANAGEMENT STYLES

France differs from Germany in its separation between human and technical resource management. This separation reflects the distinct systems of professional relationship which exist in the two countries. For example, the head of a 'technical' department in a German company devotes more than 50 per cent of his time to human resource management issues. In France, the objective of the HRM function is to relieve engineers of social responsibility so that they can concentrate on technical issues. The manner in which personnel can make representations also illustrates their cultural differences. In German companies, there is a close correspondence between immediate personal hierarchy and the management of conflict. Potential tensions are deflated before they got out of hand. The tendency in French organisations consists rather in allowing claims to rise to the upper echelons of the system and then to refer them to the administrative and regulatory departments.

The model of the French firm which we have presented above values technical skill highly and is anxious to reduce its costs. However, as has frequently been suggested, the pressure of competition and economic recession has made it a priority to improve quality as well. It has become essential to review the range of products with increasing frequency in order to keep abreast of ever shorter life-cycles. In short, flexibility has become the watchword – a harsh demand to place on companies whose tradition is one of compartmentalisation and hierarchical structures.

Thus, following Japanese models, it has become accepted in principle that horizontal coordination allows for shorter series of production with a high quality/price ratio than are possible in organisations which adhere too rigidly to hierarchical chains of command.

UNEMPLOYMENT AND THE SOCIAL RESPONSIBILITY OF THE FIRM

Over the last ten years, France has created less jobs then other European countries despite having a comparable growth rate. Between 1987 and 1990, when growth was particularly marked, many available posts remained vacant while unemployment stayed at a high level. As we have seen, the realisation of the mismatch between the qualifications required by firms and those 'available' on the market has inevitably called into question the quality of the French

---

Encadre 28: Towards a project-based management structure

Traditionally, car design is carried out sequentially – the dossier passes from the research department to the design and engineering office and from there to sales and forecasting before going forward to factory production. But sequential development is no longer manageable when the number of projects which are run in parallel increases beyond a certain point and when it becomes imperative to reduce drastically the lead in development time of a new model. Despite the growing intensity of pressure in recent times, Renault has been attempting for the last twenty years to shift to a 'project based' management structure, in other words to introduce a transversal dimension into an essentially vertical hierarchy. Midler (1993) traces the progressive reinforcement of the project manager's position, the means which have been put at his disposal and the measures which have been taken to implement a system of simultaneous engineering. The story of Renault is the story of the way in which functional structures have resisted the progressive undermining of their power. The Twingo is the first model to have been developed according to this system and it was completed in record time. Nevertheless, the resistance of hierarchical and vertical structures has still not been broken down.

---

education system (*cf.* Chapter 1) and has led in particular to criticism concerning its lack of vocational–professional focus. This is hardly a new theme. It is not difficult for industry to blame education for the shortfall in appropriately qualified recruits or for educationists to criticise industry for its inability to forecast its future needs. If anything the boot is now on the other foot. Towards the end of the 1980s, there was widespread concern about the insufficiency of the numbers of engineers with management qualifications. Since that time the situation has been rectified, partly as a result of closer cooperation between universities and business schools. It is now the recruitment capacity of companies which is unable to keep pace with supply.

The increasing precariousness of recruitment has been accompanied by a kaleidoscope of special statutes governing conditions of employment (*cf.* Chapter 6). A hard core of staff with competencies deemed to have strategic value have stable positions and are able to develop their careers according to a set structure. For the rest, fixed-term contracts and even less stable forms of employment, such as company placements, part-time jobs, franchises, etc., have become the rule. The human resource management challenge which is currently facing firms is how best to integrate these different categories of employee. The resolution of this issue is considered in the following chapters which review the way in which the HRM function is developing to cope with the fundamental transformation in the nature of the social contract between the company and its employees.

SELECTED TEXTS

Albert, M. (1991)
Crozier, M. (1963)
Crozier, M. (1994)
Crozier, M. and Friedberg, E. (1977)
D'Iribarne, P. (1989)
Bollinger, D. and Hofstede, G. (1987)

See Bibliography

USEFUL ADDRESSES

Association Nationale des Directeurs et Cadres de la fonction Personnel (ANDCP)
29 avenue Hoche
75008 Paris
Tel. (1) 45.63.55.09/45.63.79.57.

Association francophone de Gestion des Ressources Humaines (AGRH)
ESSEC – IMD, CNIT
place de la Défense
92090 Paris-la-Défense
renseignements Nicole Mourrier
Tel. (1) 45.58.39.63 Fax. (1) 45.58.36.91

Centre d'Etudes de Recherches sur les Qualifications (CEREQ)
10 place de la Joliette
13474 Marseille Cedex 02
Tel. 91.13.28.28.

Agence Nationale pour l'Amélioration des Conditions de Travail (ANACT)
7 boulevard Romain-Rollaud
92128 Montrouge Cedex
Tel. 42.31.40.40.

Centre pour le Développement de l'Information sur la Formation Permanente
Tour Europe Cedex 07
92049 Paris-la-Défense
Tel. (1) 41.25.22.22.

Association Nationale pour la Valorisation Interdisciplinaire de la recherche en sciences
de l'homme et de la société auprès des Entreprises (ANVIE)
54 boulevard Raspail
75270 Paris Cedex 06
Tel. (1) 49.54.21.16.

Ministère du Travail, de l'Emploi, et de la Formation Professionnelle
Service de Presse
1 place de Fontenoy
75007 Paris
Tel. (1) 40.56.60.00.

Office National d'Information sur les Enseignements et les Professions (ONISEP)
77423 Marne la Vallée Cedex 2
Tel. (331) 64.80.35.00.

8 Negotiation, state ownership and privatisation: the changing role of the trade unions

Guy Groux

In French companies today, as elsewhere in Europe, the HRM function is obviously not restricted to managing the workforce or to establishing policies aimed at promoting teamwork and individual motivation. In its fullest and perhaps its more traditional sense, it involves social negotiation and, in particular, the search for contractual agreements with union representatives. Whether it be in the Anglo-Saxon, German or Japanese systems, internal 'social' negotiation can be defined as the vector of the HRM function. In France, however, for a long time, negotiation within the firm was practically non-existent, especially in the private sector.

As has been seen (*cf.* Chapters 1 and 2), the French economy has traditionally been mixed, with state-run nationalised companies coexisting with firms under private ownership. The responsibility for establishing and maintaining contractual relationships was frequently located at the national level (Reynaud 1978). Confronted by a centralised network of professional relationships, within which relationships between sectors or between branches of the same profession were regulated through negotiation, the company appeared more like an area of conflict (open or latent) than like a work environment governed by contractual concord. Far from playing a controlling or preventive role, in-company negotiation consisted rather of a struggle of wills based on confrontation. Its essential function was formally to contain or temporarily to stifle existing conflicts. Attempts in the early 1970s by Jacques Delors, then adviser to the Prime Minister Jacques Chaban-Delmas, to introduce *contrats de progrès* (negotiation procedures aimed at preventing confrontation) never got off the ground. The lack of a proper negotiating structure within French firms became one of the defining features of the term 'the French exception' in the field of social relations (Birnbaum *et al.*, 1987).

However, from about the middle of the 1980s new administrative principles were established. The characteristics which made France an exceptional case partly dissolved and the French social support system became closer to other systems operating within the European Union. From then on, negotiations within companies and the part played by the human resource function in determining the outcome of negotiated agreements underwent a significant growth. In 1950, barely seventeen agreements were concluded within firms. In 1970, 658 were identified, many of these following strikes. By 1992, the number of agreements totalled 6,370, virtually all of these having been arrived at without any overt conflict having taken place (*Bllun Annuol de la Négociation Collective: Ministère du Travail*, 1993).

However, despite the extent of its development, negotiation within firms is still a problematic process. Frequently, it is marked by breakdowns and its immediate outcomes are called into question. There are several reasons for this state of affairs:

- the weakness of unions within firms at the local level;
- the ill-preparedness of human resource managers and their frequent lack of experience in the art of social negotiation;
- the relative underdevelopment within French firms of a 'culture of negotiation' such as is present within German companies;
- the fact that the negotiating function has developed in response to economic pressures which have placed new demands on the human resource function.

These shortcomings can be traced further to structural features which are traditional within French society.

PROGRESS TOWARDS A NEW FRAMEWORK

Although, since 1945, the state has played a central role in industrial relations, the role of the state is legitimised by a long historical tradition which goes back to the origins of French republicanism and beyond (*cf.* Chapter 1). In Republican eyes, the principal notion of law was as an instrument of reform and social transformation. This was a principle which was reaffirmed during the Second World War by the *Conseil National de la Résistance* (*CNR*) and by the post-war government under General de Gaulle.

The influence of the political and social heritage of the post-war period continued to the middle of the 1980s. It meant that law dominated the public regulation of company negotiation and affected individual rights as much as the most general aspects of social life. The law protected the institutional rights of employees as much as the processes and procedures of the HRM function.

It also covered social protection schemes (sickness, pensions), the state regulation of a minimum wage or of hierarchical classifications which acted as a framework for negotiation and collective agreements (1945–50). Later, in the 1960s, it was legislation which governed workers' participation in company profits, unemployment benefit, the involvement of the unions in private firms, the agreement on work conditions. In the 1980s, once again, it was through law that the obligations of firms in collective negotiation procedures were worked out, as were the rights of unions in the application of new technologies. The same applied to employees' rights of expression concerning the conditions and

---

Encadré 29: Structure of social representation within the firm

The notion of law as the initiator of social reforms based on state intervention is reflected in its different structures of representation within firms:

- delegates (*délégués du personnel*);
- works councils (*comités d'entreprise*);
- hygiene and safety committees (*comités d'hygiène et de sécurité*).

See also Encadré 26.

---

organisation of work, the basis for agreements between unions and employers as regards company training policy, the reduction of working hours to thirty-nine hours per week, etc.

THE ROLE OF THE NATIONALISED SECTOR

In the context of the traditional French model, the state is not only the guardian of the law and an agency which influences human resource management and negotiation practices within the firm. Through the nationalised sector it is a major player in the economy – an 'enterprise state' (Naville *et al.* 1971). The French state dominates the principal sectors of industrial production – the Renault factories, the major utilities, coal, electricity, gas and nuclear power as well as main public services: railways, post and telecommunications and – until the middle of the 1980s – the leading French banks (*cf.* Chapter 1).

As an entrepreneur, the state not only takes on an economic role. It uses the nationalised sector as a means of defining new forms of regulation and social reform. By expressing the 'power of the law', the nationalised sector therefore plays a central part in upholding its status in the country as a whole. Social reforms which are initiated within the nationalised industries often have direct or indirect implications for the private sector. From the 1950s to the end of the 1970s, a whole series of innovatory agreements emerged relating to employment management. Renault and EDF (Electricité de France) were the first to define training programmes for workers. In so doing, they laid the basis for change in the regulations controlling the internal labour markets.

The emergence of these policies did not come about merely as the result of initiatives taken by the management of the organisations concerned. At the *Régie Renault*, it was the product of long negotiations between employers and unions: a policy which aimed to link wages to productivity and to the introduction of new technologies. Later (1969–70) the establishment of 'progress linked contracts' (*contrats de progrès*) at EDF-GDF (Electricité et Gaz de France) and at the SNCF (Société Nationale des Chemins de Fer) brought in new styles of negotiation which involved not only rates of pay but also professional training, job definition and conditions of work.

So, at a time when private firms were rarely the arena for autonomous agreements, nationalised companies were establishing new contractual relationships. Under pressure from unions and backed by the force of the law, these often served as models for private firms. It was therefore a centralised development in which legal action preceded the setting up of professional agreements on the ground, first at group and then at local level. In private firms, the human resource functions adapted to the global context which governed conventional practice. Often deprived of any real autonomy in terms of its executive power, HRM departments were for a long time primarily filled by legal specialists whose main function was to negotiate the terms of application of rules and regulations, agreements on the texts of laws drawn up outside the organisation.

THE 1980s: A TURNING POINT

It was in the middle of the 1980s that the situation changed – radically. The state began to withdraw from the social domain, a process which was, paradoxically, implemented by the Socialist government which had been in power since 1981. As has already been pointed out in Chapter 1, civil servants, intellectuals and a large section of public opinion turned against the 'kick-start' economic policy based on promoting consumption which had been followed by François Mitterrand after his accession to the presidency in 1981. The policy, which led to pay rises, increased inflation, a growing deficit in the balance of trade and an increased national debt, was replaced in 1983 by one of wage restraint linked to severe cutbacks in the level of public spending, offset by investment in industry and public infrastructure. In a few months, the country swung from a socialism based on Keynesian principles to a hybrid form of capitalistic social democracy.

The 'rehabilitation' of the company and the upsurge of an 'enterprise culture' brought with them a relaxation of the judicial constraints which at the time restricted company practice. It also led to a decentralisation of negotiation procedures and to greater independence on the part of the agents involved at local level.

THE EMERGENCE OF NEW SOCIAL CONVENTIONS

The autonomy ceded by the state to the private sector has had a direct and lasting effect on the world of negotiation. The level of activity surrounding contracts – both between professional groups and within companies – has increased as a consequence. These have also been affected by the European regulations on company relations which formed expression in the social chapter of the Treaty of Maastricht (1991). New styles and bases of negotiation have emerged affecting the unions, the development of professional agreements and the content of the HRM function. Former conventions based on conflictual claims and the accumulation of social gains which led to the establishment of a permanent balance of opposing forces have given rise to new conventions and forms of dialogue. Leading unions – the *Confédération Française et Démocratique du Travail* (*CFDT*), and *Confédération Générale des Cadres* (*CGC*) and the *Confédération Française des Travailleurs Chrétiens* (*CFTC*) – have come to accept the need for new practices based on economic realism. Overt conflict has become less frequent. Instead, measured negotiation aims at regulating and preventing potential confrontation.

The topics of negotiation too have changed and now focus on areas which were previously the responsibility of the HRM department. Instead of collective bargaining, discussion deals more with the allocation of tasks within the firm, with individual incentives and pay increases, with the impact of medium-term strategy on training practices or the organisation of work. At the same time, as the previous sections have shown, the HRM function itself has evolved. Different competencies are required based less on knowledge of the law and more on broadly based awareness of the negotiating conventions which apply within the context of the individual firm. At the same time, despite the withdrawal of the state in the middle of the 1980s and the greater freedom to negotiate within companies, the HRM function has found it difficult to rise to the challenge, in part at least because the multiplicity of agreements has taken away the legitimacy and influence of the union as a body with which sound negotiation can take place. The unions in France have been undergoing a crisis which has been deepening for a number of years.

The present crisis facing the unions in France began well before the left came to power in 1981. Since then, however, it has become more serious and has eclipsed those of previous years (Groux and Mouriaux 1992). Even at their high point, French unions have never represented more than 22–23 per cent of the workforce. They have been politically divided and have only had a superficial impact within private firms. There are many reasons for this underlying weakness which derive from the structures, practices and ideologies within organisations. Between 1975 and 1990 the number of manual workers fell by 20 per cent. The restructuring of the workforce and the substitution of manual work by more or less highly qualified 'intellectual' functions meant that a generation of employees emerged which was traditionally not sensitive to the historical culture shared by most of the unions.

The consequent fall in union membership is due once again to certain features which are specific to French society. In order to compensate for its numerical weakness and the gaps in its representation in the private sector, French trade unionism has come increasingly to depend on the diverse institutions set up by the state. Despite the additional power which this tendency gave to workers' organisations, transforming militants into 'professionals in negotiation' and leading figures within organisations, it also served to sharpen the distance between the trade union machinery and the mass of working people. In 1990, 54 per cent of the workforce claimed to have 'no confidence' in trade unions (SOFRES 1990). Despite the role played by the unions in the sudden wave of political unrest which swept over France in November 1995, this situation is unlikely to change substantially under a right-wing presidency and national government.

Thus the withdrawal of the state has undermined certain traditional practices which had previously been dominant within French trade unionism. From 1945 up to the beginning of the 1980s, a large proportion of the activities initiated by unions were aimed at addressing the agencies of political power as much as at changing practical conventions governing work practices. The massive strikes of the 1960s sought to bring about changes in the laws governing working practices and thus to influence the content of negotiations which would subsequently take place in companies. The reduced involvement of the state meant that the unions lost one of their main bases for action precisely at a time when they were already fundamentally weakened. Over a twenty-year period the level of union membership fell from 23 per cent to 8 per cent and the number of days lost in strike action from 1,742,200 to 665,500. In company elections non-affiliated workers account for almost 35 per cent of the vote and are now well ahead of the CGT (*Confédération Générale du Travail*) which attracts less than 25 per cent.

As a consequence of these developments, union action has become fragmented. It is now marked by schisms and cleavages such as the split within the *Education Nationale* or the creation of new union groupings within the CFDT (SOFRES-Liaisons Sociales 1990). This break-up of union structures has given way to purely corporatist movements in firms. These tend to be linked to specific jobs and reflect to differing degrees the authority of the large national unions to represent them.

RENEWING NEGOTIATION PROCEDURES: A MISSED OPPORTUNITY

The crisis facing collective action serves to explain the breakdowns in the development of negotiation procedures, especially within companies. Alternatives which have been put forward by certain unions with a view to adapting collective action to suit prevailing conditions have not been able to take root. In undermining fordist practices, the economic crisis has called into question the importance of traditional claims linked to salary levels which dominated between 1950 and the late 1970s (Boyer 1986). Yet the introduction of measures designed to modify professional behaviour within organisations remains marginal. In 1992, the number of agreements affecting professional training represented 2 per cent of the total number of agreements concluded within French firms, those on strategic career development less than 1 per cent. The basic substance of negotiation and agreement within French firms remains rooted in law and the more 'social' forms of discourse have not fundamentally changed the range of abilities deployed within departments of human resource management.

Encadré 30: The AXA agreement

The agreement arrived at by the AXA insurance company affecting more than 5,000 employees was finalised on 2 July 1990. Within the context of French business, it was an agreement of major social importance which covered a number of points:

- Where collective negotiation was concerned, it was made compulsory that there be an outcome agreed by the parties involved. Where there was persistent opposition between the parties, the dispute would be taken to external arbitration.
- Each elected union representative would be designated according to a job description which would be in keeping with his/her status as a representative of a section of the personnel within the organisation. The development of his/her responsibilities would follow a proper career plan linked to an appropriate salary scale.
- More frequent recourse would be had to the financial strategy and training groups which were set up alongside the *comité d'entreprise*, so as to enable the organisation as a whole to respond to changes in the external environment.
- Finally, the agreement established a formal system for financing union organisation. Each employee would receive an annual voucher representing the equivalent of four hours' salary which the employee was free to allocate to the union of his/her choice. The total value of the vouchers received by each union would then be made over to the union by the company.

THE ECONOMIC AND LEGAL RIGHTS OF THE UNIONS

As the above review has sought to demonstrate, the former system of professional relationships in which the state played a pivotal role has given way to a more open context, the effectiveness of which is to some extent undermined by a range of factors – the crisis affecting trade unionism in France, the economic recession and the diffusion of negotiation practices within commercial organisations. In the context which has dominated since the mid-1970s, it is as if the establishment of publicly regulated negotiation procedures came too late and has not yet been replaced by a viable alternative on the ground. In the 1980s, under the Socialist government, the focus was on rehabilitating the economy – a direct outcome of the prevailing economic situation at the time.

Today the emphasis is on rehabilitating a sense of society both at the level of the company and at a more general level.

Since their accession to power, the 'right-wing' parties have taken a number of initiatives relating to social relations within the firm. The principle of a calendar of meetings between the Prime Minister and the directors of the main professional organisations in France has been established. Fresh initiatives have been taken to reduce working hours, a topic close to the hearts of union representatives. New financial and budgetary measures have been taken to defend salaried employment in the face of severe economic pressures. These measures are lending a new spirit to the processes and procedures of negotiation. Although their outcome is impossible to assess, it is certain that the measures focus attention on a question which is fundamental to the character of the French social system, that of the balance between political power and relationships which are contractually defined, between the state and the autonomy of professional negotiation.

SELECTED TEXTS

Adam, G. (1983)
Boyer, R. (ed.) (1986)
Groux, G. and Mouriaux, R. (1992)

See Bibliography

USEFUL ADDRESSES

Direction des Relations du Travail, Ministère du travail, de l'Emploi et de la Formation Professionnelle
1 place Fontenoy
F-75007
Paris
Tel. (1) 40.56.60.00.

Conseil National du Patronat Français (CNPF)
31 avenue Pierre 1er de Serbie
75016 Paris
Tel. (1) 40.69.44.44.

Association Nationale des Directeurs et Cadres de la Fonction Personnel (ANDCP)
29 avenue Hoche
75008 Paris
Tel. (1) 45.63.55.29.

Confédération Française et Démocratique du Travail (CFDT)
4 boulevard de la Villette
75019 Paris
Tel. (1) 42.03.80.00.

Confédération Générale du Travail (CGT)
263 rue de Paris
93100 Montreuil
Tel. 48.51.80.00.

Institut d'Etudes Entreprise et Personnel
69 quai de Grenelle
75015 Paris
Tel. (1) 43.92.13.00.

Institut de l'Entreprise
6 rue Clément Marot
75008 Paris
Tel. (1) 47.23.63.28.

Institut de Recherches Economiques et Sociales
16 boulevard du Mont d'Est
93192 Noisy-le-Grand Cedex
Tel. 48.15.18.90.

Institut Syndical d'Etudes et de Recherches Economique et Sociales (ISERES-CGT)
263 rue de Paris
93100 Montreuil Cedex
Tel. 48.51.80.00.

Institut Syndical Européen (Confédération Européenne des Syndicats – CES)
Boulevard Emile Jacqmain 155
1210 Brussels.

Liaisons Sociales
5 avenue de la République
75001 Paris Cedex 11
Tel. 48.05.91.05.

9 The development of the human resource function and the inadequacies of discourse

Bernard Galambaud

During the period of recession and intermittent recovery experienced since 1991, French companies have undergone a number of significant changes, as much in their functioning as in the management of their human resources. The most noteworthy of these have been the decentralisation of management and the increasing instability of employment. The expectations of managers and employees towards the executives responsible for human resource management have irreversibly altered. It is no longer the priority of company executives to create a social dynamic which enhances the extent of employees' participation in the life of the organisation. Rather, under pressures induced by the need to survive, management has found itself in the position of demanding productivity gains of personnel while, at the same time, cutting back on the number of staff. Many companies are achieving the same levels of output as ten years ago but with only half the number of employees.

On the employees' side, however, there has been no slackening in the pressures exerted on human resource managers to respect principles of justice and equity while ensuring the best possible conditions under the law for staff development and pay. Under the economic circumstances prevalent in France, as elsewhere in West Europe, it is hardly surprising that the two sets of expectations are not easily reconciled. The human resource function is a long way from having the power and authority to respond simultaneously to the demands of the workforce and of its own executive. It too has entered a state of crisis. To a greater extent than ever before, the challenge which it has to face has exposed the inadequacies and contradictions which had remained concealed during the preceding period of growth. Thus, in revealing the limitations in existing HRM practices and policies, the present economic difficulties have acted as a catalyst not simply within France but within West Europe as a whole.

THE GENERAL CONTEXT

Strategic pretensions and the pressure of reality

In the not so distant past, it was commonplace to make claims in support of HRM's significant role. Bookshops were full of works emphasising the strategic dimension of employment, training and recruitment. In line with the promotional material of universities and business schools, HRM directors never tired of repeating the refrain that 'people are the main wealth of companies'. Such claims underlined the strategic importance of the function, and simply extended a discourse which had developed in the early 1980s. This discourse viewed the greater involvement and mobilisation of employees within organisations – their personal commitment to their aims – as a response to the intensification of global competitiveness.

Fifteen years on, the situation has changed radically. It is hardly consistent to believe that people are the wealth of companies when those same companies are laying people off in droves, when plans to cut back personnel are the norm and when pressures to increase productivity are more or less systematically replacing men by machines. Staff flexibility (or physical mobility), employees' readiness to identify with the quality of the product or service and their acceptance of fixed-term contracts have become the principal factors in HRM and the basis of companies' short-term planning.

Many HRM executives are convinced that, in order to lend authority to their position, they have to serve the operational hierarchy. Senior management is so focused on financial pressures and on short-term profitability that it cannot do other than regard human resources as an adjustable variable. Thus, in French companies, as elsewhere in Europe, the old 'staff and line' view that the HRM executive is merely a function for providing advice, help and support – or an instrument for implementing unpleasant decisions – is undergoing a renaissance.

A role transformed by language

It is a striking feature of many organisations that a social discourse develops autonomously yet only maintains a loose relationship with lived reality. The propagators of such discourses tend to be individuals whose aim is to legitimise or condemn certain practices within the organisation and who are constantly seeking to convince or attract a specific audience. It is less important for the communicator that a discourse of this type be true or false than that it be effective.

The discourse of enterprise is clearly evidenced in all power games within the firm and in all ideological confrontations. The fact that human resource managers have lost the power to act means that they are forced to adopt a dialogue of persuasion. The management of people is thereby transformed into a rhetorical exercise. However, if the social dimension of HRM is accused of being excessively focused on rhetoric, it is also true that the rhetoric itself has become impoverished, or at least conceptually less clear. Even the most frequently used terms are polyvalent in their reference. The word '*poste*' for example can equally well mean the person or persons allocated to a task as a work situation defined by a particular job description. The concept '*qualification*' can refer either to the competence of employees or to their classification according to a collective convention. This lack of definition in the meaning of terms arises partly from the fact that human resource management is still approached from a Tayloristic perspective. New forms of organisational structure are coming into place. Yet the language required to identify, understand and direct these structures has not yet caught up with the rate of change.

The problem of understanding the reality of life within the firm

If HRM discourse has tended to become detached from its object, this is because the function itself finds it difficult to represent the reality of the firm. In many companies, human resource executives are preoccupied by the formal aspects of relationships in the workplace in the sense that their principal task is to manage employees' work contracts which are represented in terms of coefficients, status and terms of agreement. Historically, however, the human resources function has had many 'clients'. There is the state, whose administrative machinery and social services are required to regulate work according to the identified status and salary levels of employees. Then there are the unions who have demanded that the state establish formal rules and procedures which guarantee minimum salary levels so as to ensure a state of justice and equity in the firm. Finally, of course, there are the employees themselves who actually constitute the company's human environment. Thus, human resource funding has always had a solid judicial-administrative tradition which has tended to favour the formal over the substantive at the expense of reflecting the real attitudes of and relationships between employees (see also Chapters 5, 6 and 7).

This detachment from 'reality' means that the HRM function is not in the habit of measuring the results of its actions, for example the consequences of individualising salary increases within organisations. In general terms, it implies that the HRM executive all too easily reduces companies to judicial entities. Such entities tend to overlook part-time employees, the personnel of subcontracting firms and so on. The difficulty which the HRM function has in circumscribing the reality of life in companies leads to a situation where the authority of the function is based on the illusory strength of certain approved social practices – systematised personal evaluation, routine job analyses, the application of software packages to work costing, and so on. Such tendencies all too easily reduce the HRM task to a set of instruments which constitute a range of accessories or formal procedures rather than a social policy.

CHANGING PERSPECTIVES

The cultural relativity of personnel management

It is recognised that the chief determinant of decision-making is the belief in the future success of companies. It is difficult to conceive of a company developing a strategic view of management when its managers only believe in short-term returns. These cultural determinants represent the very nature of the firm. In *Capitalisme contre Capitalisme* (1991), Michel Albert emphasises that two opposing conceptions of the firm coexist in the minds of directors. For one of these (the Anglo-Saxon model) the company is perceived essentially as a legal entity to which employees are merely linked contractually. The logic which pervades in this model is that of the free market in which the mobility of employees and the instability of work are predominant. In the second model, defined by Albert as '*rhénan*' (appertaining to Germany, the Scandinavian countries and, in a different sense, to Japan), the company is seen as a community. In this model, salary follows a more complex logic based on loyalty and a psychology of belonging. It tends to favour functional mobility, internal to the organisation, over external mobility (Albert 1991: 19–20).

French management has always hesitated between these two models. In the early 1980s, the desire to involve employees placed the emphasis on the community dimension. This was the period when directors stated that a company was a 'culture', a community defined by its values, its norms, its plan. However, towards the end of this same decade, French management seemed to opt for an Anglo-Saxon model. Many employees found such drifts in perspective hard to accept. They felt betrayed by public statements about integration and a collective belief in improved performance which then led to downsizing and redundancies.

Encadré 31: The evangelistic mission statement (1987)

The modern company has changed from an organisation based on control to one based on corporate identity. Rules and procedures have given way to confidence, respect and faith in shared values which underpin the attitudes, objectives and choices of each employee.

1 An instinctive drive towards growth should be transformed into a natural desire to promote the company's development and into a collective will to succeed.
2 A belief in self-discipline is a reflection of the essential pressure to remain in profit and to maintain control over risks and costs.
3 A sense of the marketplace derives from the constant need to adapt products, structures and people.
4 Responsibility and decentralisation promote awareness of the value of autonomy.
5 Care for other people is dependent on collective loyalty and a sense of shared commitment to a common mission.

Source: Entreprise et Personnel, Confidential report.

Organisational uncertainty

A company is not only a set of representations, it is also a system for producing goods and services. Commercial organisations have three main functions. First, they must oversee the relationship between the market and the product. This relationship is generally conceptualised by what is known as the 'strategic positioning' of the company. This positioning has major consequences for human resource management. A company which is dependent on goods in a highly competitive market from the point of view of prices is forced to be flexible from the point of view of the volume of its workforce. This positioning leads inevitably to franchising and to instability of employment. On the other hand, a company which is in a marketplace where competitiveness depends on the company's capacity to respond to fine shifts in the nature of demand or on the maintenance of high standards of quality must sustain the loyalty and continuity of its personnel (Silver 1991).

The reality of corporate life in most companies means that it is important to succeed both in adjusting employee levels and maintaining their loyalty in key fields of competence. The present tendency in French firms is for there to be a central regrouping around a core and a range of satellite functions which are more or less distant from this centre (Gadrey and Gadrey 1991). The stable core of the company usually consists of generalists with management backgrounds and high-level specialists. The periphery contains units consisting of employees who have a lesser strategic interest for the company and who can more easily be replaced on the labour market. While mass-producers of consumer goods have tended to turn to part-time workers or employees on fixed-term contracts, it has been essential for companies producing specialist glassware, for example, to keep on the books the experts who maintain the knowledge on which the profession depends

The second role of organisations is to maintain a system of production which can be analysed in terms of structures, forms of coordination and information flows. The third main function is of course the achievement of the act of production itself. The articulation between these two last functions has direct consequences on the content of jobs, the qualification of employees and on the reality of their work. In the traditional company, the worker is to a large extent locked into concrete operations and is excluded from the functioning of the company. More recently, however, a greater or lesser proportion of the workforce has tended to become involved in the management process (Kern and Schumann 1989). Progressively, production systems have evolved from an industrial logic to a services logic which has demanded competencies linked to the ability to create relationships, to communicate, to think strategically and to take advantage of opportunities. However, these competencies are often hard to define in practical terms and are difficult to build into formal training programmes. As Roustang and Perret (1993) point out, the transition from an economic system based on industry to one based on services depends on employees' access to forms of qualification which seek to promote social integration as opposed to more traditional programmes which tend to be functionally focused.

The social system

The organisational sphere of the company is not simply founded on internal coherence. It is also linked to the cultural sphere. As Bernoux (1985) confirms, all organisations reflect a system of values. The social system brings together all the practices relating to human and financial management issues. The system fulfils three functions. The first is the acquisition of human resources. This process can be carried out by recruiting employees but can also be achieved by seeking firms to which work can be franchised or which depend primarily on part-time staff. The second function is integration. All companies demand a minimum of commitment from their personnel without which it is clearly impossible for the organisation to function properly.

Naturally, the goal of integration is achieved in different ways in different companies, typically according either to a short-term or long-term perspective. Some consultation agencies, for example, have a turnover rate of 20–5 per cent since they do not have the capacity to offer long-term career prospects to the numerous young graduates which they attract from the best schools. On the other hand, certain firms still recruit staff whom they wish to retain for twenty or thirty years. However, the duration of employment is not the only difference between the two types of organisation. Location is also an initial factor. The feeling of belonging to a group is central to any process of integration and the objects of loyalty vary.

The third function fulfilled by a company's social system is the search for efficiency. In 'traditional' firms, this goal is relatively underdeveloped since efficiency is essentially the outcome of the production system and the way in which it is organised. In the 'traditional' firm, management requires above all from the social system that it maintain reasonably harmonious relations between members of the workforce. Efficiency is the objective of the organisation itself – of its machinery and its system of production. While this has been true in the past, it has become self-evident in recent years that companies with equal levels of technological and organisational development achieve different levels of performance. Those differences are clearly the result of different human resource management policies and practices, and have placed HRM at the centre of the debate on organisational efficiency.

The breakdown of territorial boundaries

The integration of contingency into the thinking surrounding the human resource function has forced HRM out of its traditional role in order to establish a different basis for collaborating with other functions. We have attempted to show that the three spheres of the company mentioned above – organisational, cultural and social – are interdependent. Any managerial decision affects all three dimensions collectively. The traditional firm is generally perceived by its executives as a mechanism in which each element fills a function. The factory produces, the sales personnel sell, accountants manage finances and HRM staff look after personnel issues. Such is the vision of the company based on a territorial logic, one in which each is responsible for his/her own job and minds his/her own business.

Within this scheme of things, human resource issues are generally dealt with last and do not directly influence technical or production problems. This frame of reasoning is still reflected in the curricula of management schools in which sociology and psychology are inferior in status to subjects such as finance, marketing or accounting. This autonomy in the perception of human problems has meant that the human resources function has largely been excluded from responsibility in the management of organisations, a fact which has caused it to focus instead on the legal and administrative aspects of firms. Such autonomy has contributed to what may be termed the 'vicious circle of professionalism' (Berry and Matheu 1986) according to which, if a group of specialists feels dominated, they seek to emphasise their shared attributes. Thus, gradually, a technical discourse evolves and fosters a spirit of independence which makes its difficult to deal with problems which fall between two stools.

It follows that the HRM function must re-establish contact with the reality of the firm. It must be capable of establishing a foothold in the organisational and cultural spheres. In this respect it must confront the same challenge as has been faced in the management of quality. Initiative within French firms to put an end to territorial logic has been demonstrated most clearly in efforts to develop a satisfactory system for drawing up strategic forecasts of job needs and competency requirements. Clearly, it is impossible for the HRM field to make a contribution to this development if it cannot influence organisational, strategic and technical decisions.

A more managerial function

Management is the link between the choices of executives and the practices of employees which enables policies to be translated into actions. On this basis, human resource management consists in conceiving and directing a series of operational decisions in such a manner as to ensure that they conform to current political orientations. This focus on operational decision-making underlines the fact that, in an organisation which is well managed from a human point of view, the contribution which such decisions make to the company is left neither to chance nor to the good offices of an individual member of the hierarchy. Signs that a company's HRM is inadequate include the unsystematic analysis of performance, the avoidance by those responsible for the task of evaluating the performance of colleagues, the lack of follow-up to such personnel evaluation as does take place and the internal advertising of vacant posts.

The design of a human resource management system inevitably raises the question of its power. Three major types of role can be identified. The first is encountered in heavily bureaucratised organisations. Here, human resource management is close to personnel administration and is defined by a widespread series of rules which prescribe the decisions which should be taken in particular circumstances (e.g. job vacancies). The only latitude in decision-making is in areas which are not covered by these rules. In companies of this type, the HRM function is the guardian of the law according to which it can intervene in the administrative procedures of the hierarchy and, by extension, in those of the organisation as a whole. A model of this kind can be reduced essentially to a form of social regulation.

The second type of role for HRM is encountered in companies where the hierarchy is emphasised to such an extent that personnel are completely subordinated to it. In such organisations, the personnel are answerable more to the owner than to the company. He/she acts as a medium through which all relations between the staff and the company necessarily go. Respect for

---

Encadré 32: An example of mixed site management according to categories of population (*Entreprise et Personnel* 1995)

The company concerned is based on a number of sites. Its personnel is divided into executive staff (managers), technicians, foremen, white-collar and blue-collar workers. With the exception of the blue-collar workers, who are managed on a site-by-site basis, one member of staff, or 'human resource manager', is responsible for the management of each category of staff.

When it comes to arranging individual salary increases, it is the human resource manager who is responsible for the overall salary budget and who makes proposals for individual salary increases based on performance evaluations carried out by the staff member responsible.

The human resource manager meets each evaluator following an evaluation discussion between the employee and the staff member responsible. The classification of job descriptions is carried out by a committee consisting of all the staff members responsible who deal with the full range of files, not only those relating to their 'own' staff.

Procedures such as these give a central role to the human resource manager who is in overall charge of a given 'category' of staff. The decision-making process is thus in line with two major policy decisions taken by senior management – the decentralisation of decision-making so as to allow for greater hierarchical participation and the optimisation of human resource management according to category rather than to site.

hierarchical prerogative is a dogma underpinning the management of such firms. If it wishes to intervene, the human resource function is forced to rely on its capacity to influence others and on the strength of its connections. These inevitably vary according to the people and the circumstances involved. In contexts such as these, it is no longer appropriate to refer to human resource management but rather to a kind of 'adjustment' achieved more or less easily between the HRM department and the various 'operational' agents in the hierarchy. Only the third type mentioned plays an active role in policy-making and in major strategic decisions. The third type of HRM function is developing in companies which have been forced to restructure and which are now obliged to manage their human resources with greater rigour.

We have tried to show, how, in a small number of companies of different types, the human resource function has evolved and how it has attempted to participate more effectively in the running of firms by playing a more 'real' and fully integrated role in its organisation. In order to realise this objective, it has been necessary for the HRM function to mature politically so as to gain a fuller understanding of the nature of internal relationships and of the objectives which they serve.

SELECTED TEXTS

Collectif (1995)
Coriat, B. and Taddei, D. (1993)
Crozier, M. (1963)
Crozier, M. (1989)
D'Iribarne, P. (1989)
Le Boulaire, M. and Freiche, J. (1994)

See Bibliography

USEFUL ADDRESSES

Revue de Gestion des Ressources Humaines
Editions ESKA
27 rue Dunois
75013 Paris
Tel. (1) 44.06.80.42.

Revue Française de Gestion
FNEGE
2 avenue Hoche
75008 Paris
Tel. (1) 44.29.93.64.

Liaisons Sociales
1 avenue Edouard Belin
92856 Rueil-Malmaison
Tel. (1) 41.29.96.96.

Association Nationale des Directeurs et Cadres de la fonction Personnel (ANDCP)
29 avenue Hoche
75008 Paris
Tel. (1) 45.63.55.09.

Institut d'Etudes Entreprise et Personnel
69 Quai de Grenelle
75015 Paris
Tel. (1) 43.92.13.00.

Association Francophone de Gestion des Ressources Humaines (AGRH)
102 rue Saint Charles
75015 Paris

10 Competency, personal autonomy and action within the firm

Patrick Gilbert and Sandra Bellier-Michel

As has been seen in the previous chapters on human resource management, the term 'competency' (*compétence*) emerged in French and 'Anglo-Saxon' management discourse at the end of the 1980s. Until then the term had merited only a short entry in social science dictionaries and management textbooks. The *Dictionnaire Larousse* of 1930, for example, provided a definition which corresponds closely to current usage: 'In the commercial and industrial world, *compétence* is the complete set of knowledge, qualities, capacities and aptitudes which place the individual in a position to discuss, consult and decide on all matters concerning his job.' Since then, the concept has been so closely scrutinised by company directors, human resource management professionals and academics that it has been described as 'a new imperialism' (Courpasson and Livian 1991).

All large firms now pursue policies which seek to develop the 'competencies' of their staff so that the latter can become better equipped to face processes of organisational change while enhancing their productivity and self-fulfilment. These policies became headline news with the enactment of the law of 31 December 1991 which granted employees a legal entitlement to 'skills assessment leave'. Since that time, the skills notion has been taken up, in varying degrees, by all sectors of corporate activity, both public and private. In 1994, the *Agence Nationale pour l'Emploi* completely recast its *Répertoire Opérationnel des Métiers et des Emplois*, a handbook of information for helping the job-seeking public, so as to include in it the skills required for each job. The reasons for the widespread interest in the concept of 'competency' were multiple. It is generally agreed that the adoption of the concept was directly linked to changes in production methods brought about by advances in technology and imposed by the economic crisis. Thus Zarifian (1988) identified the emergence of a new model of labour management, 'management by competency', in which he saw a new set of practices replacing the outdated management techniques of Taylorism. The expression '*logique de compétence*' provided a clear illustration of this change of direction which was formalised by agreements in the steel and automotive industries. Since 1991, the idea of competency has been variously adopted in very different spheres of commercial and industrial activity – the aircraft and plastics industries, banks, public social security bodies, etc.

Not surprisingly, enterprises have responded differently to the challenge of adopting more 'person-centred' management styles. However, when examining current practice, three themes recur. The first is the increasing difficulty of defining jobs according to 'classical' criteria, i.e. as a set of prescribed tasks leading to predetermined outcomes through the use of specific methods. Faced with vague and changing job definitions, it is the person who should in principle become the anchor point of the management process. Yet, for the most part, the structures which would allow this to happen are not yet in place.

The second trend consists, as has already been noted, of the need to create a stronger individual relationship between company and employees, a tendency which may be observed to go hand in hand with the diminishing influence of trade unions. As well as seeking to promote company loyalty through finite measures such as meetings and missions statements, companies increasingly record the development of staff in terms of employees' acquisition of competencies through special courses and varied work experience. The intended outcome is that the individual should take on work which is better suited to his/her personality and aptitudes, should be motivated to show greater initiative and should play a more active role in planning his/her career. A third feature has been that administrators have taken a wider definition of the work situation than in the past, tending to move away from the specific post to a more generalised notion of the job. This was an idea suggested by the *Centre d'Etudes et de Recherches sur les Qualifications* (Mandon 1987), the aim being to increase mobility between posts which may be functionally different, yet which require similar skills and procedures.

FROM RHETORIC TO ACTION?

Although there is general acceptance that traditional line management is becoming progressively outmoded, there is little consensus in France as to which alternative model should dominate. Taking on board the principle of focusing on personal skills calls into question the established foundations of human resource management, even when the initial objective is only a limited one. An operation which sets out initially to evaluate skills inevitably raises the question of how to locate the skills, then how to recognise, define and develop them. This immediately leads on to the related problem of grading and appropriate remuneration. Talk about competency does not necessarily translate into action – except in the field of training where teaching methods have long since prepared the way for an acceptance of the competency concept. In terms of identifying training needs, competency based analysis focuses attention on the gap between the employee's existing skills and those needed for the job. In more practical areas, however, such as career development and job classification, progress made by the competency principle within French firms has been more modest, while the recruitment sector has so far remained virtually untouched.

THE OUTCOME OF FLEXIBLE SYSTEMS: THE EMPLOYEE AS 'ACTOR'

The need for companies to accommodate internal systems of grading and performance evaluation based on competencies has been made more acute by the pressure to promote greater flexibility on the part of individuals. As well as encouraging greater corporate loyalty among personnel working together in teams, it has clearly been important for French firms to continue to exploit the spirit of entrepreneurship vested in individuals who cross functional boundaries and who can act as initiators and decision-makers. In many firms, the individual entrepreneurial energy of the 1980s and the rationale of the *'projet d'entreprise'* have therefore to some extent been combined – through *force majeure* rather than as a result of deliberate policy (see Chapter 9 and, in particular, Encadrés 30 and 31).

Three aspects of the relationship between the organisation and the individual have served to focus attention on the group and on the individual as actor and decision-maker. The first is that of timescale. Companies which have succeeded in reconciling the tension between the group and the individual tend to be those which plan in the medium term. In successful companies of this kind, 'commitment' and 'consensus' go hand in hand. To be an 'actor' in the full sense of the term means having a sense of 'belonging' which goes beyond the scope of the particular post held at a given moment. For companies like these, opportunities are created for the workforce to be flexible and mobile within the framework of a long-term career development plan. The potential for integration in time is linked to that of integration in space. Whether it be at the level of the group or of the individual, the company as a whole becomes the context or terrain in which projects are implemented. The aim of the company should be to promote a sense of 'belonging' which goes beyond the level of the individual department and to create a context in which the individual is empowered to move outside the space of his/her routine job definition. He/she should exist for and within the organisation as a whole.

The third theme which serves to reinforce the link between the individual and the group is that of the individual 'project' which should ideally make a visible contribution to the wider mission of the company. Projects bring together the three strands of the individual, the group and the organisation. By definition, they imply an extension of functional roles both in time and in space. If successful, they should represent the formal acknowledgement of a set of relationships in the workplace by recognising their durability and the place of each within the organisational framework. The three themes just mentioned are mutually reinforcing. Projects can only effectively be initiated and implemented by players who feel confident of their role within an organisation. Conversely, an important consequence of projects is that those who are responsible for them normally seek to remain within the organisation so as to see them through (Michel 1989).

THE ILLUSION OF CHANGE

For a long time, access to mobility was the preserve of potential high flyers in French organisations. It was a means of managing one's career and of gaining experience of key functions which would serve as a basis for future senior responsibilities. Today, mobility has become a means of avoiding redundancy. In order to restructure and modernise while making best use of current personnel, staff are required to move geographically and professionally. It is no longer possible to remain in the same type of job all one's professional life. In practice, the principles of mobility and flexibility encounter huge practical difficulties due in large measure to personal and social loyalties. It has become necessary for staff to incorporate mobility into their career plans and for the HRM function in organisations to reconcile the horizontal and vertical dimension of staff development, that is the concept of functional and geographical change linked to levels of pay. The capacity for an organisation to change depends therefore on employees who are themselves ready to adapt in the manner outlined.

The question then arises as to how to empower staff so that they can themselves create and manage their personal career development (*cf.* Michel and Mallen 1990). Concretely, this means creating a special department in which counsellors are open to discuss employees' futures with them personally, enabling them to enfranchise themselves and take their careers in hand. As has been seen, the evaluation system is the most common means by which companies are able to empower individuals and to enable them to take full advantage of their personal potential. However, all too frequently the margin of negotiation is too narrow to allow the individual's own interests and competencies to be adequately developed. Often, particularly within French firms, the hierarchical constraints of the organisation make it impossible to implement the agreed outcomes of the evaluation, a reality which inevitably devalues the process itself.

The very concept of personal improvement – the emergence within organisations of employees capable of action and initiative – is therefore dependent on a number of factors:

- a centralisation of the HRM function such that the organisation is better able to take account of individual talents and competencies and to accommodate them within a medium-term strategy;
- a movement towards 'flatter' structures in which employees have greater power to control their work situation on a day-to-day basis – this necessarily implies a modification of the hierarchical relations which still exist within the majority of French companies;
- an ability to plan strategically in a manner which allows temporal and spatial 'domains' within the organisation to be more satisfactorily integrated to the benefit of the individual and the organisation as a whole.

The problem in the 1990s – not only in France but elsewhere in Europe too – is that the concept of individual empowerment within organisations which is embodied in the combined notions of initiation, decision-making and project management has in many cases reached employees but has not permeated the structure of companies. This is essentially because, in a climate where the first priority of firms is survival, effective human resource management is represented in terms of short-term staff reduction rather than in terms of medium-term corporate strategies founded on the action of individuals working in teams.

SELECTED TEXTS

Aubret, J., Gilbert, P. and Pigeyre, F. (1993)
Crozier, M. (1989)
Michel, S. and Mallen, M. (1990)

See Bibliography

USEFUL ADDRESSES

(Chapters 7, 8 and 9.)

11 Speculation and prognosis: the outlook for the French business environment

Robert Crawshaw

At a time when so many aspects of the political and economic future of Europe are in the melting pot, it is hazardous to attempt to sum up the state of an individual country with any confidence that the general evaluations of an amateur will stand the test of time. The contributions in this volume have done little more than provide an institutional framework for analysis, a prism which may allow a set of refracted insights into the French business environment but which does not itself represent an overview of the spectrum as a whole. From the various specialist perspectives contained within the book, it is nevertheless possible to identify a series of interim themes or features which characterise French economic culture at the end of the millenium and which perhaps point the way to the future. It is then feasible to consider to what extent they represent strengths, weaknesses, opportunities or threats to the well-being of France and of Europe as a whole.

SOCIAL PROVISION AND THE REDUCTION OF THE NATIONAL DEBT: THE PRESSURE FOR COMPROMISE

The first, overriding theme is that of the political and moral imperative for France and for Europe to strike a balance between a republican tradition of social care which is seen as a prerogative of French citizenship and the economic pressure to reduce national deficits. It hardly needs stating that both these demands, which many see as contradictory, if not irreconcilable, were cornerstones of the Maastricht Treaty of 1991. The urgent desire to minimise the destructive effects of unemployment and to guarantee equal social protection in the workplace was adopted under the EU presidency of French Socialist Jacques Delors as a guiding social principle. Needless to say, it constituted one of the main points of disagreement between the United Kingdom and her European partners. At the same time, the Treaty imposed on EU member states convergence criteria for entry to a single European currency which were all but unattainable by 1999 – not only for France with a 1996 deficit which represented more than 5 per cent of GNP, but for most other European countries as well – including Germany.

It is self-evident that Germany cannot afford to adhere to a policy of European monetary integration on terms which are unacceptable to the German electorate. A weak German mark linked to a rise in inflation would be an intolerably high price to pay for a population which is still reeling from the cost of reunification and which would scarcely be willing to carry the further economic burden of the disparities within the EU as a whole. Equally, however, Germany needs Europe, and France in particular, to lend it legitimacy as the leading European power. France for its part cannot allow the power of the *Bundesbank* to regulate the economic development of the Union without its leading economic advisors playing an active part in the decision-making process. In this way, they can safeguard the state-controlled 'liberalisation' of the French economy and the country's political power in Europe and the world. As in the days of the alliance between Adenauer and de Gaulle in the 1950s and early 1960s, the future of Europe is essentially being directed by a Franco-German axis, with the political and economic agendas of each country being inextricably entwined. As a consequence, the maintenance of high interest rates in Germany which underpins the *franc fort* policy in France limits the French government's capacity to promote growth as a means of combating unemployment.

In many ways France, as the birthplace of human rights in continental Europe and source of the post-renaissance model of the 'mother state', has most clearly encapsulated the tension between the parallel principles of social protection and economic stability. Whatever comfort might have been drawn from Michel Albert's acclaimed 1991 study into the economic benefits of a mixed economy, it was exposed to the full glare of reality when plans to tackle the 200,000 million francs deficit were drawn up in November 1995 by the right-wing Prime Minister, Alain Juppé. In 1994, the French social security system was running a debt of 54,400 million francs. The government proposed to revise the pension rights of state employees and the staff of nationalised industries and to reduce the range of health benefits then available. The measures led to social unrest and mass demonstrations on a scale reminiscent of the 'events' of May 1968, which many commentators saw as a turning point, if not a revolution, in the concept of republicanism. The French state was widely accused of having betrayed the citizens whose rights it had been set up to protect. Senior government officials were seen as safeguarding their own inner spheres of influence within a closed, hierarchically determined system of access. They were accused of condemning more vulnerable public sector employees to harsher conditions of service and cutting back on healthcare and social amenities for the population at large. In the aftermath of the upheavals, neither side could claim outright victory and each was forced to recognise that the other was right. It was impossible to reform the '*Etat Providence*' overnight. However, things could not go on as before. The economic cost of retaining adequate levels of social provision within the rigorous context of the new Europe had to be recognised.

Given the high levels of unemployment, it remains incumbent on the French government to control conditions of recruitment as well as the treatment of employees at the place of work. As the chapters on the legal environment and on human resource management have explained, the judicial structures governing conditions of employment are still a defining characteristic of business culture in France, despite the marked decline in the power of the trade unions to regulate the conditions in which negotiations take place. However much it may be in the interest of a French multinational such as BSN/Danone to merge its centres of production in France and to invest abroad, the legal machinery brought to bear by the unions involved in March 1996, could still prevent the programme of rationalisation from taking place (*Le Nouvel Economiste* 1996). Equally, it is clear that the burden of training will increasingly be the responsibility of the corporate sector itself. Close government controls oblige companies to offer student traineeships and the issue of first contracts to young people is closely regulated so as to minimise the effects of youth unemployment.

It is a great strength of French business culture and of the social fabric in France that it has maintained a structure and tradition of social protection within the firm, however much it may have been under threat in recent times. The potential weakness of the tradition is that, as in Europe as a whole, it places too great a strain on companies at a time when they have to grapple with ever-greater competitive pressure from abroad. The temptation is always present to relocate centres of production in areas of the world where costs are cheaper. The burden of protection then has to be borne in greater measure by purely national enterprises. Yet their smaller profit margins make it harder for them to subscribe to government conditions of employment. Clearly, if France wishes to avoid the progressive degradation in employment conditions experienced, for example, in the UK, the only way out of this conundrum is to promote conditions for growth by reducing taxation and interest rates in expectation of a sustained upturn in the economic cycle.

MAINTAINING THE BALANCE BETWEEN PUBLIC AND PRIVATE OWNERSHIP

Since it is the corporate sector in France which bears the fiscal burden of supporting the social security system, it has clearly been important, as was shown in Chapter 1, for the government to engage in a programme of privatisation which takes the cost of national welfare out of the public domain. The second major theme which holds the key to the future economic well-being of the country is therefore the balance of public and private ownership and the availability of capital for investment. These two factors are clearly linked. As the review of the French financial market makes clear, the growth of French firms has traditionally been hampered by undercapitalisation. Despite its huge expansion, the Paris financial market is still small by comparison with New York, Tokyo, London and Frankfurt. The re-privatisation of the banks which had been nationalised by the Socialists during the 1980s, the autonomy of the major utilities such as water and electricity and the stepped transfer of state-owned enterprises such as Renault, parts of the SNCF and France-Télécom from the public to the private sector do not in themselves represent a solution to the wider economic issues facing France.

The problem attending the privatisation programmes of the 1980s was that they did not represent a real transfer of financial responsibility or of managerial control from the state to the citizen. The main investors in the newly 'privatised' conglomerates were corporations which were themselves owned, at least in part, by the state. The state itself has never relinquished its influence over the investment plans of the major sectors of production. The senior executives of the companies concerned share a common educational background and many have served as civil servants. In one respect, as well as being one of the traditional features of the French business environment, it has often been seen as one of the country's greatest strengths. Major industrial projects have formed part of a plan over which government policy has always been able to have a more or less direct influence. The fact that interdependent and overlapping networks of companies (*noyaux durs*) were directed by a close circle of executives meant that the country would never sacrifice the 'national interest' to the control of multinationals. Even the development of a scheme such as the Eurodisney theme park north of Paris was tied into the national transport infrastructure and the interests of French hotel chains.

From another perspective, however, the state interest in the major private corporations has been and remains a self-limiting factor in French companies' capacity for growth. Pressures for what are known as 'institutional investors' such as banks and insurance agencies to bolster state-owned or recently privatised enterprises have tied down funds which might otherwise have been available to smaller companies. As the notorious example of Bull demonstrated (see Chapter 3), it has led to an incestuous situation in which the managerial weaknesses of organisations in which the state has a controlling interest are protected against the rigours of global competition, to the detriment of the taxpayer and, ultimately, of the economy as a whole. This internal weakness has, however, provided an opportunity for French companies to seek alternative sources of investment through the purchase of companies abroad so as to cross-subsidise development at home. The recent purchase by French firms of certain UK utilities and sections of the British rail network augurs well for the future of the French economy within a European free trade area as do the measures taken by a number of French-owned international groups to maintain France's competitive position within the world.

PROMOTING THE LOCAL AND INTERNATIONAL DEVELOPMENT OF SMEs

A third major factor which will determine the future of the French business environment is the development of small and medium-sized enterprises (see

Duchéneaut 1995 and Silvestre *et al.* 1995). While larger firms have the capacity to protect themselves against undercapitalisation through expansion and mergers with foreign companies, the situation facing small and medium-sized enterprises in France is much more precarious. Despite the unbearable pressure on French *'patrons de PME'* in 1993, the French public perceive SMEs as representing the main hope for the future in terms of local development and a fall in unemployment. An enormous burden of French public expectation for the future therefore rests on a dual imperative, first to develop the entrepreneurial capacity and basic skills of individuals on a regional basis and second to enhance the readiness of young people to remain in local communities rather than add to the pressures on urban structures. At one level, this view corresponds to Alain Madelin's (1995) vision of a renaissance of small businesses servicing basic local needs and thus maintaining the stability of the population, a standpoint strongly supported in the recommendations of the *Commissariat Général du Plan* in its 1992 report (Documentation Française, Décembre 1992).

At another level, the economic future of France as of other West European countries will be determined in part by the capacity of SMEs to take advantage of export opportunities, not only in Central and East Europe but in the growing economies of the Far East, most notably China. In 1993, more than 75 per cent of SMEs in France did not export at all and of those which did, only 7 per cent exported to a level which amounted to more than 30 per cent of their turnover. Not surprisingly, the main barriers to export are a lack of time and money combined with a poor knowledge of foreign languages and overseas markets. Only companies above a certain threshold can afford to employ a member of staff to take responsibility for foreign markets, yet nine out of ten SMEs see international development as essential to their future.

Despite the surge in entrepreneurship in the 1980s in France, it is still possible to detect a prejudice towards small business management among the more highly educated sectors of the French population. Few graduates of the major *Grandes Ecoles de Commerce* see themselves making a career as a *'patron de PME'*, a label which is perhaps still tainted with the connotations of *'petit commerce'*. They prefer instead to work for a major international firm or in a large state-run corporation where they can expect to gain rapid promotion. In order to safeguard the future economic and social development of the country these attitudes will need to change, so that the most highly qualified young people, especially in the area of technological innovation, will feel motivated to translate their knowledge and ideas into durable commercial opportunities.

The problem of succession is another issue which is seen as directly related to France's future economic performance and the reduction of unemployment (Duchéneaut 1995: 493ff.). In 1995 Over 30 per cent of the owners of French *PMEs* were more than fifty years old and it was clearly important to ensure that the transfer of capital and management know-how could take place smoothly. As has been seen in the chapter on the development of the French financial marketplace, the creation of new financial instruments is making it easier for private firms to broaden the base of their capital, and hence of their management structure, without the owners losing control of the company. In addition, the heavy fiscal penalties which were previously associated with transferring ownership of family firms were alleviated by the Prime Minister, Alain Juppé, in August 1995, a clear sign of the importance which the French government attached to the maintenance and development of small business in France. Ways will also need to be found to reform the tax linked to profits and the number of employees in firms (*taxe professionnelle*) which hampers the investment capacity of small companies and is presently one of the main sources of disparity in the levels of prosperity between regions (Caramel 1996: 65).

FRANCE'S REGIONAL INFRASTRUCTURE: A SOURCE OF RESIDUAL STRENGTH

In Chapter 1 and in the book as a whole, another recurring theme has been the tension between centralisation and regional identity. One of the most noteworthy features of France is the residual strength of the country's regional infrastructure. Chambers of commerce, regional business schools and research agencies funded through subscription and state grants provide centres of advice, training and expertise as well as access to international, and particularly European, networks. They also represent sources of venture capital (*capital-risque*). Local civil servants are equally adept at communicating with colleagues in Brussels and Dusseldorf as they are with government authorities in Paris. Frequently aided by support from the European Commission, these structures maintain a stability in the French business environment which it will be vital for the country to preserve. The economies of scale realised in the food and agriculture industries (*l'agro-alimentaire*) through the creation of regional co-operatives has been matched by the regional pooling of resources in research and development and technological innovation which can assist local companies to survive and grow.

At the same time, the disparities between regions remain a residual issue which must be tackled if France is not to exacerbate its social problems. In July 1996, the level of tax levied on firms varied between 2.89 per cent (Neuilly-sur-Seine) and 26.77 per cent (Toulon). The existence of such contrasts, referred to as '*dumping fiscal*' (Caramel 1996: 65), represents a vicious circle which can only reinforce existing differences. Clearly the constraints on the development of companies in less economically prosperous areas need to be relieved through grants and tax provision, particularly in rural communities, so that the depopulation of these areas can be arrested. In this respect, the importance of tourism – as a means of maintaining the stability of regional cultures, by creating a new environment for local business – cannot be overestimated.

CULTURAL HERITAGE AND THE NATURAL ENVIRONMENT

For a country which is physically the largest in Europe (550,000 km^2) and perhaps the most varied from a topographical point of view, it is impossible to ignore the socio-economic significance of the countryside for the future well-being of the nation. Of all the countries in Europe, France is having to undergo the most radical transformation from an agricultural to a mixed industrial and service-based economy. As Crozier (1994: 37) points out, while France was not well placed to take advantage of the first industrial revolution due to regional fragmentation, the lack of raw materials and a shortage of available manpower, it has excellent residual opportunities to survive in the 'post-industrial' age. Yet the stakes involved in failing to manage smoothly the further transition from an agricultural economy and way of life are inordinately high since rural diversity is still such an integral part of the fabric of French society and national identity.

In 1994, agricultural production and forestry accounted for 84 per cent of land use in the country as a whole with only 8 per cent being taken up by residence and other forms of economically productive human activity (*INSEE* 1995–6: 20). However, the number of people employed in jobs related to agriculture in 1990 (the date of the last national census) was less than a third of what it had been in 1962. It seems extremely unlikely that the direction of this fundamental change in the occupation of such an important sector of the working population will alter in the foreseeable future, though its pace may slow down. It is also improbable that the level of support to French farmers under the Common Agricultural Policy will be sustained. This, together with the growing intensity of world competition, will put ever-greater pressure on rural populations and consequently on the stability of the national way of life. While improved transport infrastructure makes it easier for those in full-time employment to live in the country and travel considerable distances to work, the dangers of lasting population movements for those with less secure jobs or no jobs at all have already been alluded to and are serious.

It seems inevitable therefore that tourism will play an increasingly important role, not simply in the management of local economies but in the whole future of the French business environment, linked to the 'green field' location of SMEs and the offices of larger firms. Like Switzerland, and to a much greater extent than physically smaller, more densely populated countries in Europe, France will need to become even more aware of itself as a reflection of the perceptions of others and to take full advantage of the economic opportunity which this implies while not losing touch with the authentic patterns of life in rural communities. Within this type of context, it will be necessary for farming to continue to be protected by the state or by the European Union, though the nature of land use will inevitably change as it becomes more orientated towards leisure activities and as traditional identities ('*patrimoine*') become progressively translated into economic commodities.

These changes are, of course, constantly taking place and the packaging of lifestyles is already having deep-seated effects on the relationships between local inhabitants and on the physical exploitation of the countryside. It can only be hoped that the lessons of the 1960s and 70s will have been learned and that the threat to natural ecologies which was witnessed for example in the Alps will not be repeated. It is a defining characteristic of France that the organisational infrastructure of region, department and *commune* allows for development which supports the economic and cultural needs of local communities while the strength of central government enables projects which are seen to be in the national interest to be ruthlessly pushed through. In a general sense, this is a positive factor in terms of the country's future economic potential. From the perspective of being able to manage the balance between economic development and the protection of local cultural integrity, the outlook for France is as good as for any country in Europe.

CORPORATE ORGANISATION AND MANAGEMENT CULTURE

The tendency towards growth through merger or foreign acquisition inevitably means that in France, as elsewhere in Europe, the cultural conventions which govern attitudes and behaviour within larger companies are modifying national stereotypes. The principles which have classically been seen to govern French organisations – respect for hierarchy, the emphasis on role and external conventions, the assertion of individual freedom within clearly defined boundaries – are having to adapt to accommodate more open-ended and less structured forms of relationship as the level of international and hence intercultural activity increases. International company cultures are increasingly superimposed on national traditions, particularly at the European level, and demand an enhanced ability on the part of managers to cope with and to manage cultural difference.

As Crozier (1989) and other organisational sociologists repeatedly remind us, change is irreversible. The contributors to the chapters on human resource management in France confirm Crozier's belief that, in capitalist societies, corporate organisations are at the forefront of social change and that, correspondingly, the redefinition of relationships in the workplace will need to be matched by more open and less formalised attitudes within French society as a whole. As a paradigm of French social attitudes within large units of production, it seems that d'Iribarne's striking portrait of life in a French firm is already being overtaken by events. Teamworking and management by project on a national and international basis are becoming a feature of many French companies. The boundaries between the traditional hierarchies are becoming blurred as management becomes more a matter of combining different forms of expertise to meet short-term deadlines than of issuing functional directives. It is reasonable to assume that more flexible forms of relationship will become more commonplace as markets become more segmented, communication more sophisticated and production systems more automatised. The need for staff to develop skills which cross functional boundaries is already current in many firms. This is due to a number of factors – the restructuring forced on companies by the global concentration of groups in the major industrial sectors, the growing dependency on external suppliers and the tendency to combine automatisation with customised products.

For the time being, as the chapters on human resource management suggest, the organisation of French firms is in a state of uncomfortable transition with personnel directors attempting to convince managers to implement changes which threaten the organisational structure of their departments if not their own jobs. For the present generation of middle managers who find themselves directly responsible for managing organisational change, the future is as uncertain as the growth prospects of their own companies. Their response, if they can afford it, is either to seek to take a share in their own companies as a means of self-protection or to set up as an independent supplier to their former employer with all the insecurity which that entails. Meantime, far from presiding over the restructuring process and playing an active role in a process of retraining, the human resource management function finds itself marginalised while the real pressure falls on line managers themselves. The latter are having to adapt or make way for a new generation of recruits who have the qualifications which they lack or are unable to develop. However, because of the difficulty for individuals to have expertise in the full range of knowledge and skills required in any given project, priority, even for new recruits, is on cooperation within and between firms in order to achieve integrated goals, a trend which is not peculiar to France but is rather a feature of Europe as a whole (*cf.* Van den Bergh 1993; Calori and de Woot 1994). While the idealised model of a 'European manager' may not represent a clearly identifiable or realistic objective, both these studies show that the fundamental priorities for education and training in preparing the countries of West Europe for a 'post-industrial' future remain the same.

THE FURTHER DEVELOPMENT OF EDUCATION AND TRAINING

Although generally judged to be less successful than Germany in the field of education and training, France is superficially better placed than most European countries to supply human resources appropriately qualified to meet the challenges of the new millenium. Unlike Germany and the UK, France has built up a strong private sector in post-secondary management education. Its *Grandes Ecoles de Commerce*, although very variable in size and reputation, are strongly vocational in orientation, offer widespread opportunities for international study and work experience, and attract highly motivated and good quality students. As instruments of the regional chambers of commerce, the business schools are designed to respond to local, as well as national, needs.

However, the recent problems facing the private sector business schools in France are a direct function of those besetting the wider economy. The dearth of jobs for graduates of higher education and the fall in disposable income of the parents of potential students have reduced the national pool of recruits and are making it increasingly difficult to maintain quality levels within the scope of a single system. The pressures of a shrinking market and the resulting fall in the standards of entry to certain schools are threatening the integrity of the association or *Chapitre des Grandes Ecoles de Commerce* and are forcing the relationship between the private and public sectors of higher education to be re-examined.

A re-examination of the provision of education and training for management in France may not, however, be a bad thing. As has been seen above, one of the problems of the private sector schools is that their culture and curricula reflect the aspirations of their students to obtain high-flying managerial posts in large organisations rather than to work in smaller companies. Moreover, the hierarchy of the schools themselves is so governed by reputation that the students, having worked exhaustively for two years to gain entry to a *grande école*, tend not to take the study process at the schools themselves sufficiently seriously. Having gained entry to the school, their graduation is more or less guaranteed provided that they satisfy minimal legal requirements based on attendance and the submission of assignments. Furthermore, in view of the breadth of competencies required by the new business environment, the curriculum is, if anything, too 'technical' with insufficient attention being given to the development of a broad-based academic foundation. One of the advantages of the current pressures on the system is that the schools are increasingly admitting students after a first university degree (*entrée parallèle*) which allows them to have a broader culture and to take a less 'career-driven' approach to their business studies. Thus the private and public sector systems are becoming progressively interrelated – to the apparent benefit of the former.

Another feature of the French higher education system of training, which may or may not be a strength but which is shared at least by Germany, is that the distinction between universities and technical institutes, *Instituts Universitaires de Technologie* (*IUT*), has been maintained. The existence of these institutions which, unlike universities, are selective at the point of entry, ensures a continuing flow of graduates with a foundation in technology management who should, in theory at least, be equipped to implement the innovations required by the entrepreneurs of the future. Nevertheless, the statistics of the higher education system as a whole, and particularly those for the university sector, paint a gloomy picture. Apart from the excessively high drop-out rate at French universities, some 250,000 graduates leave higher education after four years of study post-*baccalauréat* seeking 100,000 potential posts appropriate to their qualification (Madelin 1995: 166). It is by no means clear that more higher education necessarily means the right form of education for France's citizens and that the endless quest for *diplômes* of an ever-higher academic level is the appropriate response to the country's future social and economic needs. Thus the pressure is once again transferred to further and secondary education. Albert (1991) is not alone in emphasising the urgent need for France to revitalise apprenticeship schemes along German lines based on closer regional partnership between schools, colleges and enterprises (*cf.* Madelin 1995), schemes which should reach pupils currently leaving school at sixteen with little, if any, prospect of employment.

CONCLUSION: DEMOGRAPHY, RIGOUR AND THE POTENTIAL FOR GROWTH

It is not necessary to be an economist or a specialist in demography to be aware of the economic burden which will fall on the present generation of young people in France as in other countries of West Europe in the early years of the new millenium. Among the member states of the EU, only Ireland, where nearly 26 per cent of the population were under 15 in 1993, can claim to be to some extent protected against the medium-term effects of current demographic trends. In the year 2000, it is estimated that one in five French citizens will be over 60. By the year 2020, assuming a stable birth-rate, that figure will have risen to almost one in three. Even given the extent of saving which is characteristic of France, the purchasing power of retired citizens is bound to be lower than that of the younger sectors of the population. It is clearly in the interest of the present generation of parents in employment not only to protect themselves but also to safeguard the future of their children. Assuming that the combination of state and company-funded national insurance will be unable to sustain the present level of provision, it seems inevitable that in future a greater burden will have to be borne by the private citizen, a fact which can only have a negative impact on the average levels of disposable income.

It is clear that, in the context of a difficult present and an uncertain future, rigour and growth do not make easy bedfellows. According to the report of the World Economic Forum of April 1996 (*Le Nouvel Economiste* 1051 June 1996: 29), the average level of public spending in the fifteen member states of the EU represented 54 per cent of GNP against 39 per cent in North America and 27 per cent in the industrialised nations of the Far East (Japan, Korea, Thailand, Malaysia and Taiwan). The report's estimation of countries' potential for growth was based on a number of criteria – the degree of openness of the economy to world trade, the level of public expenditure, the maturity of financial markets, the quality of infrastructure, technological know-how, management and political and judicial institutions and, finally, the flexibility of labour. It placed France twenty-third among the countries of the world, behind Germany (twenty-second) and the UK (fifteenth). Whatever reservations more socially minded analysts may have about the soundness of these parameters or about the reliability of economic forecasting in general, it is clear that, for West Europe, there are no simple answers. Neither France nor Germany, any more than the UK, can afford any longer to ignore the shared problem of their respective national deficits. All three need a stable economic environment in Europe which will facilitate trade and allow for inward investment. This in turn means keeping production costs down to the minimum level which will allow social stability to be maintained pending an upturn in the world economy. In the short term, the French government is therefore confronted with the need to reduce expenditure on social provision and to cut back on infrastructure projects, bearing in mind that the latter provide short-term employment while laying the basis for future growth, thus safeguarding one of France's greatest residual assets.

As long as close relations with Germany are maintained, France's future position in Europe and the world is relatively secure. European Monetary Union is inconceivable without at least those two countries having achieved a satisfactory degree of economic convergence. Together they can dictate the pace of European development, which will give France the breathing space it needs to accommodate the problem of its budget deficit. Meanwhile, in general terms, the outlook for France and for Europe is serious given the high expectations of its population, the marginalisation of a high proportion of its young people and the increasing availability of cheap, mass produced goods on the world market. In the context of enhanced global competition and oligopolistic markets, the growth of micro-enterprises within close local networks (bottom-up entrepreneurship) is a form of development for which France is particularly well suited, provided that the dispersal of the population, the effectiveness of regional infrastructure and the tradition of local government can be maintained. However, these alone will scarcely be enough to see the country – and Europe – through a very difficult period. France's international groups must remain competitive on the world market and the facilitation of French companies' access to private capital must continue. It can only be hoped that sustained improvements in the quality of education and training, the continuing vigilance and realism of governments, individual entrepreneurship and the belief of France's citizens in the future of its institutions and those of the EU will be sufficient to protect the country's culture and standard of living in an uncertain world.

Glossary

This semi-specialised lexicon seeks to provide an English-speaking reader of business and economics with a restricted set of terms which can act as a point of reference both for understanding written French and for written composition.

Many common terms have been excluded, with preference being given to expressions which might seem less familiar to an English speaker. Highly specialised terms which feature in the body of the text, generally in *encadrés*, have not been included in the glossary.

In compiling the list, the text of the manuscript itself was the primary source. This was combined with comprehensive reference to existing dictionaries, in particular the *Dictionnaire de l'anglais économique et commercial*, compiled by Marcheteau *et al.* and published in 1985 by Garnier (Paris) in the *Langues pour tous* collection. I am grateful to the authors of this excellent reference book for their permission to draw on their material.

absorber (v)	to merge or take over (of companies/groups)
acquit (nm)	receipt
acquittement (nm)	settlement, clearing (of debt)
actif (nm)	assets (of statement of accounts)
action (nf)	share (hence *actionnaire*: shareholder)
affaire (nf)	deal (of business)
affecter (v)	to earmark or make over (a sum of money)
affermage (nm)	leasing or letting
afficher (v)	to post or advertise
affréter (v)	to charter
agio (nm)	premium or charge (on financial transactions)
agiotage (nm)	risky speculation; fixing the market
agréer (v)	to accept, approve, agree (commonly used in business correspondence)
agronomie (nf)	agronomy, i.e. the study of rural economics, agricultural science
ajournement (nm)	postponement; adjournment
ajourner (v)	to delay; postpone
alignement (nm)	adjustment, bringing into line
alimentation (nf)	food (as in retail sector or type of outlet/shop)

allègement (nm)	lightening or relief (hence *allègement des impôts*: tax relief)
allocation (nf)	allowance or benefit for unemployment, family entitlement, etc.
aménagement (nm)	planning or land management (hence *aménagement du territoire*: town and country planning); layout (of office or building)
amortissement (nm)	redemption (of loan, debt, etc.); amortisation; depreciation (of the value of goods or the amount of a loan)
ampleur (nf)	size (of a market)
amputer (v)	to curtail, reduce
analyse (nf)	analysis (hence *analyse des données*: data analysis)
ancienneté (nf)	seniority, years of service in an organisation
animation (nf)	co-ordination, organisation
annexe (nf)	appendix, attached document
annonce (nf)	announcement, statement, advertisement
annuler (v)	to cancel, annul
anticipé (adj)	in advance (e.g. of payment)
appareil (nm)	apparatus or structure (e.g. of administration)
appel (nm)	appeal or recourse
appointements (nmpl)	salary
apport (nm)	assets (brought into a business)
approbation (nf)	formal or legal approval (e.g. of accounts)
approvisionnement (nm)	supply (e.g. of stocks)
appui (nm)	support, backing
appuyer (v)	to audit, agree (of account); wipe out, settle (of debt)
arbitrage (nm)	arbitrage (of bank); arbitration (general)
arrérages (nmpl)	arrears
arrêté (nm)	cover note (of insurance); order (of ministry)
arrhes (nmpl)	deposit
assainissement (nm)	reorganisation, reconstruction (e.g. of organisation or financial system)
associé (nm)	partner, associate (of business)
assurance (nf)	insurance
attaché commercial (nm)	sales representative
avance (nf)	advance or loan (hence *avance sur découvert*: overdraft)
aviser (v)	to inform, advise, notify
avoir (nm)	assets, property
bail (nm)	lease
bailleur (nm)	lender or broker (of money: *de fonds*)
balance (nf)	balance (e.g. of trade or payments, etc.)
bénéfice (nm)	profit
biens (nmpl)	goods, assets (e.g. *de consommation*)
biens corporels (nmpl)	tangible assets
bilan (nm)	balance sheet; (*déposer son bilan*: to file for bankruptcy)
blocage (nm)	freezing (of prices)
bon (nm)	certificate, form (hence *bon de commande*: order form; *bon de trésor*: treasury bond)

bonification (nf)	allowance
bordereau (nm)	list or statement; file
bourse (nf)	stock exchange
boursier (nm)	a trader on the stock exchange
brevet (nm)	patent (hence *brevet d'invention*)
cadre (nm)	executive manager (denotes a person having managerial status within a French firm)
Caisse d'Epargne (nf)	national savings bank
capital-risque (nm)	venture capital
caution (nf)	a guarantee or deposit
certificat de dépôt (nm)	warrant (e.g. for stock)
certificats d'investissement (nmpl)	share certificates (e.g. in investment trust)
cessation (nf)	suspension (of business i.e. closure or of payments)
cession (nf)	transfer (e.g. of shares)
chapitre (nm)	chapter or association, e.g. of *Grandes Ecoles de Commerce*
charges (nf)	(fixed) expenses or charges
charte (nf)	charter
chef (nm)	head (e.g. of company or department)
chevaucher (v)	to overlap
chiffre d'affaires (nm)	turnover
clôture (nf)	closure (of books, of an account, of the stock exchange)
Code Civil (nm)	civil law
Code Commercial (nm)	commercial law
Code du Travail (nm)	labour law
collectivité (nf)	group (in the general sense)
combler (v)	to fill (e.g. a deficit)
comité de direction (nm)	the board (of a company)
commander (v)	to order
commanditaire (nmf)	sleeping partner
commandite (nf)	limited partnership (of company)
commissaire aux comptes (nm)	an official (state-approved) auditor
compétence (nf)	ability (general); in a more technical sense competency, i.e. a specific set of skills
composant (nm)	part (of machine or system)
comptant (nm)	cash (of payment)
compte (nm)	account
compte courant (nm)	current account
compte de dépôt (nm)	deposit account
compte d'épargne (nm)	savings account
compte de profits et pertes (nm)	profit and loss account
compte de résultats (nm)	income statement
compte d'exploitation (nm)	trading account
compte rendu (nm)	minutes (of a meeting)
comptes approuvés (nmpl)	certified, approved account
conception (nf)	design (of a product or project)
concession (nf)	franchise
concessionnaire (nm)	the holder of a franchise, dealer
concours (nm)	a competition (e.g. for admission to *grandes écoles*)
concurrence déloyale (nf)	unfair competition (in a legal sense)
congédier (v)	to make redundant ('sack')

conjoncture (nf)	the present state (of the market, of the economy)
connaissement (nm)	bill of lading
Conseil des Prud'hommes (nm)	special regional arbitration board to which unresolved company disputes are referred
Conseil d'Etat	the senior council of state for administrative and legal matters
consigner (v)	to deposit
contester (v)	to dispute (a claim)
contrat à durée déterminée (nm)	fixed-term contract
contremaître (nm)	foreman
contrôle (nm)	a formal inspection (normally financial)
convention (nf)	a formal agreement
convertibles (nmpl)	convertible (stock)
convocation (nf)	the calling (convening) of a meeting
copropriété (nf)	joint ownership
corporel (adj)	tangible (e.g. of goods, property, etc.)
Corps d'Etat (nm)	the senior echelons of the major departments of the French state
cotation (nf)	quotation (normally of share prices on the stock exchange)
cote (nf)	quoted rate of exchange or value (of shares)
cotisation (nf)	subscription
Cour des Comptes (nm)	the senior advisory council which monitors state expenditure in France
courbe (nf)	curve (e.g. of a graph)
cours (nm)	rate (hence *cours de change*: rate of exchange)
courtier (nm)	broker (on the stock exchange)
coûts (nmpl)	costs
créances nfpl.	debts or claims
cursus (nm)	programme of study
cycle de vie (nm)	life-cycle (of product)
débauchage (nm)	laying off, discharge (of employees)
débaucher (v)	to lay off, dismiss, discharge
débiter (v)	to retail
débouché (nm)	market outlet
débours (nm)	outlay, disbursement
décomposition (nf)	breakdown, splitting up (of work); analysis
décompte (nm)	deduction; tally; detailed breakdown
découvert (nm)	deficit; overdraft
dédouanement (nm)	customs clearance
déduction (nf)	deduction; allowance
défaillance (nf)	failure or default (e.g. of repayment on loan)
déficit (nm)	shortfall; deficit
déficitaire (adj)	uneconomical, loss-making
défrayer (v)	to defray (of expenses)
dégrèvement (nm)	relief (hence *dégrèvement fiscal*: tax relief)
délai (nm)	time limit, lead time
délégué (nm)	representative (hence *délégué d'atelier*: shop steward)
démissionner (v)	to resign
dépassement (nm)	overrun
dépense (nf)	expense, expenditure

déplacement (nm)	shift in prices
dépositaire (nm)	trustee
dépôt (nm)	placement (in the sense of registration) (hence *dépôt de brevet*: register or patent; *dépôt de bilan*: bankruptcy)
dépouillement (nm)	analysis (of collected data, e.g. via questionnaire or recording)
détaillant (nm)	retailer
détaxe (nf)	remission of tax obligations, i.e. amount returned as a result of reduced liabilities
détournement (nm)	embezzlement, misappropriation of funds
détourner (v)	to embezzle
devise (nf)	currency
dirigisme (nm)	policy based on central state regulation of economy or the administration of public affairs
dispositif (nm)	system or framework
dossier (nm)	file or brief (i.e. an issue)
dotation (nf)	allocation (financial) or endowment
droit (nm)	law
dû(e) (adj)	due or owing (e.g. of debt)
dynamisme (d'un marché) (nm)	buoyancy
ébaucher (v)	to outline, sketch out
écart (nm)	gap or margin
échantillon (nm)	sample
échantillonner (v)	to sample
échéance (nf)	deadline or date of maturity (of a policy or investment)
échelle (nf)	scale
échelon (nm)	rung or level in terms of status or responsibility
échelonner (v)	to stagger (in the sense of setting out intervals)
échoir (v)	to fall due or mature
économiser (v)	to save
écoulement (nm)	flow or turnover (of goods)
écouler (v)	to sell or dispose of
effectuer (v)	to carry out (a task), make (a payment)
effet (nm)	bill or draft
élasticité (nf)	elasticity (e.g. of demand)
emballage (nm)	packaging
emballer (v)	to pack or wrap up
émetteur (adj)	issuing (as of agency)
émetteur (nm)	sender (of goods, mail, etc.)
émettre (v)	to issue (of shares)
emmagasinage (nm)	storage, warehousing
emprunt (nm)	loan
encaisser (v)	to cash
enchère (nf)	bid (*vente aux enchères*: sale by auction)
encourir (v)	to incur
endosser (v)	to endorse
enquête (nf)	investigation; survey or study
enquêter (v)	to research, carry out a study
enregistrer (v)	to show (of profit); to file on record
entrepôt (nm)	warehouse, depot

entrepreneur (nm)	businessman/woman
entreprise (nf)	a commercial enterprise or company; the quality of entrepreneurship
équilibrer (v)	to balance
escompte (nm)	discount
escompter (v)	to discount
escroc (nm)	swindler or crook
escroquer (v)	to defraud
escroquerie (nf)	swindle, fraud or racket
étalage (nm)	display, shop window
étatisation (nf)	nationalisation or transfer of private agencies to state control
étude (nf)	research study or survey
excédent (nm)	excess or surplus
excédentaire (adj)	excess
excéder (v)	to exceed
exercise (nm)	trading year or summary presentation i.e. financial statement relating to it (as of tax return or official company report)
exploitation (nf)	operation or trading (of company); the trading organisation (i.e. company itself)
fabricant (nm)	manufacturer
fabrication (nf)	manufacture
fabrique (nf)	factory or works (hence *fabriquer* (v): to manufacture)
facture (nf)	bill, invoice (hence *facturer* (v): to bill, invoice)
facultatif (adj)	optional, voluntary
faillite (nf)	failure, bankruptcy
fidéliser (v)	to develop customer loyalty
filiale (nf)	subsidiary
filière (nf)	stream or strand (e.g. in education)
fisc (nm)	Inland Revenue, i.e. the state tax authority in France
fiscalité (nf)	tax system
flux (nm)	flow (of capital)
foncier (adj)	landed (of estate or property)
fonctionnaire (nm)	civil servant
fonds (nmpl)	capital, money
forfait (nm)	flat fee or sum; rate agreed by contract
fourchette (nf)	bracket, margin
frais (nm)	expenditure, charge, cost
franchise (nf)	freedom of exemption (e.g. from tax)
franco (adv)	pre-paid, free of charge at point of delivery (hence *franco à bord*: free on board – FOB)
fusionnement (nm)	merger (hence *fusionner* (v): to merge)
gamme (nf)	series, range
générique (adj)	generic (of products), i.e. sold without brand name
gérance (nf)	management (normally of a small or branch unit)
gérer (v)	to manage
gestion (nf)	management, general administration (more narrowly financial management)
grand livre (nm)	general ledger

grandes écoles nfpl.	specialised and highly selective schools forming a privileged section of the French higher education system
grande surface	supermarket or shopping centre normally developed on the outskirts of towns.
grands magasins (nmpl)	department store – originally developed in Paris in the late nineteenth century
grève (nf)	strike
greviste (nmf)	striker
grossiste (nm)	wholesaler
groupe (nm)	group (of companies)
habiliter (v)	to entitle, authorise
hausse (nf)	rise, increase
hors cote (adj)	over-the-counter, i.e. outside the financial trading market
hors service (adj)	out of order
hors taxe (adj)	before (exclusive of) tax
hypothèque (nf)	mortgage (hence *hypothéquer* (v): to mortgage; *hypothécaire* (adj): mortgage)
immatériel (adj)	intangible (also *incorporel, intangible*)
immobilier (nm)	real estate, property
immobilisation (nf)	fixed capital
impayé (adj/nm)	unpaid; outstanding account
implantation (nf)	installation, location of site (e.g. for company office or centre of production)
implanter (v)	to set up or establish (a centre of operations of a company)
impôt (nm)	tax (hence *imposer* (v): to tax; *imposable* (adj): taxable)
incitation (nf)	incentive
indemnité (nf)	allowance, benefit
indice (nm)	index (of shares or consumer prices)
intéressement (nm)	profit-sharing
intérêt (nm)	interest
intérimaire (adj)	temporary, provisional (of labour or job)
interlocuteur (nm)	speaker or participant
interprofessionnel (adj)	relating to different forms of work
inventaire (nm)	inventory or stock list
Keynésien (adj)	Keynesian (of economic theory)
krach (nm)	crash, collapse (of stock exchange)
label (nm)	trademark
lacune (nf)	gap (in the market)
laissé-pour-compte (nm)	reject, outcast (as of marginalised person)
libre (adj)	free (e.g. of trade, exchange or enterprise)
licenciement (nm)	dismissal (hence *licencier* (v): to dismiss)
linéaire (nm)	shelf (of supermarket)
liquidation (nf)	liquidation, closure, winding up (hence *liquider* (v): to go into liquidation)
liquidité (nf)	liquidity; liquid assets
livraison (nf)	delivery
livrer (v)	to deliver
locaux (nmpl)	premises

main-d'oeuvre (nf)	labour force, manpower
mainmise (nf)	seizure; grasp, understanding, control (of problem or situation)
maîtrise (nf)	mastery; supervisor (of workforce or unit of production in factory, masters level university qualification)
maîtriser (v)	to master
majoration (nf)	increase, rise (in price, taxation, etc.)
majorer (v)	to increase or raise (rate or price, etc.)
majoritaire (adj)	majority (e.g. shareholder)
mandat (nm)	mandate, set of instructions; tenure
mandataire (nm)	authorised agent, trustee
manoeuvre (nf)	manoeuvre or operation; unskilled worker or labourer
manque (nm)	lack or deficiency
manquement (nm)	breach or violation (of discipline or procedure)
manufacturer (v)	to manufacture
manutention (nf)	handling
maquiller (nf)	model (of design or simulation)
marchandage (nm)	bargaining (hence *marchander* (v): to bargain)
marchandise (nf)	commodity (-ies) or goods
marche (nf)	running (i.e. system or organisation)
marge	margin (e.g. of profit or loss)
marge brute d'autofinancement (nf)	cash flow
marque (nf)	brand; make
marquer (v)	to show or record (e.g. a fall or increase in price)
masse (nf)	mass; body or supply (e.g. of money: *masse monitaire*; of pay: *masse salariale*)
matériel (adj)	material, i.e. physical or tangible (e.g. of advantages or damage)
matériel (nm)	material or equipment
matière première (nf)	raw material
menu (adj)	petty, small (of change or expenditure)
mesure (nf)	measure, step, action
mettre (v)	to put, place
mettre à la porte (v)	to sack
mettre au courant (v)	to inform
mettre au point (v)	to develop or perfect
mettre en cause (v)	to call into question, challenge
mettre en oeuvre (v)	to implement, put into effect
mettre en place (v)	to set up (of an institution, activity or organisation)
mettre en vente (v)	to put up for sale
mise (nf)	placing
mise à jour (nf)	updating
mise à la retraite (nf)	retirement
mise à profit (nf)	taking advantage of
mise au point (nf)	perfecting, fine tuning
mise en chantier (nf)	starting work on
mise en page (nf)	layout
mise en valeur (nf)	emphasis, turning to good effect
miser (v)	to bank on, stake, commit oneself to
mobiliser (v)	to mobilise, make available, call up (of resources – mental or physical)

modalité (nf)	means, method
moins-value (nf)	depreciation, fall in value
monétaire (adj)	monetary (of market, unit or system)
monnaie (nf)	money or current; change
monnayable (adj)	negotiable, capable of being exchanged
monnayer (v)	to make money out of, cash in, take advantage of
monopole (nm)	monopoly (hence *monopoliser* (v): to monopolise)
montage (nm)	assembly
montant (nm)	amount, total
moyennant (prep/adv)	against, i.e. in consideration of (a given amount of money, time or commitment), while taking account of
moyenne (adj)	average
mutation (nf)	change, shift (e.g. in circumstances)
mutuelle (nf)	insurance company
navette (nf)	shuttle, i.e. between two places (hence *faire la navette*)
négoce (nm)	business, trade, trading (hence *négocier* (v): to trade)
négociable (adj)	negotiable, transferable
négociation (nf)	negotiation, bargaining, transaction
net (adj)	net (of profit, tax or proceeds)
note (nf)	bill or invoice; note (e.g. of expenses) or memorandum
noyau (nm)	nucleus; core (of inner integrated group of French companies or groups: *noyaux durs*)
nuisance(s) (nf)	harmful effect(s)
nuisible (adj)	detrimental, harmful, prejudicial
objectif (nm)	objective, aim, goal
objet (nm)	purpose, subject (e.g. of document, initiative, etc.)
obligation (nf)	legal agreement or bond
occasion (nf)	opportunity, chance
occasionnel (adj)	occasional (i.e. counting on, dependent on circumstances); casual (of type of work)
occupation (nf)	occupancy or use of land or property (hence *plan d'occupation des sols*: zoning laws governing approved land use)
office (nm)	function, duty, job
officiel (adj)	official, formal
officieux (adj)	semi-official, informed; officious, interfering
offre (nf)	offer or bid (hence *offre publique d'achat* – *OPA*: takeover bid)
oligopole (nm)	oligopoly (i.e. a saturated market in which any new product must by definition replace or displace existing products)
optimisation (nf)	optimisation, maximisation
ordonnance (nf)	order, regulation (legal); ordinance, decree (political)
ordonnancement (nm)	scheduling (e.g. of debt repayment hence *ordonnancer* (v): to schedule)
ordre (nm)	order
ordre de grandeur (nm)	scale or scope

ordre du jour (nm)	agenda
ordre permanent (nm)	standing order (bank)
organigramme (nm)	organisation chart, flowchart
orientation (nf)	direction, flows, trend
ouvrable (adj)	working (i.e. when work is normally undertaken hence *jour ouvrable*, working day)
ouvrier (nm)	worker (hence *ouvrier spécialisé – OS*: unskilled, assembly line worker)
pacotille (nf)	shoddy goods, junk
paiement (nm)	payment
paiement à la livraison (nm)	payment on delivery
paiement à tempérament (nm)	payment by instalments
paiement au comptant (nm)	payment in cash
paiement en nature (nm)	payment in kind
panne (nf)	breakdown (e.g. of plans or negotiations) (hence *tomber en panne*)
panneau (nm)	board, boarding
parc (nm)	range, number of products within a specific market sector (hence *le parc automobile*)
paritaire (adj)	joint, i.e. shared equally
parquet (nm)	the floor (of stock exchange); the court or office of the public prosecutor (*procureur général*)
parrain (nm)	supporter, backer
parrainage (nm)	sponsoring, sponsorship (hence *parrainer* (v): to sponsor)
part (nf)	share, portion (hence *part de marché*: market share)
participation (nf)	share(s); joint venture
partie (nf)	party (of law) (hence *partie civile*: plaintiff)
passage (nm)	passage or passing (of document or information)
passation (nf)	drawing up or official signing (of act or agreement)
passer (v)	to conclude, enter into (of contract); place (of order); to run (of article, programme or advertisement)
passif (nm)	liabilities
patente (nf)	licence
patron (nm)	boss, tycoon, owner of company; 'employers'
patronage (nm)	sponsorship, patronage
pécuniaire (adj)	pecuniary, financial
pension (nf)	annuity
perception (nf)	collection (e.g. of tax, rent, payment due)
percevoir (v)	to collect or levy
périmé (adj)	out of date
personnel (nm)	personnel, staff, employees, labour force
petite(s) et moyenne(s) entreprise(s) (PME) (nf)	small and medium-sized enterprise(s) (SME), i.e. companies having less than 150 and 500 employees respectively
pièce (nf)	piece
pièce de monnaie (nf)	coin
pièce de rechange (nf)	replacement part (of machine)
pige (nf)	piecework, freelancing
pigiste (nm)	freelance worker (e.g. journalist)
piquet de grève (nm)	strike picket

place (nf)	(in a specialised sense) trading place (hence *place boursière*: stock exchange)
placement (nm)	investment
placer (v)	to invest
plafond (nm)	ceiling, limit
plafonner (v)	to reach an upper threshold
plainte (nf)	complaint
plan (nm)	plan or general strategy (hence *Le Plan*: the strategic forecast for the French economy)
plancher (nf)	floor, lowest price
planification (nf)	planning
plus-value (nf)	increase in value, appreciation
police (nf)	policy (of insurance, etc.)
politique (nf)	policy (of political party towards employment, economy in general, etc.)
ponctuel (adj)	precise
pondération (nf)	weighting (e.g. attached to a given factor or statistics)
port (nm)	carriage, transport
porte-parole (nm)	spokesperson
porter sur (v)	to bear on, centre on (of issue)
position (nf)	position (e.g. of finance or bank account or product in marketplace)
positionnement (nm)	positioning (of produce in market sector)
poste (nm)	post or position (e.g. of person in organisation); job
pourvoir (v)	to provide, supply
pouvoir d'achat (nm)	purchasing power
pré-retraite (nf)	early retirement
prédire (v)	to forecast, predict
prélèvement (nm)	deduction (e.g. of taxes)
prendre (v)	to take
prendre effet (v)	to come into force
prendre en change (v)	to take responsibility for
préséance (nf)	precedence, priority
président (nm)	chairman and managing director (hence *président directeur général* – *PDG*: chief executive officer – CEO)
prévision (nf)	forecast
prévoir (v)	to foresee, expect, forecast
prévoyance (nf)	foresight (hence *Caisse de Prévoyance*: national insurance scheme)
prime (nf)	bonus; premium
prix (nm)	price
prix d'achat (nm)	purchase price
prix de vente (nm)	selling price
procuration (nf)	proxy
procureur (nm)	legal prosecutor
produit (nm)	product (hence *produit national brut* – *PNB*: gross national product – GNP)
profil (nm)	profile or job description
profit (nm)	profit (hence *mettre à profit*: to take best advantage of)
promotion (nf)	promotion (of person or product)

propre (adj)	own, specific (hence *fonds propres*: equity)
protocole (nm)	memorandum or formal minute (e.g. of agreement)
provision (nf)	cover or provision (hence *cheque sans provision*: bouncing cheque)
publicité (nf)	advertising
publicité mensongère (nf)	misleading advertising
publicité produit (nf)	product/brand advertising
quittance (nf)	discharge, receipt (hence *quittancer* (v): to receipt)
quitte (adj)	to be discharged (from a debt)
rabais (nm)	reduction, discount (hence *rabaisser* (v): to reduce *au rabais* (adj): reduced)
rabattre (v)	to reduce, knock down (of price)
rachat (nm)	to buy back; buy out; redeem (of loan)
rapporteur (nm)	secretary or official reporter (of political commission)
rayon (nm)	department or shelf in a department store
réaliser (v)	to carry out (of project); to realise (of financial investment)
recensement (nm)	census (of population); inventory (of goods or merchandise)
recenser (v)	to take a census, carry out an inventory
recette(s) (nf)	return(s), receipt(s) (of money)
réclamation (nf)	claim, complaint (hence *réclamer* (v): to complain)
réclame (nf)	advertisement
reconductible (adj)	renewable
reconduire (v)	to renew
reconvertir (v)	to retrain
recourir à (v)	to have recourse to
recours (nm)	recourse, resort (hence *avoir recours à*)
recouvrement (nm)	recovery, collection (of debt)
redevable (adj)	indebted, liable
redevance (nf)	rent, rental, royalty
redressement (nm)	rectification (of debt); recovery, upturn (of the economy)
redresser (v)	to rectify
redresser (se) (v)	to recover, improve (of economy)
référer (se) à (v)	to refer, report to (e.g. of manager)
régie (nf)	state control, state ownership (of company or group)
réinstaller (v)	to relocate
relance (nf)	revival, recovery, reflation (of economy)
relevé (nm)	statement, return (e.g. of bank)
relèvement (nm)	raising, increase, revival (of wages, of economy)
remaniement (nm)	restructuring, reshuffle (of personnel)
remboursement (nm)	repayment, refund, redemption (e.g. of debt)
remercier (v)	to thank; to dismiss (of staff)
remise (nf)	postponement; reduction (in price)
rémunération (nf)	payment, salary
renchérir (v)	to raise, increase (of price)
rendement (nm)	output
renflouer (v)	to assist (bail out, refloat) a company in difficulty
rentabiliser (v)	to make profitable

rentabilité (nf)	profitability, return (e.g. on capital)
rentable (adj)	profitable
rentrée (nf)	return
renvoi (nm)	postponement; dismissal (of staff)
renvoyer (v)	to postpone, put off; to dismiss, discharge (of staff)
réparation (nf)	redress (of legal situation)
répartir (v)	to distribute, divide, share with (of tasks, responsibilities)
répartition (nf)	distribution, allotment
répercuter (se) (v)	to pass on to (i.e. impact by ricochet e.g. of prices passed on to consumers)
répertorier (v)	to index
replier sur (se) (v)	to fall back on
report (nm)	carrying over, deferment (hence *reporter*: to defer, postpone)
reprise (nf)	recovery, revival, upturn (of economic activity)
résilier (v)	to cancel, terminate, annul (of contract)
résorber (v)	to absorb (e.g. of deficit)
ressortissant (nm)	national, citizen (of a country, state)
rétablissement (nm)	recovery, restoration (of fortunes or state or person)
retombée (nf)	consequence, aftermath (of event, economic or other measure, etc.)
retrait (nm)	withdrawal (of funds)
retraite (nf)	retirement, superannuation
revendication (nf)	claim, demand (hence *revendiquer* (v): to claim)
revenu (nm)	income, revenue
revers (nm)	setback
revient (nm)	basic or initial cost (hence *prix de revient*: cost price)
revirement (nm)	reversal, turnabout in circumstances
révoquer (v)	to cancel or rescind
rigueur (nf)	austerity, restraint (typically in controlling money supply in economic policy)
ristourne (nf)	rebate, allowance
saisie (nf)	seizure (of property, assets); access and analysis (of data normally on computer hence *saisie des données*)
salarié (nm)	employee
saturé (adj)	saturated (of market)
schématiser (v)	to outline
scolarité (nf)	tuition
séance (nf)	session, meeting
secteur (nm)	sector, industry
segmentation (nf)	segmentation; sampling (of market)
sensible (adj)	substantial, marked, significant (e.g. of improvement or increase/decrease)
serie (nf)	set or batch
service (nm)	department; service
sidérurgie (nf)	iron and steel industry
siège (nm)	head office
sigle (nm)	acronym
signalétique (adj)	descriptive (of note, memorandum or report)

sinistre (nm)	accident, damage (of person, property, etc.)
social (adj)	relating to the human administration of organisations (hence *le bilan social*: the state of the company/country as seen from a human perspective)
société (nf)	company or enterprise
solde (nm)	balance (of funds or assets)
solder (v)	to settle or sell off (normally at a discount)
solder (se) (v)	to end up (hence *se solder par une réussite*: to end on a successful note)
solliciter (v)	to ask for
solvabilité (nf)	solvency, creditworthiness
sondage (nm)	poll, survey
sortie (nf)	outgoings, disbursement
soumission (nf)	tender, bid
soutenir (v)	to support, back (financially or morally)
stabiliser (v)	to stabilise, control, level off (of rate of exchange or price of stock)
stock(s) (nm)	stock, inventory of goods
subvention (nf)	subsidy, grant (e.g. from government)
succéder (v)	to succeed, take over (e.g. of staff)
succursale (nf)	branch, sub-office
suivi (nm)	monitoring, control (e.g. of orders, administrative project, etc.)
surcharge (nf)	overload; excess (of tax); overrun (of computer)
surcoût (nm)	additional cost
surcroît (nm)	increase, addition (e.g. of workload)
sureffectif(s) (nm)	overmanning (i.e. excess personnel)
surenchère (nf)	higher bid or overbid (i.e. in excess of real or apparent value of goods or stock)
sûreté (nf)	safety, security, surety (e.g. for debt)
surmenage (nm)	overwork
surpeuplé (adj)	overpopulated
surseoir (v)	to postpone, defer, put off
sursis (nm)	delay, deferment, reprieve
suspendre (v)	discontinue or interrupt (e.g. a project)
(en) suspens (adj)	in abeyance
syndical (adj)	appertaining to a union or similar organisation
syndicalisme (nm)	(trade) unionism
syndicat (nm)	(trade) union
syndiquer (v)	to unionise (of organisation)
tableau (nm)	chart, table (of an arrangement, presentation or document)
taille (nf)	size
tarif (nm)	rate, price, change (e.g. for a service)
tassement (nm)	levelling out
taux (nm)	rate, ratio
taxe (nf)	tax or duty (hence *taxe à la valeur ajoutée – TVA*: value added tax)
temporiser (v)	to play for time; to temper or calm down (of situation)
terme (nm)	end, limit, conclusion (hence *mener à terme*: to complete; *marché à terme*: futures market)

terrain (nm)	land; site (of building)
tirer (v)	to draw (of cheque, profit, etc.)
tissu (nm)	fabric (of society, of cities)
trafic (nm)	traffic, i.e. transport of goods (connotations of illegality)
traite (nf)	bill of exchange, draft
traitement (nm)	salary
traiter (v)	to transact (of monies), deal with (jobs in hand)
tranche (nf)	section, group, block
troc (nm)	barter, exchange in kind
troquer (v)	to barter, exchange
truquer (v)	to fake, manipulate, rig
ultérieur (adj)	subsequent
urbanisme (nm)	(town) planning
usage (nm)	custom, practice (e.g. within organisation)
usiner (v)	to machine
vacation (nf)	service paid on piecework basis (normally hourly)
valider (v)	to validate, authenticate
valoriser (v)	to lend value to; to rate highly
versement (nm)	payment, settlement, remittance
virement (nm)	transfer (of funds)
visée(s) (nf)	goal, vision for the future
viser (v)	to aim at
voie (nf)	way, means, channel, measure, process
vrac (nm)	bulk (hence *en vrac*: in bulk)
warrant (nm)	warrant (esp. of goods stored in warehouse)
zonage (nm)	urban planning or zoning
zone (nf)	zone, area

ABBREVIATIONS AND ACRONYMS

AFB	Association Française des Banques
AFEC	Association Française des Etablissements de Crédit
AFSB	Association Française des Sociétés de Bourse
AGTT	Accord Général des Taxes et des Tarifs
AGRH	Association francophone de Gestion des Ressources Humaines
ANACT	Agence Nationale des Conditions de Travail
ANDCP	Association Nationale des Directeurs et Cadres de la fonction Personnel
ANVAR	Agence Nationale pour la Valorisation de la Recherche
BEP	Brevet d'Etudes Professionnelles
BEPC	Brevet d'Etudes du Premier Cycle
BISF	bons des institutions et sociétés financières
BNP	Banque Nationale Populaire
BON	billets à ordre négociables
BT	billets de trésorerie
BTN	bons de trésor négociables
CAF	coût, assurance, fret
CBV	Conseil des Bourses de Valeurs
CCB	Commission de Contrôle des Banques
CCF	Crédit Commercial de France
CCI	chambre de commerce et d'industrie
CD	certificats de dépôt

CDC	Caisse des Dépôts et Consignations
CDD	contrats à durée déterminée
CDIFP	Centre pour le Développement de l'Information sur la Formation Permanente
CEA	Commissariat a l'Energie Atomique
CEC	Comité des Etablissements de Crédit
CEO	Compagnie des Eaux et de l'Ozone
CEP	Certificat d'Etudes Primaires
CEREQ	Centre d'Etudes de Recherches sur les Qualifications
CESP	Centre d'Etudes sur les Supports de Publicité
CFCE	Centre Français du Commerce Extérieur
CFDT	Confédération Française et Démocratique du Travail
CFTC	Confédération Française des Travailleurs Chrétiens
CGC	Confédération Générale des Cadres
CGE	Compagnie Générale d'Electricité
CGT	Confédération Générale du Travail
CIC	Crédit Industriel Commercial
CL	Crédit Lyonnais
CNAM	Conservatoire National des Arts et Métiers
CNCC	Commission Nationale des Commissaires aux Comptes
CNPF	Conseil National du Patronat Français
CNR	Conseil National de la Résistance
CNRS	Centre National de la Recherche Scientifique
COB	Commission des Opérations de Bourse
CRB	Comité de la Réglementation Bancaire
CREDOC	Centre de Recherche, d'Etudes et de Documentation sur les Conditions de vie
CVT	correspondants en valeur du trésor
DIRD	dépense intérieure de recherche-développement
DNRD	dépense nationale de recherche-développement
EDF	Electricité de France
ENA	Ecole Nationale d'Administration
ENS	Ecole Normale Supérieure
ESCP	Ecole Supérieure de Commerce de Paris
ESSEC	Ecole Supérieure des Sciences Economiques et Commerciales
FCC	fonds de crédit commercial
FCP	fonds commun de placement
FCPE	fonds commun de placement d'entreprise
FCPR	fonds communs de placement à risque
FIFO	*first in first out*
FIMAT	fonds commun d'intervention sur les marchés à terme
FIST	France Innovation Scientifique et Transfert
GDF	Gas de France
HEC	Ecole des Hautes Etudes Commerciales
INPI	Institut National de la Protection Industrielle
INSEE	Institut National de la Statistique et des Etudes Economiques
IRE	Institut de Recherche en Entreprise
LEST	Laboratoire d'Economie et de Sociologie du Travail
LIFO	*last in first out*
MATIF	marché à terme international de France
MONEP	marché des options négociables de Paris
MRES	Ministère de la Recherche et de l'Enseignement Supérieur

NASDAQ	*National Association of Security Dealers Automated Quotation*
OBSA	obligations avec bons de souscription en actions
OECCA	Ordre des Experts-Comptables et des Comptables Agréés
ONISEP	Office National d'Information sur les Enseignements et les Professions
OPCVM	organismes de placement collectif de valeurs mobilières
OPM	opérateurs principaux du marché
PIBOR	*Paris Interbank Offered Rate*
PME	petites et moyennes entreprises
PMI	petites et moyennes industries
PNB	produit national brut
PTT	Poste, Télégraphe et Télécommunications
RATP	Régie Autonome des Transports Parisiens
SA	société anonyme
SARL	société anonyme à responsabilité limitée
SBF	Société des Bourses Françaises
SCA	société en commandite par actions
SCS	société en commandite simple
SEAQ	*Stock Exchange Automated Quotations*
SG	Société Générale
SICAV	société d'investissement à capital variable
SME	Système Monétaire Européen
SMIC	salaire minimum interprofessionnel de croissance
SNC	société en nom collectif
SNCF	Société Nationale des Chemins de Fer
SOFRES	Société Française d'Enquête par Sondage
SVT	spécialistes en valeurs du trésor
TAM	taux annuel monétaire
TCN	taux de crédit national
TGV	train de grande vitesse
TMM	taux moyen mensuel
TMO	taux moyen des obligations
UET	unité elémentaire de travail

Bibliography

Adam, G. (1983) *Le Pouvoir Syndical*, Paris: Dunod

Albert, M. (1991) *Capitalisme contre Capitalisme*, Paris: du Seuil

Alexander, D. (1993) 'A European true and fair view', *The European Accounting Review*, Vol 2; No. 1, May: 59–80

Alexander, D. and Archer, G.S.H. (eds) (1992) *The European Accounting Guide*, London: Academic Press

Amadieu, J-F. (1992) 'Changements concertés de l'organisation du travail', in J. Rojot and P. Tergeist (eds) *Nouvelles orientations dans l'organisation du travail: la dynamique des relations professionnelles*, Paris: OECD pp. 67–97

Aoki, M. (1988) *Information, incentives and bargaining in the Japanese economy*, New York: Cambridge University Press

Ardagh, J. (1973) *The New France*, London: Penguin

Ariès, P. (1973) *L'Enfant et la vie familiale sous l'ancien régime*, Paris: du Seuil

Arnould, D. (1995) *Les Marchés de Capitaux en France*, Paris: Armand Colin

Attali, J. (1994) *Europes*, Paris: Fayard

Aubret, J. and Gilbert, P. (1994) *Reconnaissance et validation des acquis*, Paris: PUF

Aubret, J., Gilbert, P. and Pigeyre, F. (1993) *Savoir et pouvoir: les compétences en question*, Paris: PUF

Badot, O. and Cova, B. (1992) 'Des marketing en mouvement, vers un néo-marketing', *Revue Française de Marketing*, No. 136. Vol. 1: 5–24

Banque de France (1995) *Banque de France, la monnaie et les systèmes de paiement en 1994*, Paris: Banque de France

Barsoux, J.-L. and Lawrence, P. (1990) *Management in France*, London: Cassell

Barthes, R. (1957) *Mythologies*, Paris: du Seuil

Baudrillard, J. (1968) *La société de consommation*, Paris: Gallimard

Bauer, M. and Bertin-Mourot, B. (1993) 'Quelle alternative à la tyrannie du diplôme initial?', *Education Permanente* No. 114/1: 43–49

Bensahel, L., Fontanel, J. and Vigezzi, M. (1992) *L'Economie contemporaine de la France*, Paris: PUF

Bernoux, P. (1985) *La Sociologie des Organisations*, Paris: du Seuil

Berry, M. and Matheu, M. (1986) 'Pratique et morale de l'irrévérence', *Revue Française de Gestion*, No. 58: 40–42

Bertrel, J.-P. (1996) *Droit de l'entreprise*, Paris: Lamy

Bertrel, J.-P., de Couliboeuf, P. and Saint-Alary, B. (1992) *Relations Entreprises-Banques*, Paris: Editions Francis Lefebvre

Birnbaum, P. (1993) *La France aux Français*, Paris: du Seuil

Blake, J. & Amat, O. (1993) *European Accounting*, London: Pitman

Bollinger, D. and Hofstede, G. (1987) *Les différences culturelles. Comment chaque pays gère-t-il les hommes?* Paris: Editions d'Organisation

Boss, J.-F. (1993) 'L'evolution du secteur des études', *Revue Française de Marketing*, No. 142–3/Vol. 2–3: 15–30

Bourdieu, P. (1979) *La distinction, critique sociale du jugement*, Paris: Editions de Minuit
—— (1989) *La Noblesse d'Etat*, Paris: Editions de Minuit

Boyer, R. (ed.) (1986) *La Flexibilité du Travail en Europe*, Paris: La Découverte

Bremond, J. and Bremond, G. (1990) *L'Economie Française*, Paris: Editions de Minuit

Calori, R. and de Woot, P. (eds) (1994) *A European Management Model: beyond diversity*, New York: Prentice Hall

Cannac, Y. (1992) *Pour un Etat Moderne*, Paris: Plon

Caramel, L. (1996) 'Taxe professionnel: un jour peut-être' in *Le Nouvel Economiste* No. 1055, July, p. 65

Cayrol, R. (1994) *Le Grand Malentendu: les Français et la Politique*, Paris: du Seuil

Closets, F. (1984) *Tous ensemble*, Paris: du Seuil

Collectif (1995) *Les Mondes Sociaux de l'Entreprise*, Paris: Desclée de Brower

Collins, L. (1992) 'Audit implication in early warning systems – the French experience', *The European Accounting Review*, Vol. 1, No. 2, December: 447–452

Commissariat Général du Plan (1992) *France: le choix de la performance globale*

Commission des Opérations de Bourse (COB) *Rapports annuels*

Conseil National de Crédit (CNC) *Rapports annuels*

Conseil National de la Comptabilité (1993) *Tenue des comptabilités sur ordinateurs*, Paris: Juris Classeurs

Cooper, P. (1991) 'Internationalisation des études qualitatives', *Revue Française de Marketing* No. 134/4: 69–80

Coriat, B. and Taddei, D. (1993) *Made in France*, Paris: Livre de Poche

Courpasson, D. and Livian, Y.-F. (1991) 'Le développement récent de la notion de compétence: glissement sémantique ou idéologie?', *Gestion des Ressources Humaines* No. 1, October: 3–10

Crawshaw, R. H. (1995) *The European Dimension in Management Education*, Luxembourg: Publication Office of the European Communities, DG XXII Studies No. 8

CREDOC (1993) 'Où en est la consommation aujourd'hui? Une enquête sur la consommateur des années '90', *Cahiers de Recherche*, April

CREDOC (1995) *L'Etat de la France*, Paris: La Découverte

Crozier, M. (1963) *Le Phénomène Bureaucratique*, Paris: du Seuil

Crozier, M. (1989) *L'Entreprise à l'Ecoute*, Paris. Interéditions

Crozier, M. and Friedberg, E. (1977) *L'Acteur et le Système*, Paris: du Seuil

Dahrendorf, R. (1972) *Classes et conflits de classes dans la société industrielle*, Paris/La Haye: Mouton

Dany, F. and Lemetais, N. (1994) *Les Dirigeants des PME face aux Grandes Ecoles*, Lyon: Institut de Recherche en Entreprise

Dauberville, B., Gilbert, P. and Pigeyre, F. (1996) *Les sciences humaines dans l'entreprise*, Paris: Economica

Dayan, A. (1990) *Le Marketing*, Paris: Que sais-je?

Delpit, B. and Schwartz, M. (1993) *Le système financier français*, Paris: Montchrestien

De Maricourt, R. (1996) 'Paternalisme au Japon et en Occident', in *Etudes* No. 3842, February

De Tocqueville, A. (1856/1904) *L'Ancien Régime*, Oxford: Clarendon Press

D'Iribarne, P. (1989) *La Logique de l'Honneur*, Paris: du Seuil

D'Iribarne, P. (1991) 'Culture et effet sociétal', *Revue Française de Sociologie* xxx11-4, pp. 599–614

Donnadieu, G. and Denimal, P. (1993) *Classification-Qualification. De l'Evaluation des Emplois à la Gestion des Compétences*, Paris: Editions Liaisons
Dormagen, J.-C. (1990) *La Comptabilité Intégrée*, Paris: la Villeguérin
Duchéneaut, B. (1995) *Enquête sur les PME*, Paris: Darmattan
Dunlop, J. (1958) *Industrial relations systems*, Southern Illinois University Press
Dupuis, M. (1991) 'Avantage compétitif et roue de la distribution', *Revue Française du Marketing* No. 135, Vol. 5: 33–45
Enriques, E. (1983) *De la Horde à l'Etat*, Paris: Gallimard
Ferrandier, R. and Koen, V. (1994) *Marchés de capitaux et techniques financiers*, Paris: Montchrestien
Finkielkraut, A. (1987) *La défaite de la pensée*, Paris: Gallimard
Floch, J.-M. (1990) *Sémiotique, marketing et communication. Sous les signes, les stratégies*, Paris: PUF
Flottes-Lerolle, A. (1992) *Analyser les compétences: la méthode en question*, Paris: Editions ANACT
Fortin, D. (1993) 'Les Français et leur voiture: le divorce', *L'Expansion* No. 462, 21 November: 48–53
Fournet, F. (1991) 'Comptabilité et audit dans un environnement sans papier', *Revue Française de Comptabilité* No. 220: 35–37
Fraisse, R. and Foucauld, J.-B. de (eds) (1996) *La France en prospective*, Paris: Odile Jacob
Gadrey, J. and Gadrey N. (1991) *La Gestion des ressources humaines dans les services et le commerce*, Paris: l'Harmattan
Galambaud, B. (1993) *Les employés administratifs: crise d'identité et gestion sans ambition*, Paris: Entreprise et Personnel
Galambaud, B. (1994a) *Des hommes à gérer*, Paris: ESF
Galambaud, B. (1994b) *Une nouvelle configuration humaine de l'entreprise*, Paris: ESF
Gallo, G. (1990) *Le marketing des entreprises du commerce de détail*, Paris: Rapport ICC
Géradon de Véra, O. (1993) 'Le nouveau tableau de bord du décideur', *Revue Française de Marketing* No. 142–143/2–3: 39–44
Gollac, M. (1989) 'L'organisation du travail dans l'entreprise', in *Economie et Statistique* Vol. 224, Paris: INSEE pp. 15–44
Gordon, C. (1995) *The Business Culture in France*, Oxford: Butterworth Heinemann
Groux, G. (1989) 'French industrial relations: from crisis to today', in J. Howorth and G. Ross (eds) *Contemporary France*, London: Pinter pp. 52–70
Groux, G. and Mouriaux, R. (1992) *La CGT. Crises et Alternatives*, Paris: Economica
Guerin, F. (1991) *Comprendre le travail pour le transformer*, Paris: Editions Anact
Guéry, G. (1994) *Pratique du droit des affaires*, Paris: Dunod
Guigou, E. (1994) *Pour les Européens*, Paris: Flammarion
Hall, E. T and Hall, M. R. (1987) *Hidden differences – doing business with the Japanese*, New York: Doubleday
Herter, P. (1993) *La France en crise 1970–1993*, Paris: Editions de la Roche noire
Herzberg, F. (1966) *Work and the Nature of Man*, New York: World Publishing
Hunout, P. (1992) 'Les méthodes d'évaluation des emplois: du classement des emplois à la mesure des compétences', *Formation et Emploi* No. 39, July–September: 35–43
Imprimerie Nationale (1992) *Projet de Loi de Finances: Etat de la Recherche et du Développement Technologique*, Paris
INSEE (1995/96) *Tableaux de l'Economie Française (TEF)*, Paris: INSEE
Kern, H. and Schumann, M. (1989) *La fin de la division du travail?*, Paris: Maison des Sciences de l'Homme
Laboratoire d'Economie et de Sociologie du Travail (1979) 'Productions de la hierarchie dans l'entreprise. Recherche d'un effet societal Allemagne-France', *Article paru dans Travail et Emploi* No. 2, September

Lallemand, M. and Jardin, D. (1993) 'Témoignage: la collecte d'information d'ici à l'an 2000', *Revue Française du Marketing*, No. 142–143/2–3: 33–38

La Bruyère, J. de (1965) *Les Caractères*, Paris: Garnier

La Documentation Française (Decembre 1992) *France: le choix du la performance globale*, Rapport de la Commission 'Compétitivité Française' pour la préparation du XIe plan.

Le Boulaire, M. and Freiche, J. (1994) *L'emploi et l'entreprise: l'apprentissage des ruptures*, Paris: Liaisons

Le Nouvel Economiste, Paris: Publications du Nouvel Economiste

Leroy-Ladurie, E. (1975) *Montaillou, Village Occitan*

Lipovetsky, G. (1983) *L'Ere du vide. Essais sur l'individualisme contemporain*, Paris: Gallimard

—— (1987) *L'Empire de l'éphémère. La mode et son destin dans les sociétés modernes*, Paris: Gallimard

Lyon-Caen, G. (1985) *Droit au travail*, Paris: Dalloz

Madelin, A. (1995) *Quand les Autruches relèveront la tête*, Paris: Robert Laffont

Maffesoli, M. (1988) *Le temps des tribus: le déclin de l'individualisme dans les sociétés de masse*, Paris: Klincksieck

Mandon, N. (1987) 'Dimensions de l'activité professionnelle et compétences mises en oeuvre', *L'analyse des contenus d'activité*, Paris: CEREQ June, *Document de Travail*, No. 30: 31–42

Maslow, A. (1970) *Motivation and Personality*, New York: Harper & Row

Maurice, M., Sellier, F. and Silvestre, J.-J. (1982) *Politique d'éducation et organisation industrielle en France et en Allemagne*, Paris: PUF

Maurus, V. (1993) 'France, terre ouverte', *Le Monde*, 5 October

Mermet, G. (1995) *Francoscopie*, Paris: Larousse

—— (1996) *Tendances 1996. Le nouveau consommateur*, Paris: Larousse

Michel, S. (1989) *Peut-on gérer les motivations?*, Paris: PUF

—— (1993) *Sens et contresens des bilans de compétences*, Paris: Editions Liaisons

Michel, S. and Ledru, M. (1991) *Capital Compétences*, Paris: ESF

Michel, S. and Mallen, M. (1990) *Le Bilan Professionnel*, Paris: Editions d'Organisation

Midler, C. (1993) *L'auto qui n'existait pas*, Paris: Interéditions

Most, K. (1993) 'The great accounting conspiracy', *Accountancy*, October pp. 91–95

Naville, P. (1971) *L'Etat Entrepreneur*, Paris: Anthropos

Nobes, C. and Parker, R. H. (1998) *Comparative International Accounting*, London: Philip Allan

Pebereau, M. (1992) *La Politique économique de la France*, Paris: Armand Colin

Pérec, G. (1965) *Les choses: une histoire des années soixante*, Paris: Union Générale d'Editions

Peyrefitte, A. (1974) *Le Mal Français*, Paris: Plon

Ray, J.F. (1993) *Droit du travail – Droit vivant*, Paris: Editions Liaisons

Ripert, G. and Roblot, R. (1993) *Traité élémentaire de droit commercial* – Paris: LGDG

Reynaud, J. (1978) *Les Syndicats, les Patrons et l'Etat*, Paris: Editions Ouvrières

Ripert, G. and Roblot, R. (1993) *Traité elémentaire de droit commercial*, Paris: LGDG

Rochefort, R. (1995) *La société des consommateurs*, Paris: Odile Jacob

Rojot, J. and Tergeist, P. (1992) *Nouvelles orientiations dans l'organisation du travail: la dynamique des relations humaines*, Paris: OECD

Rosanvallon, P. (1988) *La Question Syndicale*, Paris: Calmann-Lévy

Ross, G. (1984) 'The CGT, economic crisis and political change', in M. Kesselman *et al.* (eds.) *The French Workers' Movement*, London: Allen Unwin

Rouquette, G. (1992) 'L'EDI et la comptabilité', *Revue Française de Comptabilité* No. 231, February: 13–15

Roustang, G. and Perret, B. (1993) *L'Economie contre la Société*, Paris: du Seuil

Rueff, J. (1959) transl. Clement, J. (1967) *Balance of payments: proposals for the resolution of the most pressing world economic problem of our time*, London: Macmillan

Schama, S. (1989) *Citizens*, London: Penguin

Scheid, J.-C. and Walton, P. (1992) *European Financial Reporting: France*, London: Routledge

Séguéla, J. (1982) *Hollywood: lave plus blanc*, Paris: Flammarion

—— (1983) *Fils de Pub*, Paris; Flammarion

Silver, H. (1991) 'Vers une gestion flexible des services professionnels', in J. and N. Gadrey (eds) *La gestion des ressources humaines dans les services et le commerce*, Paris: L'Harmattan

Silvestre, H., Goujet, R. and Pastorello, M.-H. *Tissu industriel des PMI indépendantes*, Lyon: Institut de Recherche en Entreprise

SOFRES (1990) *Liaisons sociales*, Paris

Solow, R. (1956) 'A contribution to the theory of economic growth', *Quarterly Journal of Economics* Vol. 70 Part I: 65–94

Suleiman, E. (1974) *Politics, power and bureaucracy in France: the administrative élite*, Princeton University Press

Szarka, J. (1988) *Business in France*, London: Pitman

Terrsac, G. de (1992) *Autonomie dans le Travail*, Paris: PUF

Teyssié, B. (1993) *Droit du travail*, Paris: LITEC

Théret, B. (1991) 'Le rawlisme à la française: le marché contre l'égalité démocratique?', *Futur Antérieur* No. 8/hiver, Paris: L'Harmattan pp. 39–75

Thierry, D., Sauret, C. and Monod, N. (1993) *La gestion prévisionnelle et préventive des emplois et des compétences*, Paris: L'Harmattan

Thorsrud, E. (1969) *A strategy for research and social change in industry: a report on the industrial democracy project in Norway*, Oslo: Mimco

Tribalat, M. (1993) 'Les immigrés et les populations liés à leur installation en France au recensement de 1990', *Population* No. 6

Van den Bergh, W. (1994) *Quality and Relevance*, Luxembourg: IRDAC/Publication Office of the European Communities

Warwick University Small Business Research Unit (1993) *SME Observatory*, Brussels: Commission of the European Communities DGXXIII

Weil, P. (1991) *La France et les Etrangers*, Paris: Calmann-Lévy

Zarifian, P. (1988) 'L'emergence du modèle de la compétence', in F. Stankiewicz *Les stratégies d'entreprise face aux ressources humaines*, Paris: Economica

Zeldin, T. (1983) *The French*, London: Collins

Index

The European Business  Environment:
France

Series List

Series Editors: Robert Crawshaw and Stephen Fox (Lancaster)

The European Business Environment: France
Volume Editor: Robert Crawshaw
French co-ordinator: Jean-Yves Eglem
ISBN: 0–415–10535–8

The European Business Environment: United Kingdom
Volume Editor: Stephen Fox
ISBN: 0–415–12128–0